MAJOR INDUSTRIAL RESEARCH UNIT STUDIES

No. 66

UNION CORPORATE CAMPAIGNS

by

CHARLES R. PERRY

INDUSTRIAL RESEARCH UNIT
The Wharton School, Vance Hall
University of Pennsylvania
Philadelphia, Pennsylvania 19104-6358

Copyright © 1987 by the Trustees of the University of Pennsylvania
Library of Congress Catalog Card Number 86-082727
MANUFACTURED IN THE UNITED STATES OF AMERICA
ISBN: 0-89546-065-3
ISSN: 0083-9094

FOREWORD

Union membership as a percentage of the American labor force has been on a steady decline since 1945, and union membership has declined absolutely as well as relatively since 1980. In the period since 1983 we have witnessed union decline in a period of prosperity, the first time this has occurred since the 1920s. With these facts, and the knowledge based upon a public opinion poll, which the AFL-CIO itself underwrote, that a majority of nonunion workers do not see unions as contributing to their welfare or security or do not believe that union officials act in the interest of the membership but rather in the interest of the officials themselves, it is not surprising that unions have been looking for new methods or organization. The current method which unions have emphasized is the so-called "corporate campaign." This is a system under which pressure is placed upon not only the employer, but in addition upon stockholders, boards of directors, financial institutions which deal with the company, customers, others who have relationships with the company, and on legislators to pressure the company either to recognize unions or to agree to union demands. Thus the objective of this union tactic is to achieve the results desired by the unions by secondary pressure—that is, pressure on others to induce them to compel the company management to agree to union demands.

The first widely publicized union corporate campaign involved the textile manufacturer, J. P. Stevens. It resulted in a symbolic union victory in that the company did sign a union agreement, but only for already unionized plants covering just 3,500 of the company's 40,000 employees. Union attempts to organize more J. P. Stevens employees have been unsuccessful, and the textile industry continues as a nonunion bastion. As in this case, claims and counterclaims about the success or failure of union corporate campaigns are often more propaganda than fact.

Professor Charles R. Perry's study, *Union Corporate Campaigns*, is the first objective analysis of this phenomenon. To accomplish this he has carefully researched and evaluated information concerning such campaigns which have involved the following companies: BASF, Beverly Industries, Campbell Soup, Consolidated Foods (now Sara Lee), General Dynamics, Litton Industries, Louisiana-Pacific, Phelps Dodge, and Seattle First National Bank. After explaining the nature of the campaign and how it works, he then analyzes the issues. He evaluates the success and failure of such campaigns and why some are successful and some have failed. In the Appendices, he summarizes the history of several of these campaigns on a company by company basis.

Union Corporate Campaigns, No. 66 in the Major Industrial Research Unit Studies series, is a careful examination of union tactics. Dr. Perry brings to it long experience in industrial relations work and studies. His most recent books have been *Collective Bargaining and the Decline of the United Mine Workers, Deregulation and the Decline of the Unionized Trucking Industry,* and *Operating During Strikes.* The last is in many ways the counterpart of *Union Corporate Campaigns* because, whereas *Operating During Strikes* is an examination of new corporate tactics in the collective bargaining arena, *Union Corporate Campaigns* is an equally incisive analysis of new union tactics. Company and union practitioners anxious to learn more about tactics and policies in the modern collective bargaining world, as well as students of the subject, will do well to examine these studies carefully.

Dr. Perry is Associate Professor of Management and Industrial Relations in the Wharton School and Senior Faculty Research Associate in the Industrial Research Unit. A former student, Peter H. Glick, assisted in the research of some of the case studies. This book was edited by Kathryn E. Pearcy, chief editor of the Industrial Research Unit. She also compiled the index. It was word processed by Ms. Sherrie L. Waitsman. Administrative matters were handled by the Unit's business manager, Mrs. Marthenia A. Perrin. Research was funded by membership contributions of the Wharton Industrial Research Unit's Industry Research Advisory Group, and by unrestricted grants from the Roland M. Gerstacker, General Mills, and William Penn foundations, and from Mobil Oil Corporation and William R. Griffith, a dedicated alumnus, plus special contributions from the Eaton, Lane, PPG Industries, Weyerhaeuser, and Whirlpool foundations. Publication was assisted by grants from the Alcoa and IBP foundations.

As in all Wharton Industrial Research Unit publications, the author is solely responsible for the research and for all views expressed, which should not be attributed to the University of Pennsylvania, or any grantor.

Herbert R. Northrup
Industrial Research Unit
The Wharton School
University of Pennsylvania

Philadelphia
March, 1987

TABLE OF CONTENTS

CHAPTER I

The Name of the Game

The first half of the 1980s produced many notable changes in the character and conduct of union-management relations in the United States. One of those changes was the emergence of something called a "corporate campaign" as an increasingly prominent and popular part of the union arsenal of weapons in its battles with management. Indeed, one self-interested consultant, Ray Rogers of Corporate Campaign Inc., reportedly has suggested that such campaigns can become the basic weapon in that arsenal by virtue of their power to enable unions to win without walkouts.[1] The Industrial Union Department (IUD) of the AFL-CIO, however, has taken the position that "[s]uch a campaign should reinforce—not replace—traditional union strengths" including "a well-prepared and well-conducted strike when necessary."[2]

The corporate campaign is not an invention of the 1980s. There is general agreement that the first such campaign was conducted during the latter half of the 1970s by the Amalgamated Clothing and Textile Workers Union (ACTWU) against the J. P. Stevens Company. That campaign probably had its origins in a relatively successful boycott and public relations campaign conducted by the Amalgamated Clothing Workers against Farah Manufacturing Company in the early 1970s. The Stevens "campaign," much like the union approach to Farah, involved what has been described as:

> . . . a three pronged effort consisting of legal charges of unfair labor practices, a consumer boycott of Stevens' products, and a *corporate campaign designed to isolate Stevens from the rest of the business and financial community.*[3] (Emphasis added.)

---

[1]Bill Keller, "For Union Ally, It's All in the Name," *New York Times*, May 2, 1984, p. A 24.

[2]Industrial Union Department, AFL-CIO, *Developing New Tactics: Winning With Coordinated Corporate Campaigns* (Washington, D.C.: Industrial Union Department, AFL-CIO, 1985), p.1.

[3]Terry W. Mullins and Paul Luebke, "Symbolic Victory and Political Reality in the Southern Textile Industry: The Meaning of the J. P. Stevens Settlement for Southern Labor Relations," *Journal of Labor Research*, Vol. III, No. 1 (Winter 1982), p. 82.

The Stevens campaign ended in 1980, but its concept was kept alive by Rogers who had been on the staff of ACTWU during the campaign and then left to form his own consulting firm, Corporate Campaign Inc. Rogers, who claims to have coined the phrase "corporate campaign," brought added fame to that phrase when, in 1984, he filed for a trademark on it, setting off a major public relations and legal battle with a rival consulting firm, The Kamber Group.[4] The Kamber Group filed formal objections to Corporate Campaign Inc.'s application with the trademark office in which it claimed that

> ... the term is "descriptive" and that The Kamber Group, its clients, and others should be free to continue to use it when describing their *strategic programs to counter corporate policies that are against "unions and other public interests."*[5] (Emphasis added.)

By the time the Rogers-Kamber battle was resolved in early 1985, the AFL-CIO had entered the business in the form of a copyrighted IUD guide entitled *Developing New Tactics: Winning with Coordinated Corporate Campaigns.* That guide sought to identify "less conventional means to deal more effectively with intransigent anti-union employers."[6] In the words of that guide:

> A coordinated corporate campaign applies pressure to many points of vulnerability to convince the company to deal fairly and equitably with the union.... It means seeking *vulnerabilities in all of the company's political and economic relationships—with other unions, shareholders, customers, creditors, and government agencies*—to achieve union goals.[7] (Emphasis added.)

An alternative view of coordinated corporate campaigns was provided in a charge of failure to bargain in good faith filed by BASF Corporation against the Oil, Chemical and Atomic Workers (OCAW) as a result of OCAW's campaign against the company. That charge, filed with the New Orleans Regional Office of the National Labor Relations Board (NLRB) in May 1986, stated, in part:

> Since in or about June, 1984, and continuing to the present, OCAW has engaged in an intensive course of conduct maliciously intended to injure and interfere with BASF in its business, trade and reputation. This course of action has been described by OCAW as a "coordinated campaign" or "corporate campaign." Its express purpose, as stated by OCAW President Joseph W. [*sic*] Misbrener, is to make the conse-

---

[4]Keller, "For Union Ally..." p. A 24.

[5]"Two Firms Settle Dispute Over Use of Term 'Corporate Campaign'," *Daily Labor Report*, No. 63 (April 2, 1985), p. A-3.

[6]Industrial Union Department, *Developing New Tactics*, p. i.

[7]*Ibid.*, p. 1.

quences to BASF for the lockout "as unpleasant, disagreeable and expensive as possible." OCAW has stated its intent to precipitate "a crisis . . . in employee, customer and public confidence—and loyalty."[8]

THE NATURE OF THE GAME

The growing prominence and popularity of the corporate campaign as a union power tactic in confronting employers raises three obvious but interesting questions. The first is why the need to play this new power game—the role of the game in the broader scheme of union-management relations. The second is how the power game is played in practice—the rules of the game and response of management and government to this innovation in union-management relations. The third is how effectively the game is played—the results of the game and their implications for the basic balance of power in union-management relations.

The Role of the Game

The IUD Guide to *Winning With Coordinated Corporate Campaigns* begins with a description of what it terms "Today's Crisis" and clearly suggests that the need for new tactics is related to the growing resistance of management to unions in organizing campaigns at the bargaining table and on the picket line, and to the seemingly growing ineffectiveness of the government in controlling such resistance. In that context, it indicates three situations in which corporate campaigns may be useful: 1) operating during strikes; 2) resistance in organizing campaigns and/or refusal to bargain in good faith over a first contract; and 3) demands for concessions with or without threats to move or close operations.[9]

The prospect that corporate campaigns can and will be used effectively to challenge management's right to operate during a strike is a particularly intriguing one to this author who, as co-author of an earlier work, explored that very subject. In that work, the authors predicted that a significant acceleration of the trend toward plant operation during strikes would undoubtedly produce a response from the labor movement, but did not foresee the corporate cam-

---

[8]Letter from Mr. William R. D'Armond of Kean, Miller, Hawthorne, D'Armond, McCowan and Jarman, attorneys at law, to Mr. Hugh Frank Malone, Regional Director, National Labor Relations Board Region 15, dated May 17, 1986, Appendix I. p. 131.

[9]Industrial Union Department, *Developing New Tactics*, p. 1.

paign, per se, as one of the legion of possible responses.[10]

The use of corporate campaigns to deal with employer resistance to union organizing drives or successes is hardly new. The Farah and Stevens cases which spawned the phenomenon centered on just such issues. The fundamental question with respect to such situations is whether or not corporate campaigns can and will impose upon employers who resist unionization and collective bargaining the kind of punitive damages currently unavailable under the National Labor Relations Act (NLRA) which were such an integral part of the labor movement's drive for "labor law reform" in the late 1970s. In short, it may be that the corporate campaign may prove to be the 1980s equivalent to the neutrality clause[11] of the 1970s in the search of unions for self-protection rather than government protection against hostile managements.

The possibility that corporate campaigns can and will be used to gain a measure of control by unions over management decisions not currently subject to the obligation to bargain in good faith, except as to their effects, is potentially far more significant than the other two possible roles for corporate campaigns in union-management relations. Should that potential be realized, it would provide unions a far greater measure of control over managerial capital investment/disinvestment decisions than they enjoy under the current definition of the scope of the obligation to bargain in good faith.

The Rules of the Game

When a union calls a strike, it commits itself to a well defined and well understood course of action. The same is not the case when a union announces that it is undertaking a corporate campaign. A corporate campaign may entail any of a wide array of actions used in varying numbers, combinations, and sequences to fulfill whatever role that campaign is designed to serve. In short, it seems that the corporate campaign is a type of cafeteria plan of confrontational tactics from which unions are free to choose in conducting a "campaign." Thus, there is no definitive answer to the question, "What is a corporate campaign?" other than "Whatever a union says it is!"

---

[10]Charles R. Perry, Andrew W. Kramer, and Thomas J. Schneider, *Operating During Strikes: Company Experiences, NLRB Policies, and Governmental Regulation* (Philadelphia: Industrial Research Unit, The Wharton School, University of Pennsylvania, 1982), p. 126.

[11]Andrew M. Kramer, "Labor's New Offensive: Neutrality Agreements," in Herbert R. Northrup and Richard L. Rowan, *Employee Relations and Regulation in the '80s* (Philadelphia: Industrial Research Unit, The Wharton School, University of Pennsylvania, 1982), pp. 203–221.

The IUD, in its published manual on coordinated corporate campaigns, lists ten specific "tactics which have been used successfully in coordinated corporate campaigns."[12] Those tactics are: 1) coalition building; 2) press and public relations; 3) legislative initiatives; 4) actions by regulatory agencies; 5) using the courts; 6) consumer actions; 7) pressuring lenders and creditors; 8) using fund assets; 9) stockholder actions; and 10) in-plant tactics. That same manual also states:

> The large, well-known campaigns, such as those against J. P. Stevens, General Dynamics, Louisiana-Pacific, Litton Industries and Beverly Nursing Homes, are noted for their utilization of a wide variety of tactics.
> The elements of a campaign can, however, be used in more limited situations where a full-scale campaign may not be wanted or needed. "Mini-Campaigns"—utilizing one or two techniques—can be waged, and are sometimes the wisest course of action.[13]

The use of such tactics as part of a "corporate power strategy" has been viewed as having four major targets or points of corporate vulnerability: 1) pressure/harassment of business associates; 2) confrontation with owners/management; 3) financial pressures; and 4) product market pressure.[14] In this context, the "corporate power strategy" appears to be little more or less than a multifaceted effort to disrupt access of the target company to its established sources of supply and demand by inducing others to cease doing business with it—the classic definition of boycott activity. Indeed, many of the tactics which might be used to pressure/harass business associates or to exert financial pressures might well constitute unlawful secondary boycott activity under the National Labor Relations Act, a question currently awaiting at least an initial answer in a pending case involving a campaign against Hormel at its Austin, Minnesota facility.[15]

The fact that the corporate campaign is not a tactically well-defined union power asset does not necessarily diminish, and may actually enhance, its potential effectiveness. When a union calls a strike, management generally must assume that the union will be able to pull workers off the job and therefore can plan, with reason-

---

[12]Industrial Union Department, *Developing New Tactics*, pp. 4–10.
[13]*Ibid.*, p. 11.
[14]James A. Craft and Marian M. Extejt, "New Strategies in Union Organizing," *Journal of Labor Research*, Vol. IV, No. 1 (Winter 1983), pp. 22–24.
[15]"UFCW Local Unlawfully Picketed Banks in Dispute with Hormel, NLRB Rules," *Daily Labor Report*, No. 53 (March 19, 1986), p. A-2.

able certainty, to deal with that prospect. When a union announces a corporate campaign, management cannot know what to expect or whether, as is true for most boycotts, the actions taken will have their intended effect, which makes it difficult to plan counter measures to limit such effect. In this context, it may well be that the threat of a campaign is a more potent weapon than an actual campaign because it forces management to deal with more unknowns with respect to its conduct of business as usual than is the case once the union has either tipped its hand or tried its luck in boycott activities.

The Results of the Game

It is as difficult to determine the effectiveness of a corporate campaign as it is to define what constitutes a corporate campaign. For the most part, corporate campaigns have not been used in conventional substantive disputes over terms and conditions of employment—disputes traditionally resolved by threat of or recourse to the strike. Instead, corporate campaigns typically have been conducted in the context of procedural disputes over management policies or practices—disputes in which recourse to the strike is or has proven to be ineffective.

The full-scale corporate campaigns cited by the IUD in its manual were all undertaken in an effort to "regulate" managerial behavior in areas where, from the union point of view, the NLRA and NLRB do not do so adequately. In that context, the challenge of measuring the effectiveness of corporate campaigns is not much more difficult or controversial than that of determining the effectiveness of the NLRA and NLRB in controlling "anti-union" management behavior. Indeed, the ultimate test of the effectiveness of the corporate campaign as a union power asset may be its ability to supplement or supplant government regulation as a basis for worker/union participation in the formulation of corporate human resource and related policies. In the shorter run, however, some less ambitious test of the results of corporate campaigns is in order.

The fact that the corporate campaign has not been widely used in conventional contract disputes has not meant that unions have not sought a conventional closure to such confrontations with management in the form of an "agreement," as was the case in the campaign against J. P. Stevens. Such an agreement might entail a commitment by management either to do something or to stop doing something, or both, depending on the circumstances of the union's complaint. Any such agreement must be viewed as a symbolic victory for the union in a battle with management over procedure (behavior) as opposed to substance (bargaining). Whether or not that symbolic victory leads to a subsequent substantive victory, however, is another question which has been left largely unanswered by the existing popular and partisan reports of the results of corporate campaigns. In short, little is known of the practical consequences of any managerial decisions or commitments to do things differently as a result of a corporate campaign, either generally, or specifically in relation to the union or unions which conducted the campaign.

THE CONDUCT OF THE GAME

The purpose of this study is to provide more detailed insight into the nature of corporate campaigns through an examination of the experiences of companies that have been the target of such campaigns. In the absence of any good data on the number and identity of all such target companies, ten such companies were chosen primarily on the basis of campaign visibility and secondarily on the basis of corporate accessibility. The former phenomenon proved to be a function of the campaigner's willingness to talk publicly about its actions; the latter, a function of the target's willingness to talk privately about its reaction.

Although the sample of campaigns is small, it is highly diverse and thereby hopefully representative of much of the potential universe of corporate campaigns. The sample of campaigns includes four mounted in conjunction with organizing drives and six arising out of confrontations at the bargaining table, four of which involved company operation during a strike or lockout. The IUD was involved in three of the campaigns, one of which was initiated by a non-AFL-CIO union, and Ray Rogers was involved in three others, all conducted by local unions. Three of the campaigns were conducted by AFL-CIO member national unions without extensive IUD involvement but not without federation support. The final campaign was launched by two nuns who, in the view of the target company, were doing the unions' work. Four of the target companies were consumer goods or service producers. The other six were primarily producer goods companies with two of those being heavily dependent on defense contracts.

The first step on the way to "winning with coordinated corporate campaigns," in the view of the IUD, is an analysis of the target company to identify its potential points of vulnerability or, more traditionally, costs of disagreement. In terms of bargaining power, those vulnerabilities or costs must be weighed against the target company's stake in that dispute, its costs of agreement—a fact which the IUD largely ignored in its otherwise thorough manual, *Winning With Coordinated Corporate Campaigns*. The understanding of the character of the target company and its stake in the instant dispute, which should be part of the preparation for the conduct of a campaign, is no less important in preparation for the analysis of the course and conclusion of a campaign.

BASF

BASF Corporation (formerly BASF-Wyandotte) is the American subsidiary of BASF A.G. headquartered in Ludwigshafen, West Germany, one of the world's largest chemical companies. The parent company was once a segment of I. G. Farben which was a key part of the military-industrial complex of the Third Reich. BASF in the United States is a producer of chemicals and fibers ranging from glycols and polystyrene to acrylics, nylon fibers, and printing inks.

The corporate campaign against BASF grew out of a labor dispute at its Geismar, Louisiana facility. That facility is a composite of several different operations, one of which produces isocyanates, the same family of compounds made at the Bhopal, India plant of Union Carbide. At the time the dispute began, the facility employed a total of about 400 hourly employees represented by the Oil, Chemical, and Atomic Workers (OCAW). On June 14, 1984, the company locked out those 400 employees after an impasse was reached in contract negotiations with OCAW and used contract labor as temporary replacements to continue operating. Two and one-half years later, in December 1986, that situation was unchanged.

The 1984 union-management confrontation at Geismar was only the second such event since the union was certified in 1958. The first confrontation occurred in 1970 when OCAW struck the facility after an impasse was reached in contract negotiations. In addition to its strike action, the union took its case to BASF A.G. asking it to intervene in the dispute in order to avoid the adverse publicity which would accompany a prolonged strike. As a result of that appeal, BASF A.G. directed BASF Corporation to settle the strike. When that was not done immediately, German board members came to the United States, discharged the company's vice-president of industrial relations and settled the strike themselves on terms very favorable to the union. The same union representative who led the 1970 strike has been in charge of the 1984–1986 OCAW activity at Geismar.

Beverly Enterprises

Beverly Enterprises is the largest nursing home operator in the

United States. In 1983, the year in which the campaign was launched, it controlled some 780 homes with 69,000 employees in 43 states and the District of Columbia. By 1985, the number of homes operated by the company had grown to over 900 and by 1986 exceeded 1,000, continuing a pattern of rapid growth which began in the late 1970s. According to a "Corporate Profile" of the company prepared by the Food and Beverage Trades Department (FBTD) of the AFL-CIO, much of the company's growth came through the leveraged acquisition of existing facilities with, in many cases, as much as two-thirds of the cash required for such acquisitions coming from the state and federal governments.[16] That same profile also noted that the company is regulated by not only the Securities and Exchange Commission but also the Social Security Administration (Medicare), the Health Care Financing Administration (Medicaid), the Veterans Administration, and various state agencies.[17]

The campaign against Beverly Enterprises was launched in January 1983 in conjunction with a joint Service Employees International Union (SEIU)-United Food and Commercial Workers Union (UFCW) national organizing campaign aimed at Beverly facilities. At that time, the SEIU represented employees at twenty-one Beverly facilities in four states and the UFCW represented employees of ten facilities in five states. The goal of both the corporate and organizing campaigns was to overcome the company's policy of opposing unions because "We like to deal and communicate directly with our employees. We do not believe a third party organization should come between Beverly and its employees."[18] That policy, in the view of the unions, was supported by the best benefits package in the industry and a preventative labor relations program to teach administrators to detect early signs of organizing activity.[19] In addition to such efforts to resist organization, the SEIU and UFCW reportedly were experiencing difficulty "in securing collective bargaining agreements with Beverly, both following a successful NLRB election or when Beverly acquired a health care facility that had been previously organized by one of the two unions."[20]

---

[16]Food and Beverage Trades Department, AFL-CIO, "Beverly Enterprises: A Corporate Review," released January 1983, p. 7.

[17]*Ibid.*, p. 19.

[18]*Ibid.*, p. 11.

[19]*Ibid.*, p. 11.

[20]"Beverly Enterprises, UFCW and SEIU Announce Accord Aimed at Cooperation," *Daily Labor Report*, No. 43 (March 5, 1984), p. A-6.

Campbell Soup Company

The Campbell Soup Company, headquartered in Camden, New Jersey, is the nation's leading producer of canned soups and related food products, most of which are marketed under the clearly identified and well-known Campbell brand. In addition, the company also produces other food products for the consumer market under brand names other than Campbell, including Vlasic Pickles. The company's processing/production facilities in the United States are largely unionized and it "enjoys good relations with the 9 unions in the U.S. with which it has 34 contracts covering more than 12,000 Campbell Soup employees."[21]

The corporate campaign against Campbell Soup was not conducted or supported by any of its nine unions. Instead, it was mounted by a small independent union, the Farm Labor Organizing Committee (FLOC) headquartered in Toledo, Ohio, with the advice of Ray Rogers. The goal of FLOC was to organize farm workers, in general, and migrant farm workers, in particular, in the tomato and cucumber fields of Ohio and Michigan. A number of the growers of those two crops were under contract to supply produce to Campbell Soup/Vlasic Pickles. When a FLOC-led strike against those and other growers failed to force recognition of the union, FLOC turned its attention to Campbell Soup. As a result, the company found itself the target of a campaign in which the basic issue was, in the words of the company, FLOC's demand "that Campbell enter into three-way negotiations with the farmers and FLOC . . . to tell the farmers the company will buy tomatoes from them only if their migrant employees belong to a union, and that FLOC is the union to which they must belong."[22]

Consolidated Foods Corporation

Consolidated Foods Corporation (now Sara Lee) produces a wide array of consumer food products marketed under a wide variety of brand names. In addition to its food products, it also produces and markets other consumer goods, most notably the hosiery and other knit goods of its Hanes subsidiary which was the cause of the campaign. The central issue in that campaign was the high reported incidence of tendinitis and related disorders (TRD) in Hanes facilities and the adequacy of the corrective actions undertaken to deal with

---

[21]Campbell Soup Company, Corporate News, "Campbell Soup Company and FLOC," no date, p. 2.
[22]*Ibid.*

the problem under the terms of a 1981 voluntary agreement between Hanes and the Occupational Safety and Health Administration (OSHA)—corrective actions which the company claimed "were underway at Hanes long before the OSHA agreement."[23]

In 1979, Hanes' 10 plants with a total of 16,000 employees became a major organizing target of the ACTWU. By November of that year, the union had won a representation election at the Hanes plant in Galax, Virginia, by a vote of 569 to 504. The company challenged that victory charging that the union had committed numerous unfair labor practices and pursued its case beyond the NLRB to the Fourth Circuit Court of Appeals. That action produced a threat from the union to mount a boycott against the company which, in turn, led to an agreement between the company and the union to await and abide by the decision of the circuit court. That decision was handed down in May 1982 and invalidated the union's victory.[24] Less than six months later, Hanes and its parent company found themselves the targets of a corporate campaign.

The corporate campaign against Consolidated Foods was not, strictly speaking, a union corporate campaign. The campaign was launched by two nuns, members of the Sisters of Divine Providence of San Antonio, Texas, who were at the time assigned to community work in Bennettsville, South Carolina, as members of the Connective Ministry Across the South—an organization the company charged was financed by the ACTWU. At the same time, the two "Bennettsville Sisters" were on the volunteer staff of the Southerners for Economic Justice, an organization formed in 1976 by the ACTWU to generate community support for its organizing efforts at J. P. Stevens. Those two institutional connections between the nuns and the union, coupled with employee reports that "the Bennettsville Sisters were contacting Hanes employees and among other things offering to help [them] contact union organizers," led one Hanes manager to allege openly that the Sisters were working with, if not for, the ACTWU.[25]

---

[23]Letter from John H. Bryan, Jr., Consolidated Foods Corporation to Sister Imelda Maurer, CDF, Connective Ministry Across the South, dated November 4, 1982, p. 1.

[24]Hanes Corp. Petitioner v. N.L.R.B. Respondent, 677 F.2d 1008 (4th Cir. 1982).

[25]Letter from Philip R. Currier, President of Hanes Hosiery, to Sister Mary Margaret Hughes, Superior General of the Sisters of Divine Providence, dated January 12, 1983.

General Dynamics

General Dynamics, headquartered in St. Louis, is one of the, if not the, leading defense contractors in the United States. Almost 90 percent of its sales are to the federal government. It is also a company whose production operations are substantially unionized by such unions as the International Association of Machinists and Aerospace Workers (IAM) and the United Automobile, Aerospace and Agricultural Implement Workers (UAW) which represents, among others, some 5,600 workers producing M-1 tanks under one of the company's largest defense contracts.[26] General Dynamics, like most other major defense contractors, has been the target of accusations of overcharging the government. It also bore the stigma of having one of its top executives flee the country in 1982 after being indicted on seventeen counts of illegal kickbacks from subcontractors.[27]

The corporate campaign against General Dynamics was conducted by the UAW and began in early 1984. The basic cause of the campaign was the company's decision to hire replacements for 2,200 striking UAW-represented draftsmen at its Electric Boat Division in 1983. That decision apparently prompted some, but far from all, of the strikers to return to work. When the company then began to hire replacements, the basic issue became one of the job rights of the remaining striking workers, as is generally the case in such situations. In February 1984, the company stated that it had only 500 openings for any such striking workers and by March had reduced that number to 200.[28]

Hormel

The George A. Hormel Company, like the Campbell Soup Company, is a producer of processed food products (in this case, meat products) sold to consumers under the company name. Also like Campbell, Hormel's production facilities are, for the most part, unionized and the company generally has enjoyed good relations with its unions or more accurately, its union—the UFCW. Again like Campbell, that union did not conduct or support the campaign against the company which was conducted by one of its own obviously more independent local unions with the advice and encouragement of Ray Rogers.

---

[26]"A Harder UAW Push on General Dynamics," *Business Week*, March 26, 1984, p. 36.

[27]"General Dynamics: The Tangled Tale of Taki Veliotis," *Business Week*, June 25, 1984, pp. 114–125.

[28]"A Harder UAW Push on General Dynamics," p. 35.

The campaign against Hormel, which was conducted by Local P-9 of the UFCW without the blessing or support of its international union, began in August 1985, when the local union struck the company's Austin, Minnesota facility after rejecting a company contract offer to match the industry-UFCW wage and benefit pattern. That action pitted Local P-9 against not only the company but also its own international union in a test of both institutional will and economic power. Therefore, the strike and ensuing corporate campaign against Hormel had two equally significant and ultimately unyielding targets—the company and the UFCW. The result was a campaign which drew widespread public attention as a result of the media's fascination with the David and Goliath theme of a local union battling not only "greedy management" but its own "ungrateful international union" and with the Daniel-in-the-lion's-den type exploits of its consultant, Ray Rogers.

Litton Industries

Litton Industries has been characterized in the academic literature as a "Conglomerate Multinational Firm"[29] but, in the words of the IUD, "describes itself as a high technology company... whose various businesses are tied together by the common thread of technological innovations and advanced products, processes and services."[30] Litton Industries, like BASF, is essentially a producer of goods for industrial and commercial customers in that consumer products—basically microwave ovens—accounted for only about 5 percent of its sales in 1981, the year before the campaign against it was launched. Litton, like General Dynamics, does a substantial amount of business with the U.S. Department of Defense, from which it derived about 25 percent of its revenues in 1981 (as compared with almost 90 percent for General Dynamics). Litton Industries, unlike General Dynamics, is not heavily unionized; only thirty of its eighty plants in the United States were organized in 1981, the largest of which was Ingalls Shipbuilding facility in Pascagoula, Mississippi, which employed over 10,000 of Litton's approximately 21,000 unionized employees.[31]

---

[29]Charles Craypo, "Collective Bargaining in the Conglomerate Multi-national Firm: Litton's Shutdown of Royal Typewriter," *Industrial and Labor Relations Review*, Vol. 29, No. 1. (October 1975), pp. 3–25.

[30]Industrial Union Department, AFL-CIO, "Litton Industries, Inc.," analysis distributed at a meeting in Columbus, Ohio, October 30, 1981, p. 1.

[31]*Ibid.*, pp. 11–12.

The Litton campaign was the product of the frustration of a union in its efforts to secure an initial collective bargaining agreement at one of Litton's eighty plants in the United States. The union was the United Electrical, Radio and Machine Workers (UE), a union expelled from the CIO in 1950 for communist domination, and the plant was Litton's Sioux Falls, South Dakota, microwave oven production plant. That plant, which opened in 1977, was the target of an organizing drive by the UE which represented workers at the company's only other microwave oven production plant in Minneapolis. That organizing drive bore fruit in September 1980 when the UE won an NLRB representation election at the Sioux Falls plant. Negotiations over an initial contract began in October 1980. When no real progress toward such a contract had been made by the end of January 1981, the union's negotiators told their company counterparts of the union's intention to "do a number on the company" and the campaign began.

Louisiana-Pacific

Louisiana-Pacific, headquartered in Portland, Oregon, is the nation's second largest producer of lumber products ranging from two-by-fours to waferboard. The company's major market is the construction industry which in 1983 was depressed by a low level of new housing construction. The company's 100 production facilities are spread across the country and typically are located close to forest land in small rural communities where they are a major and often high-wage employer.

The cause of the campaign, which was launched by the United Brotherhood of Carpenters and Joiners of America (UBC) in December, 1983, was an impasse in contract negotiations between the company and the Western Council of Lumber Production Workers, an affiliate of the UBC. Those negotiations involved the company's western operations—twenty production operations located in northern California, Oregon, and Washington. Prior to 1983, the company was party to multi-employer bargaining between the big seven (the seven largest unionized producers) and the Western Council. The company withdrew from multi-employer bargaining prior to the 1983 negotiations and informed its unions that it not only would not be party to multi-employer bargaining but also would not be party to multi-plant bargaining in its western operations. When an agreement was reached by the union and other companies in multi-employer negotiations, Louisiana-Pacific refused to follow the pattern set by that agreement. The result was a strike which began in June of 1983. In July of 1983, the company began to hire permanent replacements and resume operations.

Phelps Dodge

Phelps Dodge today is probably the nation's largest producer of copper. The company is headquartered in New York City but its production operations are located in the Southwest, primarily in Arizona where, in towns like Ajo and Morenci, "Mother Dodge" is the only game in town. In 1983, those production facilities were operating far below capacity due to an abundant supply of copper from developing countries.

The cause of the campaign against Phelps Dodge was the refusal of the company to follow an industry pattern set elsewhere in the 1983 round of copper negotiations. In 1983, contracts covering some thirty bargaining units at five company operations in Arizona (four) and Texas (one) expired. In conducting negotiations over new contracts for those thirty units, the company was party to coalition bargaining in which the United Steelworkers (USW) played the lead role, as it did in the campaign. The company's refusal to follow the industry pattern and insistence on concessions caused the USW and its coalition partners to strike the company in June of 1983, despite having been informed of the company's intention to continue to operate. In July, the company began to hire permanent replacements and by the end of August had achieved its desired staffing levels, although not without serious problems including considerable violence on the picket line.

Seattle First National Bank

Seattle First National Bank (SeaFirst) is a large, multi-branch, full-service bank serving northwest Washington state, which is now owned by Bank of America. In 1978, it enjoyed the distinction of having the largest unit of unionized employees in the banking industry in the United States—some 4,800 clerical and sales personnel represented by the Firstbank Independent Employees Association. In February of that year, that association voted to affiliate with the Retail Clerks International Union (RCIU) which subsequently merged with the Amalgamated Meatcutters and Butcher Workmen to form the United Food and Commercial Workers (UFCW). In the affiliation vote, only members of the association were permitted to cast ballots. As a result, only 2,691 of the 4,790 bargaining unit employees were eligible to vote. Of those 2,691 eligible voters, less than 2,000 actually voted with only about 60 percent of those voting in favor of affiliation.

Following the affiliation vote, the bank received a request from the union, now the Financial Institution Employees of America, Local 1182 of the Retail Clerks, to begin negotiations. The bank, noting that less than 25 percent of all bargaining unit employees had voted in favor of affiliation, refused that request. Specifically, in April 1978, the bank informed the union that it did not recognize the union as bargaining representative of any group of bank employees and was, therefore, in no position to commence bargaining. The bank's refusal to recognize and bargain with the union was challenged by the union in two ways. The first was through the NLRB and the courts in a legal battle to force the bank to deal with the union which was still going on eight years later. The second was a corporate campaign conducted with the counsel of Ray Rogers to encourage the bank to voluntarily recognize and bargain with the union.

THE ACCOUNT OF THE GAME

For each of the ten campaigns studied, a chronology of major public events and a narrative account of major private developments was constructed using three basic sources. The first source was published reports of events and statements associated with the campaign as found in both the popular and union press. The second source was interviews with the managerial personnel responsible for dealing with the campaign, most of whom were willing to discuss their experiences although a few insisted on doing so "off-the-record." The third source was the campaign files which many of the managerial personnel interviewed made available to the author—files which in some cases filled whole filing cabinets. The need for parallel private interview and file information from campaigners was largely obviated by the fact that they, unlike their targets, typically were anxious to be interviewed and ready to release either publicly or privately, on request, copies of studies made in preparation for or use during their campaign. Thus, it was possible to construct or reconstruct what was taking place on both sides of the campaign in all but the very few cases in which the target company was unable or unwilling to explain, even privately, "what hit them."

The Organization of the Account

The fact that the corporate campaign game lacks well-defined rules and requirements permits wide variation in the way that game is played. That variation raises the difficult question of whether, in doing an account of such campaigns, it is better to focus on their differences or their similarities. The former approach suggests a series of chronological, descriptive case studies of individual campaigns. The latter approach requires a series of cross-sectional analyses of the basic component elements—the games within the game—of the set of campaigns studied. This latter approach comprises the core of this study. For those seeking insight into the details and/or dynamics of individual campaigns, however, six appendices devoted to specific campaigns have been included. The first of those appendices contains the full text of the BASF unfair labor practice charge against OCAW which enumerates the variety of tactics used by OCAW in that campaign. The next four are case studies of campaigns cited by the IUD as "large, well-known campaigns . . . noted for their utilization of a wide variety of tactics"—those against Beverly Enterprises, General Dynamics, Litton Industries, and Louisiana-Pacific. The final appendix describes the campaign against Consolidated Foods-Hanes Division conducted by segments of the religious community.

The use of a cross-sectional approach requires the identification of a limited number of basic points of corporate vulnerability open to exploitation in the course of a corporate campaign. The basic function of a campaign is to expand the scope, of and thereby raise the cost of, a labor dispute to the target company. In pursuing that purpose, the campaigner may seek to expand the scope of conflict either horizontally in search of allies, or vertically in search of sanctions, or both. In attempting such a course or courses of action, there is a limited set of tactical targets: 1) the general public and its constituent special interest groups; 2) the various levels and branches of government; 3) the corporate governing structure including directors and shareholders; 4) the corporation's customers; and 5) the corporation's creditors. The following five chapters explore the efforts of the campaigners in the ten cases studied to appeal to these corporate publics for support in their battle with management in what constitute the games of principle, politics, protest, pressure, and principal. The seventh chapter is devoted to an analysis of the outcome of the various combinations of games played against the ten target companies—an analysis designed to determine the extent to which the whole game is larger than the sum of its sub-games. The final chapter is devoted to summarization of the current role and speculation as to the future role of corporate campaigns in labor-management relationships in the United States.

CHAPTER II

The Game of Principle

A central element in most full-scale coordinated corporate campaigns has been an attempt publicly to paint the target company as a corporate outlaw or villain. That was clearly evident in the J. P. Stevens campaign in the union movement's characterization of that company as, among other things, the nation's number one labor law violator—an honor subsequently passed on to Litton Industries. Such campaigns of corporate exposure or vilification (depending on one's viewpoint) clearly are designed to cast the union or unions in question in the role of good in the battle of good and evil, and fall into the IUD's tactical category of press and public relations. Such campaigns, however, also serve a second tactical function—the building of coalitions with other interest/pressure groups on the basis of common concern over broad social issues.

The goal of this aspect of a campaign is to "seize the high ground" in the union's battle with management by defining or redefining issues in ways which present the union in the most favorable public relations light. It is an exercise in issue and conflict expansion or escalation which traditionally has been foreign to collective bargaining in the private sector in this country. A notable exception is the relatively rare situation in which bargaining is conducted in the context of clear expectation of government intervention in and resolution of an impasse. That has rarely been the case for collective bargaining in the public sector where government involvement in impasses is automatic and where unions have long played and often outplayed management at the game of issue definition and conflict expansion—a game more studied and better understood in political science than in the dismal science.

The initiative in the game of issue definition and conflict expansion typically rests with the union, which gives it an advantage in gaining the high ground. In that context, management has three reactive strategic options: 1) seek some still higher ground on which to establish its battle position; 2) contest the union's possession of the high ground from the low ground; or 3) refuse to do battle on the ground in question. The first option entails an implicit plea of guilty but for good reason, which is often a difficult case to prove to the public. The second option involves an explicit plea of not guilty which leads to a full-scale trial in the court of public opinion where the principle of innocent until proven guilty does not always prevail. The third option implies no response to the charges made which is the public relations equivalent of a plea of no contest with all of its presumptions of culpability.

CONFLICT ESCALATION

The goal of conflict escalation is to expand the scope of a labor-management dispute vertically by redefining the issue in dispute from one of narrow self-interest to one of broad social significance. The dynamics of conflict escalation are relatively simple. The party in question seeks to define or redefine the issue in dispute so as to draw the sympathy and support of the general public and special interest groups. This is accomplished by manipulation of symbolic values and typically depends on media coverage if it is to be effective. Media coverage generally is not a problem because conflict and confrontation are news and charges or claims (issue definitions) made in that context are likely to be reported as just that—news—without inquiry into the validity of such issue definitions, at least in the first instance.

Conflict containment is the opposite of conflict escalation and involves efforts to reduce the dispute to its narrowest and most immediate terms. The outcome of a clash of these two strategies is an unjoined debate in which the conflict escalator speaks of general principles and the conflict container of specific facts. In such a debate, the advantage of factual accuracy most often lies with the conflict container, but that advantage must be weighed against the advantage of emotional appeal which most often lies with the conflict escalator. The balance between those two potential advantages depends less on the validity of than on the credibility of issue definitions to the publics in question.

Unfair to Organized Labor

One theme of issue definition common to the campaigns studied was that of corporate unfairness to organized labor. That is hardly surprising, given the fact that these campaigns were set off by some union setback at the hands of management, whether in the form of resistance to union organizing efforts (Beverly, Campbell, Hanes, SeaFirst), bargaining demands (BASF, Litton), or strike actions (General Dynamics, Hormel, Louisiana-Pacific, Phelps Dodge). What is surprising is that in almost half of these campaigns the process of conflict escalation did not go beyond the issue of fairness to organized labor.

The obvious public targeted by the unfairness issue is the larger labor movement. In and of itself, however, that issue appeared to have little appeal to other publics, judging by the course of the five campaigns in which fairness was the only issue. In the SeaFirst campaign, the fairness issue generated little sympathy and support even from within the labor movement and was eventually left to the NLRB and courts. In the Hormel campaign, the fairness issue drew substantial negative interest and attention from the labor movement because it was raised in open defiance of the national policy of the UFCW. That campaign did succeed, however, in gaining widespread public attention, if not sympathy, as a result of media fascination with the David and Goliath image of a local union battling not only management but its own international union and with the Daniel-type exploits of the outsider, Ray Rogers, who designed the campaign. The romanticization of that campaign by the media constitutes an extreme example of their potential vulnerability to being used in a corporate campaign as a result of their need for news.

The remaining two campaigns in which fairness was the basic issue involved company decisions to operate during strikes—the cases of Louisiana-Pacific and Phelps Dodge. The "unfairness" of such actions did generate considerable moral and, in the case of Phelps Dodge, some financial support for the affected workers, but little tangible sympathy or support from the general public. That lack of public response may have been a product of the fact that such actions seemed to have become an accepted if not routine part of collective bargaining in this country during the first half of the 1980s.

The limited degree of conflict escalation and resulting public interest in these four campaigns created little pressure on the companies to undertake conflict containment. For the most part they chose only to point out that they were simply exercising their legal rights and operating within the accepted framework of U.S. labor law.

The unfairness issue also played a prominent role in the campaign against BASF, although not to the exclusion of other conflict escalation initiatives. Calvin Moore, vice president of the Oil, Chemical and Atomic Workers (OCAW), charged that "BASF is waging an undeclared war on U.S. workers and has set out to systematically destroy all unions at its U.S. locations."[1] In support of that charge, the union had only to point to the fact that the company had reduced the num-

---

[1]"Oil Workers to Go Abroad to Pursue Dispute Against German Chemical Firm," *Daily Labor Report,* No. 12 (January 17, 1985), p. A-9.

ber of its unions and unionized plants from seventeen to three since 1975 and that two United Steelworkers (USW), one OCAW, and one Teamster bargaining units had been decertified recently. In addition, in the words of the corporation's unfair labor practice charge,

> OCAW has sought to arouse public animosity, distrust, suspicion and hatred of BASF by causing BASF to be listed on the so-called "Labor's Dishonor Role" [sic] by the Industrial Union Department of the AFL-CIO, and by causing the publication of such listing in the local and national news media, including the *Wall Street Journal.*[2]

The apparent annoyance of BASF at being placed on the Dishonor Roll—a dishonor shared by Louisiana-Pacific, Phelps Dodge, and Litton Industries—was a product of the fact that its parent company was located in West Germany where being anti-union and operating during strikes are not accepted parts of the national labor relations culture to the extent they are in the United States. Thus, while BASF could and did take the same position as Louisiana-Pacific and Phelps Dodge—that it was exercising its legal rights and operating within the framework of U.S. labor law—it faced a far more difficult challenge in selling that position to its parent company than did the others to their U.S. publics. Thus, it is hardly surprising that the BASF unfair labor charge also alleged:

> OCAW has sought to arouse public animosity, distrust, suspicion and fear of BASF both *internationally* and domestically by publicly and repeatedly asserting that BASF is engaging in an international and extensive course of anti-union conduct in violation of Federal law.[3] (Emphasis added.)

Corporate Outlaw

A second theme of issue definition which emerged in a number of the campaigns studied was that of corporate violations of the law. Allegations of such violations occurred in all but two of the campaigns, but were central only in the campaigns against Litton and General Dynamics and to a lesser extent in that against BASF. In the other five campaigns these issues were raised largely as unsubstantiated references to past, present, or potential problems ranging from safety and EEO violations (Hormel and Hanes), to environmental noncompliance (Louisiana-Pacific and Phelps Dodge), to excess administrative charges (Beverly).

---

[2]Letter from Mr. William R. D'Armond of Kean, Miller, Hawthorne, D'Armond, McCowan and Jarman, attorneys at law, to Mr. Hugh Frank Malone, Regional Director, National Labor Relations Board Region 15, dated May 17, 1986, Appendix I. p. 132.
[3]*Ibid.*

The escalation of union-management conflict into a question of corporate lawlessness was a central element in the campaign against J. P. Stevens in which the company was branded as the nation's number one labor law violator whose deliberate and consistent disregard for the nation's labor relations law posed a sufficient threat to the integrity of that law to warrant labor law reform. That dubious distinction was subsequently passed on to Litton Industries in the course of the campaign against it. Clearly, the award of such a dishonor requires some credible basis if it is to succeed in enlisting the interest of the public. In the case of the Litton campaign, that credible basis was provided by the largely unpublished work of an academician prepared in conjunction with his support of the AFL-CIO's abortive campaign for what was termed "Labor Law Reform."

The background and building of the case against Litton Industries deserves attention as an example of skillful conflict escalation. The lack of success of the United Electrical, Radio and Machine Workers (UE) in concluding its first set of contract negotiations at Litton's Sioux Falls, South Dakota plant clearly did not constitute a basis for an allegation of legally reprehensible corporate conduct. What was needed was a basis for suggesting far more pervasive and perverse corporate misconduct. Fortunately for the UE, the unpublished work of a Professor Charles Craypo provided allegations of just such behavior—allegations which constituted a vehicle for solidifying the UE's alliance with the larger labor movement, building an alliance with religious groups, and establishing a plausible public interest issue.

In 1975, Charles Craypo, then Associate Professor of Labor Studies at Pennsylvania State University, published an article entitled "Collective Bargaining in the Conglomerate, Multinational Firm: Litton's Shutdown of Royal Typewriter," in which he concluded that unions were at a severe disadvantage in bargaining with such firms.[4] In 1976, Professor Craypo testified before the House Subcommittee on Labor-Management Relations in support of the "Labor Reform Bill" and submitted a report in a conjunction with that testimony entitled "Litton Industries as a Repeat Violator of the National Labor Relations Act."[5] In that report he stated that an examination

---

[4]Charles Craypo, "Collective Bargaining in the Conglomerate Multinational Firm: Litton's Shutdown of Royal Typewriter," *Industrial and Labor Relations Review,* Vol. 29, No. 1 (October 1975), pp. 3–25.

[5]Charles Craypo, "Litton Industries as a Repeat Violator of the National Labor Relations Act," paper submitted to the Subcommittee on Labor-Management Relations of the U.S. House of Representatives Committee on Labor, February 19, 1976.

of twenty-six NLRB complaints filed against various Litton divisions since 1963

> ... leads to the inescapable conclusion that since the early 1960s Litton has pursued a policy of flagrant, systematic and calculated lawlessness in its aggressively anti-union policy.[6]

In 1982, Professor Craypo, then Associate Professor of Economics at Notre Dame, revised and updated that report in the form of a working paper of the economics department of that university. In that working paper, Professor Craypo reported that between 1963 and 1981 the NLRB issued forty-two complaints against Litton operations, resulting in nineteen findings of violations of the law, thirteen voluntary settlements and ten dismissed complaints.[7] On the basis of those figures Professor Craypo reiterated his earlier conclusion regarding Litton's behavior. It was this latter conclusion and academic affiliation which was cited in all leaflets used in the campaign thereafter. In addition, Professor Craypo's figures were widely cited in the press coverage of the Litton campaign. Such citations, in turn, were cited by the union and, on one occasion by Professor Craypo himself, as independent confirming sources of the company's record.[8]

The company prepared its own analysis of the data in Professor Craypo's working paper and uncovered several major factual, technical and conceptual errors.[9] It then had to decide whether to debate the detailed facts of the case or its broader allegations. Given the expected low level of media interest in and understanding of the facts of the case as opposed to the conclusions of the Craypo report, the company chose the latter course of action. Thus, its public response was to point out that there were few, if any, ongoing labor disputes at Litton subsidiaries and that such subsidiaries had successfully negotiated or renegotiated contracts at twenty locations over the past two years.

The other campaign in which the corporate outlaw theme was central was that conducted by the United Automobile Workers (UAW) against General Dynamics. That campaign formerly was focused on

---

[6]*Ibid.*

[7]Charles Craypo, "Litton Industries as a Repeat Violator of the National Labor Relations Act," working paper, Economics Department, Notre Dame University, February 1982.

[8]Charles Craypo, Jerold Paar, and Mary Lehman, "Litton Industries' Pattern of Labor Law Violations," report submitted to the Subcommittee on Labor-Management Relations of the U.S. House of Representatives Committee on Labor, April 20, 1983, p. 6.

[9]See Attachment 1 to Appendix IV.

the alleged anti-labor and anti-taxpayer posture of the company. UAW president Owen F. Bieber stated that the campaign would "expose the chronicle of General Dynamic's greed and abuse to the American people, and to the workers at General Dynamic's installations all across the country."[10] He also charged the company:

> [with] massive ripoffs of American taxpayers through the sale of materials to the Pentagon at outrageous and unjustifiable prices; of chronic abuse of the Defense Department's procurement bidding process; of acquiescence in the questionable practices of GD executives; of needless endangerment of workers' lives at GD facilities; and of grossly irresponsible conduct in collective bargaining . . .[11]

The union's charges were given some credibility by a number of specific developments which were receiving considerable press and governmental attention. The "massive ripoff" charge was given credence by charges that "12-cent allen wrenches [were sold] to the Air Force for more than $9606.00 each."[12] The questionable practices charge fit nicely with the flight of one top former General Dynamics executive to Greece in 1982 after being indicted on seventeen counts of illegal kickbacks to subcontractors.[13] Finally, the endangerment charges were given credence by the death of a worker for which the State of Michigan was to charge the company with involuntary manslaughter and willful violation of state safety standards.[14] In light of those circumstances, it is perhaps not surprising that the company chose not to deal with the specifics of the union's charges but to respond to them in the following general terms:

> [The statements attributed to Mr. Bieber are] outrageous, slanderous, irresponsible and completely without merit . . . [Bieber's] statements certainly do not indicate in any sense the determination to negotiate in good faith the difficult issues surrounding the unfortunate marine draftsmen's strike at Electric Boat.[15]

The campaign against BASF produced an unusual, if not particularly tasteful, allegation of corporate lawlessness. That allegation was described in the company's unfair labor practice charge in the following terms.

---

[10]"News from the UAW," February 1, 1984, p. 1.
[11]*Ibid.*, p. 1.
[12]*Ibid.*, p. 2.
[13].*Ibid.*
[14].*Ibid.*, p. 3.
[15]"UAW Announces Campaign Against General Dynamics, Citing Boat Strike, Safety Abuses, High Prices, *Daily Labor Report,* No. 22 (February 2, 1984), p. A-7.

OCAW has appealed to prejudice and sought to arouse the animosity of the community by publicly and repeatedly referring to the German ownership of BASF's parent corporation, alleging "foreign oppression," linking BASF with the Nazi party by use of the swastikas and other means, referring to BASF as "co-conspirators of the Third Reich," alleging that BASF "helped to bring you World War II," accusing BASF of "oppressing" the rights of "American Workers," and similar conduct.[16]

Human Misery

The third model of conflict escalation observed in the campaigns studied was one in which the target corporation was charged not with crimes against the labor movement or the state, but with crimes against humanity. This typically involves charges of exploitation of some relatively defenseless population such as the elderly (in the case of Beverly Enterprises), migrant farm workers (in the case of Campbell Soup), and women (in the case of Hanes). In its most extreme form it involves allusions to disasters of the magnitude of Bhopal, India or Chernobyl, USSR, as was done in the campaign against BASF in which:

OCAW has sought to arouse public animosity, distrust, fear and suspicion of BASF by repeatedly and publicly asserting that BASF is a safety hazard to the Geismar community and other communities. OCAW has charged both a) that BASF is operating its plant unsafely and with inadequately trained workers during the lockout, as a result of which the safety of the workers and the community is put in jeopardy, and b) that conditions which prevailed before the lockout and which will remain after the lockout ends (e.g., hazardous waste disposal practices, use of certain chemicals in plant operations) present great hazards. OCAW has sought to inflame the passions of the public against BASF by repeatedly comparing the Geismar operations to the disaster at Bhopal, India, by referring to the plant as a "ticking time bomb," and by other inflammatory statements.[17]

In the campaign against Beverly, the United Food and Commercial Workers (UFCW) and the Service Employees International Union (SEIU) sought with considerable success to assume the role of champions of better patient care in the company's then more than 700 nursing homes across the nation. At the opening of that campaign, the president of the UFCW stated the reason for the unions' efforts in the following terms:

We have pleaded for the kinds of staffing ratios, equipment, and supplies which would allow our members to deliver decent patient care . . .

---

[16]Letter from Mr. William R. D'Armond. . . . Appendix I. p. 132.
[17]*Ibid.*

Quality care is sometimes difficult to provide in the best of circumstances. In the worst of circumstances, when discouraged workers are under-staffed, under-equipped and under-paid, it is impossible.[18]

Those concerns were supported by a report entitled "Beverly Enterprises Patient Care Record: Preliminary Findings" issued by the Food and Beverage Trades Department of the AFL-CIO, which suggested that Beverly's "spectacular corporate track record has not been matched by growth in quality of care in Beverly homes."[19] The report focused on homes in Arkansas, California, and Texas and was based on statements of deficiences (inspection reports), Medicaid cost reports, civil court records and other public documents. The subjects covered included expenditure patterns, patient care deficiencies, administrative fines and civil suits. The report indicated that Beverly spent a smaller percentage of its per day expenditures on patient care than did the industry as a whole and that "significant problems" existed with insufficient staffing and outside service providers.[20] In support of that latter contention, the report presented extensive and often lurid anecdotal evidence and some questionable statistics which were only partially explained.

That report was followed by another entitled "Beverly Enterprises in Michigan—a Case Study of Corporate Takeover of Health Care Resources," also prepared by the Food and Beverage Trades Department of the AFL-CIO.[21] That report focused on Beverly's "monopoly power in Michigan," power which gave the firm "the ability to control access to care to the detriment of Michigan residents most in need of nursing home care,"[22] its "profiteering on public money" and its "deficiencies in patient care." The president of the SEIU characterized the results of this study as follows:

> In Michigan, as in four other states we have studied, we've documented that Beverly Enterprises has perfected techniques of manipulating the state medicaid system and skimping on patient care in order to make obscene profits at taxpayer expense and to build vast personal fortunes for its officers.
>
> But this report tells more than the story of one large company's

---

[18]"SEIU, UFCW Launch Drive at Some 400 Beverly Nursing Homes," *Daily Labor Report,* No. 20 (January 28, 1983) p. A-7.

[19]Food and Beverage Trades Department, AFL-CIO, "Beverly Enterprises Patient Care Record: Preliminary Findings, January 27, 1983," released January 27, 1983, p. 1.

[20]*Ibid.,* p. 20.

[21]Food and Beverage Trades Department, AFL-CIO, "Beverly Enterprises in Michigan: A Case Study of Corporate Takeover of Health Care Resources," released September 26, 1983.

[22]*Ibid.,* p. 17.

continuing greed. It begins to tell the saga of the corporatization of
health care in the country...

The impact of the corporatization of health care will be as dramatic
as if the State of Michigan sold its public schools to big business.[23]

The corporation's response to the unions' allegations was to point
out that segments of the AFL-CIO "have spent millions of their
members' dues dollars during the past several years in their overtures to the employees of Beverly" with little tangible result. Thus,
"failing significant success, they desperately attempt to create a
false portrait of Beverly in order to gather support from a public
genuinely sympathetic to the plight of the nation's elderly."[24] The
company also felt compelled to respond on the issue of patient care
in the following terms:

> Every resource available to Beverly is dedicated to providing the best
> possible health care and environment to elderly Americans. No other
> organization in the nation can boast a record of such consistent qual-
> ity and innovation in health and nursing care.[25]

The basic issue underlying the Farm Labor Organization Committee (FLOC) campaign against Campbell Soup was, in the words of
the company, FLOC's demand that Campbell "tell the farmers the
company will buy tomatoes from them only if their migrant employees belong to a union, and that FLOC is the union to which they
must belong."[26] When the company refused that demand, it found
itself drawn into a "controversy concerning migrant workers
in Northwest Ohio" which involved the following "five basic
concerns":

1) The charge is frequently made that migrant workers on farms with
   which Campbell contracts are paid less than $2.00 per hour.
2) It has been frequently implied by FLOC supporters that Campbell
   Soup company is anti-union.
3) Pictures of one room plywood shacks in which migrants live for the
   two month harvest season abound. The implication is that this
   housing is on farms from which Campbell Soup buys produce.
4) One of the most unfair, and unkind charges frequently made
   against Campbell by FLOC is that "Campbell Soup Company is
   profiting from the use of child labor in the state of Ohio."
5) The charge has been made that pesticides are applied to crops while

[23]Statement by John J. Sweeney, President, Service Employees International
Union, Lansing, Michigan, September 9, 1983, p. 1.

[24]"SEIU, UFCW Launch Organizing Drive ...," p. A-7.

[25]*Ibid.*

[26]Campbell Soup Company Corporate News, "Campbell Soup Company and
FLOC," no date, p. 2.

migrants are working the field on farms with which Campbell Soup contracts.[27]

The company prepared and released a detailed point-by-point response to each of these concerns. In that response, the company pointed out that concerns such as wages, housing, and pesticide application were the subject of federal or state standard or regulation. In addition, the company pointed out that it "enjoys good relations with the 9 unions in the U.S. with which it has 34 contracts covering more than 12,000 Campbell Soup employees" and that it "has a long history of involvement with day care centers, and presently underwrites the entire cost of three such centers in Northwest Ohio for the children of migrant workers."[28] Finally, it also noted that "of the 90 farmers in Northwest Ohio from whom Campbell buys tomatoes, only seven house and hire migrants" and that FLOC's contention that workers are paid an hourly wage of $1.96 is based on:

> ... a *1976* study when the federal minimum wage was $2.00. It was made by three students under the auspices of the American Friends Service Committee. In that study, the students clearly state that their findings were not definitive and that the study was not scientifically done.[29]

The key public relations events in the Consolidated Foods-Hanes campaign were the creation of the aforementioned "Citizens Commission on Justice at Hanes" and the holding of its first meeting. That meeting was held in Chicago, the headquarters of Consolidated Foods, and was well covered by the press who had been invited to attend. At that meeting, the commission members were presented with a report on the Hanes/Consolidated Food situation apparently prepared by Sister Maurer of the Sisters of Divine Providence.[30] In that report, the blame for the problems at Hanes was focused on the management of Consolidated Foods which was characterized as lacking in "concern for the communities or people affected by CFC-owned companies" and as relegating "people to mere objects in a vast money-making machine."[31] The report concluded with the following "action recommendations."

---

[27]*Ibid.,* pp. 1–3.
[28]*Ibid.,* pp. 2–3.
[29]*Ibid.,* p. 1.
[30]"Report to the Citizens Commission on Justice at Hanes, March 21, 1983, Chicago, Illinois," prepared by Sister Imelda Maurer, Connective Ministry Across the South (Bennettsville, SC).
[31]*Ibid.,* p. 5.

1) A full-scale fact finding mission that includes a series of on-site investigations in the towns with Hanes plants and that includes the participation of workers, local churches and groups, company personnel and community representatives...

2) A broad-based campaign to educate the general public—especially women's, religious, civil rights, consumer, labor and health organizations—about repetitive trauma disorders at Hanes...

3) A well-focused effort to dialogue with, and work in cooperation with, a selection of the company's major stockholders who are also concerned about issues of health and safety.[32]

The company's public response to this activity was one of denial. The company's formal position on the charges made in the report and previously at an annual meeting was "that there is simply no basis in fact to the charges made."[33] The CEO of Consolidated Foods declined the invitation to attend the meeting of the commission. Privately, however, the corporation decided to pursue a strategy of dialogue as opposed to denial or debate in responding to the campaign against it.

The first step in that counteroffensive was to deal with the potential adverse image effects of a "Citizens Commission on Justice at Hanes." To that end, the corporation retained a prominent black consultant whose first initiative was to contact the minority organizations and individuals on the commission and invite them to visit Hanes plants. His second initiative was to do the same with a number of prominent southern community leaders in an effort to secure their active interest and involvement in the Hanes situation. As a result of this latter effort, an "advisory council" to the company composed of prominent southern private citizens was formed less than three months after the first commission meeting.

The second step in that process was to open a dialogue with the religious organizations, as opposed to their individual members, that were involved in the campaign. The opportunity to pursue that strategy came in the form of a letter from the director of the Social Justice Office of the Sisters of Divine Providence requesting a description of measures taken and planned to eliminate stressful motion; a study of the incidence of repetitive motion trauma diseases at all Hanes plants, the results of which to be shared with her congregation; and a report on the relative earnings of male and female route sales personnel.[34] The corporation aggressively pursued that

---

[32]*Ibid.*, p. 11.

[33]Letter from John H. Bryan, Jr., Consolidated Foods Corporation, to Sister Imelda Maurer, Connective Ministry Across the South, dated November 4, 1982, p. 3.

[34]Letter from Sister Theresa Billeaud, Sisters of Divine Providence to John H. Bryan, Jr., Consolidated Foods Corporation, dated March 28, 1983.

opportunity and was able to establish a private dialogue with the organization, but not without some difficulty. That dialogue began with an initial meeting in San Antonio, the headquarters of the Sisters of Divine Providence, after which the company announced formation of a medical task force composed of nine doctors with specialized knowledge in the area of TRD to undertake an extensive study of the situation in Hanes plants and to issue a comprehensive report of its findings. Also subsequent to that meeting, the company launched a study of the earnings of route sales personnel which revealed, fortuitously, that on average women earned slightly more than men.

The Hanes campaign suggests that, although it may not be easy, companies like unions may be able to identify allies and engage in a measure of coalition building in the context of a coordinated campaign. It also suggests that it may be possible for companies to de-escalate conflict through actions designed to reduce emotional issues to empirical ones, at least where those actions are consistent with the stated concerns of the other party. There are substantial potential costs and risks associated with the "dialogue" strategy pursued by Hanes which make it unlikely that many companies will pursue that strategy as opposed to one of debate (Campbell) or denial (Beverly) until or unless the experience of others proves dialogue to be a cost-effective response to a coordinated corporate campaign.

COALITION FORMATION

The goal of coalition building is to expand the scope of a labor-management dispute horizontally by enlisting the support of individuals and institutions with no apparent immediate self-interest in the outcome of that dispute in condemning the philosophies, policies, and/or practices of the target company. At a minimum, the goal of this process is to add voices to the chorus of condemnation. The ideal result, however, is to place a disinterested party in the role of choir director in lieu of the interested party. This ideal result was achieved in the Litton campaign where the UE succeeded in getting the AFL-CIO, to which it does not belong, to lead a campaign which arose out of a contract dispute at one UE plant, and in the Hanes campaign where the Amalgamated Clothing and Textile Workers Union (ACTWU) allegedly was able to involve a religious order in a campaign in which the union's only apparent role was that of interested bystander.

The success of coalition building depends on the existence of influential individuals and institutions willing to be drawn into a union-management dispute on the union side. The ten cases studied clearly suggest there is no dearth of potential union allies who may be rallied to the cause in a corporate campaign. These cases also suggest that those potential allies fall into three categories: 1) other unions, including the AFL-CIO; 2) religious groups and organizations; 3) other special interest/activist groups and organizations. These three sets of union allies differ with respect to their apparent disinterest in the outcome of any union-management dispute, with unions being the least disinterested and other special interest groups seemingly the most disinterested. In light of that ranking, it is not surprising that religious groups and organizations were the most visibly active of the union's potential allies in the campaigns studied.

The Union Movement

The most obvious and accessible of the potential allies to a union undertaking a coordinated corporate campaign are the other member institutions and individuals of the American labor movement and possibly of foreign labor movements in the case of multinational companies. That does not mean that they are the most useful or powerful allies in the game of principle which is essentially a public relations game. The AFL-CIO maintains and publicizes "do not buy" and "dishonor roll of labor law violators" lists on which many of the target companies studied appeared at one time, but those lists directly reach only a limited and shrinking audience and normally are not the subject of interest by the mass media, with the apparent exception of the case of BASF.

The most effective support which unions can give to one another is secondary boycott or secondary bargaining activity, both of which are subject to relatively stringent restrictions at least under U.S. labor relations law. Given those restrictions, much of what unions have been able to do for one another in the context of corporate campaigns has been limited to moral support in the form of rallies and fund raisers. The epitome of such an event may well have been the premiere showing of the United Steelworkers (USW) videotape "We're Not Leaving" regarding its dispute with Phelps Dodge, which was developed for use in raising funds and sympathy for the replaced employees within the larger labor movement, at the AFL-CIO headquarters in March 1985 (cash bar, donations accepted).

The only campaign studied in which coalition building within the union movement played a major role was that conducted by the UE against Litton Industries in conjunction with a contract dispute at Litton's Sioux Falls microwave oven plant. That campaign began in February 1982 when union negotiators, having failed after 14 months of negotiations to reach agreement on an initial contract, told their company counterparts of the UE's intention to "do a number on the company." The UE's campaign over the following six months was concentrated in Sioux Falls, but extended to other communities in which the union had locals. The union launched a postcard campaign, asking members of its own locals to send preprinted postcards to the chairman and chief executive officer of the corporation, urging the company to adopt a more conciliatory stance in its negotiations with the union. In the course of this effort, the UE sought the support of local unions at other (non-UE) plants, generally without notable success. In the course of that effort, however, it did uncover other unions that had experienced organizing or bargaining setbacks at Litton locations. That common experience served as the foundation for the UE's successful effort to enlist the AFL-CIO, from which it was an outcast, as an ally in its battle with Litton.

The first step in that process took place on October 31, 1981 at an AFL-CIO Industrial Union Department (IUD)-Litton conference in Columbus, Ohio, reportedly attended by representatives of six AFL-CIO unions and two independent unions—the participants in the IUD's coalition bargaining efforts at Litton. The participants at that conference were presented with a report on Litton's labor policy apparently prepared by the UE which alleged that:

> Litton Industries has a long history of abusive labor policies and labor law violations. Over the years, a pattern of conduct has emerged that makes one thing clear: no group of Litton workers, even where there is currently a stable relationship, is safe from company union-busting.[35]

That conference and allegation was the first step in what was to be the UE's successful lobbying campaign to have organized labor make Litton's labor practices a major focus of union activities in the 1980s. The first evidence of the success of that effort was the informal agreement of the six AFL-CIO unions attending the conference to lend their individual moral support to a national UE corporate campaign against Litton Industries. The final step in that campaign came in November 1983 when the IUD assumed control and leader-

---

[35]"Report To Delegates, IUD-Litton Conference, October 30, 1981, Litton's Labor Policy," p. 1.

ship of the national campaign against Litton Industries on behalf of the now nine AFL-CIO unions supporting the UE's campaign. The decision of the IUD to take over the leadership of the campaign from the UE came shortly before Litton's 1983 shareholders' meeting and reportedly was the product of the fact that "over the past few months ... Litton angered other unions," as a result of which "several AFL-CIO unions asked the IUD to take charge."[36] Subsequent events, most notably at the shareholders' meeting, suggest that this decision may have been prompted more by the fact that the scope and direction of the campaign under the UE's leadership was embarrassing the AFL-CIO and possibly angering some of its affiliates, most notably its Metal Trades Council which held bargaining rights for 10,000 Litton workers at Ingalls Shipbuilding.

The apparent success of the UE in coalition building from a relatively small and isolated base into a much larger and broader labor movement contrasts quite dramatically with the experience of two other unions involved in the campaigns studied. The first of those is Local P-9 of the UFCW which was unable to secure any international union support for its corporate campaign against Hormel and which, when it was successful in drawing some support from members of other UFCW locals in the form of refusing to cross roving picket lines, only intensified its problems with its parent union. The second of those is OCAW which, as a part of its campaign against BASF has sought to enlist the assistance of unions representing workers and represented on the supervisory board at its parent German corporation. That effort apparently was not well served by OCAW's decision to compare the parent corporation and its American subsidiary to the "Nazi" company, which was their historical origin, as part of its effort to discredit the company at the Geismar, Louisiana site of its dispute with the company.

The Religious Community

The most consistent and often most persistent of the allies of unions in the campaigns studied were churches, church organizations, and church members. Support for union efforts came from a number of denominations, but particularly from the Catholic church whose representatives drew on the principles of Pope John Paul II's statement "On Human Work." Support for union causes came from both clergymen and laymen, but generally appeared to come primarily from the pulpit rather than the pews.

---

[36]"Labor Escalates Its Campaign Against Litton," *Business Week*, November 21, 1983, p. 51.

The other campaign in which a union allegedly was able to get another party to lead its cause was that against Consolidated Foods. The company's allegations that the Bennettsville Sisters were doing the union's as well as God's work, however, brought a sharp rebuttal from the head of their order in which she insisted that the sisters were simply

> ... concerned about the issues of industrial health and about women's, consumers' and workers' rights ... concerns of our Congregation for all people [which] are consistent with the teaching of our Church and, we believe, with the moral values of all persons of ethical conviction of whatever religious denomination.[37]

The widening of the Consolidated Foods campaign to other denominations in this case came about primarily through the involvement of the Interfaith Center on Corporate Responsibility (ICCR) whose membership includes some "17 protestant denominations and more than 170 Catholic communities," including the Sisters of Divine Providence.[38] Those members "agree that as investors in companies they are also part owners and therefore have the right and obligation to monitor social responsibility of corporations and act where necessary to correct corporate policies or practices causing social injury," primarily through shareholder resolutions.[39]

The leadership role played by religious organizations in the Hanes campaign is one of three such roles discernible in the campaigns studied. The second such role is that of partnership as found in the campaign against Litton Industries. That partnership began on a limited scale in the summer of 1982 when first the Catholic Archdiocese of Minneapolis and later the Greater Minneapolis Council of Churches expressed their concern over Litton's labor relations policies. By December of that year the ICCR had entered the picture and claimed to have played an important role in seeing that a shareholder proposal regarding corporate labor policy was on the agenda for the corporation's 1982 annual meeting. The partnership became far stronger in the summer of 1983 when Msgr. George C. Higgins of Catholic University published an article in the Catholic magazine, *America*, lauding the Litton campaign as "the best opportunity ... to give concrete support to working people in their struggle to organize and at the same time contribute to the longer-range goals of

---

[37]Letter from Sister Mary Margaret Hughes, Sisters of Divine Providence to Mr. John H. Bryan, Jr., Consolidated Foods Corporation, dated December 4, 1982, p. 1.
[38]Interfaith Center on Corporate Responsibility Information Brochure, p. 2.
[39]*Ibid.*, p. 2.

labor law justice and corporate social responsibility."[40] In light of that view, it is not surprising that at the November 1983 press conference at which the IUD was joined by Msgr. Higgins, "longtime official of the National Catholic Conference" in announcing that "representatives of labor and the religious community have joined together in . . . plans for new activities designed to highlight the anti-worker actions of Litton Industries."[41]

Msgr. Higgins was not the only member of the religious community to play a visible role in the Litton campaign, but his was by far the most important to the UE and the IUD. Evidence of that importance came to light after the end of the campaign in a case study of the public relations aspects of the campaign written by a master's degree student in journalism, Ms. Mary Ann Elliott, entitled "Dinosaur War: Litton Industries v. United Electrical Workers of America." In that case study, Ms. Elliott reconstructs an interview she held with Msgr. Higgins and reports that he indicated that he wrote the article for *America* because

> the unions wanted it. They wanted someone in the Catholic community because they wanted clergy involvement in the Sioux Falls thing. They felt it would be a breakthrough if the story were told in a responsible Catholic publication. The approach was that they could then use reprints in their publicity campaign.[42]

In that same case study, the author reported that when asked how he was so familiar with the Litton situation, Msgr. Higgins replied, "Actually Lance [Lance Compa, UE Washington representative] did most of the work. I had asked what I could do to help get the word around."[43]

The third possible role for the religious community in the context of a corporate campaign is that of apparently disinterested peacemaker. Such a role does not involve an open alliance with a union, only actions designed to keep lines of communication and avenues for compromise open, usually in the face of management rather than union resistance. It was this type of role which religious groups played in the FLOC campaign against Campbell Soup. In the long course of FLOC's efforts to involve Campbell Soup in the union's efforts to organize employees of Campbell's suppliers, the Catholic

---

[40]George C. Higgins, "The Litton Campaign: Unions United," *America*, August 27, 1983, p. 88.

[41]Industrial Union Department, AFL-CIO, National Litton Campaign, News Release, November 16, 1983.

[42]Mary Ann Elliott, "Dinosaur War: Litton Industries v. United Electrical Workers of America," unpublished term paper, copy supplied to company.

[43]*Ibid.*

church in general, and its Boston Archdiocese in particular, was instrumental in convincing the company to enter into and continue informal private discussions with the leader of FLOC. When those discussions produced no concrete results and the scene of confrontation moved from the farms of Ohio and Michigan to Campbell's headquarters in Camden, the Quaker church allegedly provided the union with office space from which to carry on its increasingly public dialogue with the corporation. Finally, the National Council of Churches offered to mediate the dispute. That offer was accepted and led to an agreement that a commission be established to "find a basis to resolve the various differences" between FLOC and Campbell whose members "shall be prominent Americans representing the Protestant church, the Catholic church, Hispanics, agriculture, labor, business, academia and economics."[44] In this context, it is interesting to note that the commission concluded its first report as follows:

> The Commission commends the various religious organizations for their concern with the social and economic status of migrant workers in our society and their dedication to the improvement of the condition of life and work of migrants and their families. The Commission calls upon these religious organizations and other interested parties to maintain their interest and financial support.[45]

The Social Activists

There is no dearth of social activist or special interest groups or individuals who might be willing to ally themselves with a union in a campaign against a corporation. The fact that such groups or individuals typically represent some special interest or constituency may limit their usefulness in such a campaign, unless that special interest or constituency also has special significance to the target corporation. Thus, it is not surprising that while various of these individuals and groups have been involved in coordinated campaigns, they have not played a central role in the campaigns studied.

The most ambitious attempts to secure the support of social activist and special interest groups took place in the campaign against Hanes/Consolidated Foods. Early in the course of that campaign, the Bennettsville Sisters announced the formation of a Citizen's Commission of Justice at Hanes composed of such noted activists as Bella Abzug, Julian Bond, Gloria Steinem, and Studs Terkel, as well

---

[44]Understanding Establishing a Commission to Resolve Differences, dated May 6, 1985, p. 1.

[45]Commission Report, dated February 19, 1986, p. 3.

as representatives of such activist groups as the Southern Christian Leadership Conference, the National Council of Negro Women, and the National Organization of Women Against Pornography. That Commission, which seems to have been patterned after the Southerners for Economic Justice utilized in the J. P. Stevens campaign, held its initial meeting in Chicago, the corporate headquarters of Consolidated Foods, in March 1983. The Commission itself, however, does not appear to have played much more than a public relations role in the campaign. In May 1983, an article in the *Winston-Salem Journal* noted that "a panel of prominent social activists formed to focus attention on working conditions at Hanes Corp.'s Southern textile plants apparently hasn't been up to much since it was launched two months ago" and went on to indicate that "so far a consensus seems to be far from developing among the commission members . . . [whose] attitudes range from strident to indifferent."[46]

The unions involved in the other campaigns studied did not pursue a similarly ambitious and overt strategy of soliciting the support of social activists. Whether solicited or unsolicited, welcome or unwelcome, many of those campaigns attracted the attention of special interest groups. The UE, in its Litton campaign, held a series of rallies on college campuses aimed at the corporation's academic directors to which it invited and welcomed all interested parties. The result of these and other rallies, in the view of the union, was to demonstrate "the potential to unite trade unions, the women's movement, the civil rights movement, the peace movement and other activist forces in a struggle against the unchecked exercise of corporate power."[47] While the UE welcomed the support of the peace movement, that was not a particularly comfortable alliance for the IUD in its Litton campaign or for the UAW in its campaign against General Dynamics. By contrast, the support of environmental groups was welcomed by the unions in the campaigns against Louisiana-Pacific and Phelps Dodge as was the case with respect to the interest shown by senior citizen groups in the campaign against Beverly Enterprises.

---

[46]John Byrd, "Panel Slow in Investigating Work Conditions At Hanes," *Winston-Salem Journal*, May 22, 1983, p. G-1.

[47]Lance Compa "How To Fight a Unionbusting Conglomerate," *The Nation*, July 16, 1983, p. 41.

CHAPTER III

The Game of Politics

The treatise of the AFL-CIO Industrial Union Department (IUD) on coordinated corporate campaigns envisions a potentially significant role for appeals to the various branches of government (executive, legislative, and judicial) at all levels (federal, state, and local) as a means to "embarrass" a target company or to make it "uncomfortable." Specifically, that work refers to actions by regulatory agencies "which monitor nearly every aspect of corporate behavior," legislative initiatives including "oversight hearings, petitions and public referendums," and using the courts.[1] In the campaigns studied there were numerous instances of appeals to the executive and legislative branches of government but not to the courts—a tactic whose practical value remains to be tested.

The game of politics, as played in the campaigns studied, has been much like the game of principle. The goal of both games has been to raise an issue and force the target company to emerge from anonymity to defend itself against charges of misconduct. In the case of the game of politics the misconduct in question becomes a matter for not only social disapproval but also governmental action in the public interest. In that sense, it may be viewed as a special case of coalition building and conflict escalation—one which, if successful, places the target company in an adversarial relationship to the government. Such a relationship, however familiar, is likely to be burdensome, unproductive, and unwelcome.

THE EXECUTIVE BRANCH

In viewing the executive branch of government as a possible ally in coordinated corporate campaigns, the IUD focuses attention on regulatory agencies and largely ignores the possibility of non-regulatory executive branch intervention in labor disputes. Specifically, it ignores the possibility that top elected or appointed execu-

---

[1]Industrial Union Department, AFL-CIO, *Developing New Tactics: Winning With Coordinated Corporate Campaigns* (Washington, D.C.: Industrial Union Department, AFL-CIO, 1985), pp. 6–7.

tive branch officials might provide a source of sympathy or support in a campaign. It may be that this is not a serious oversight given the political tenor of the times in the nation's capital, as the United Automobile Workers (UAW) learned when its appeal to the Secretary of Defense to ask General Dynamics to pursue a more conciliatory course went unheeded,[2] but it overlooks the possibility of ad hoc intervention by governors or mayors in labor disputes within their political jurisdiction, as did occur in a few of the cases studied.

It is not uncommon for the governor of a state to be drawn into a labor dispute, particularly where a company's decision to operate during a strike produces threats of mass picketing and violence which necessitate the use of state police and national guard to establish and ensure ingress and egress at the site. This was the case in the disputes at Phelps Dodge and Hormel. In both of those disputes, the governors in question did utilize the national guard to keep peace, but in the course of that peace-keeping process they were also prevailed upon to arrange "cooling-off periods" during which the company agreed to suspend operations. In both cases, they were also asked to make peace by the unions in the form of involving themselves in the merits of the union's demands and company's offer. In both cases, they declined that invitation. That was not the case at BASF where when the governor was pressed by the union for a statement on the situation at Geismar, Louisiana, and, when informed of the wages employees there earned, reportedly decided the company's offer was fair and recommended that the union accept it.[3]

If unions have drawn only limited support from state governors on the front line of the confrontations underlying campaigns, they have fared slightly better behind the lines. When the issue of community safety was raised in the BASF campaign, the lieutenant governor of the state reportedly indicated that he would "oppose any measure to get tax exemptions for BASF unless they changed."[4] In the campaign against Beverly Enterprises the governor of the state of Michigan was willing to receive the aforementioned report, "Beverly Enterprises in Michigan—a Case Study of Corporate Takeover of Health Care Resources," and its related requests for changes in the state's licensing, certification, and reimbursement policies for nursing homes, but made no statement of support for those changes.

---

[2]"News from the UBC," press release issued June 26, 1984, p. 2.

[3]"Wyandotte Continues Lockout," *The Baton Rouge Morning Advocate*, June 27, 1984, p. 2-B.

[4]"BASF Wyandotte a Hazard, Says Striking Union," *The Baton Rouge Morning Advocate*, February 19, 1985.

The National Labor Relations Board

The National Labor Relations Board (NLRB) is one regulatory agency which almost routinely becomes involved in the types of labor disputes underlying corporate campaigns, typically through the filing of unfair labor practice charges by unions and/or managements. Beyond that, it would seem that the NLRB would have little role to play in a broader corporate campaign. That was not the case, however, in the original campaign against Stevens or the subsequent campaign against Litton, both of which involved a question of whether the target company should be treated as a single- or multiple-employer by the NLRB—a question of some significance in assessing liability for unfair labor practices and in ascertaining whether an employer falls within the secondary boycott protections of the National Labor Relations (Taft-Hartley) Act. The secondary boycott protections of that act more recently have served to involve the NLRB in another campaign—that against Hormel—but on the side of the company at least to this point.

The United Electrical, Radio and Machine Workers (UE), armed with the allegations contained in the Craypo report, began a campaign in the summer of 1982 to try to convince the NLRB that Litton Industries should be treated as a single, centrally-controlled enterprise under the NLRA rather than as an array of independent employers. In July and August of that year, the UE claimed that "union supporters rallied at N.L.R.B. regional offices throughout the country to back up a formal union request that the board institute a strong company-wide approach in dealing with Litton."[5] Whether such rallies indeed did occur throughout the country is an open question, but they did occur in Hartford and Minneapolis. In any event, on August 5, 1982, "representatives of a number of labor organizations met with members of the [Board's] General Counsel staff regarding Litton Industries, Inc." to express their view "that the Board's handling of Litton cases is inadequate."[6]

The August meeting produced no tangible result until March 10, 1983, when the NLRB's general counsel issued instructions to the Board's regional offices to search their files for all Litton cases for a special study of the corporation's record. In May of that year the staff of the general counsel of the NLRB completed its review of

---

[5]Lance Compa, "How to Fight a Unionbusting Conglomerate," *The Nation*, July 16, 1983, p. 40.

[6]NLRB internal memorandum from Richard A. Siegel, Deputy Assistant General Counsel to Joseph E. DeSio, Associate General Counsel, subject: Litton Industries, May 17, 1983, p. 1.

Litton cases identified by the regional offices and concluded it was not

> ... possible to reach any firm conclusions regarding the control exercised by Litton Industries, Inc., over the labor relations of its subsidiaries or divisions. Nor is it possible to conclude either that Litton Industries, Inc., is virulently anti-union or is a notorious labor law violator as the Unions claim.[7]

That staff report, also stated that, "our review of the cases does, however, raise certain suspicions ..."[8] On the basis of those suspicions, the staff recommended in September the institution of special procedures to monitor and respond to the concerns and requests of labor organizations. Such special procedures were instituted by the general counsel in a memorandum to NLRB regional offices dated October 31, 1983.[9] The following day the term of office of that general counsel ended and nothing more was heard of the Litton matter. Throughout that matter, the company's public response to the NLRB's actions was that its record before the Board was nothing special and that the general counsel's memoranda were "not anything all that new."[10] Privately, however, the company did file a Freedom of Information Act request with the NLRB for all materials in its file—a request which produced much of the information cited above.

The general counsel of the NLRB also played a role in the Louisiana-Pacific campaign. The company's decision to hire permanent replacements to operate its struck facilities left the union vulnerable to decertification elections. In an effort to forestall or prevent such elections, the union sought and secured a standing order from the general counsel of the NLRB to regional directors to file an unfair labor practice complaint against Louisiana-Pacific for "bad faith bargaining."[11] In May 1984, after the general counsel's term in office had expired, the acting general counsel of the NLRB revoked that order, paving the way for decertification elections at nine facilities. The union threatened to challenge the acting general counsel's action in court, but was unsuccessful in so doing.[12] Eventually,

---

[7]*Ibid.*, p. 6.

[8]*Ibid.*

[9]NLRB Office of the General Counsel memorandum to all Regional Directors, subject: Litton Industries, memorandum GC 83-18, October 31, 1983.

[10]"Labor Escalates Its Campaign Against Litton," *Business Week*, November 21, 1983, p. 51.

[11]"News from the UBC," press release issued June 26, 1984, p. 2.

[12]"Electric Boat Hires 400 Replacements for Draftsmen at Connecticut Shipyard," *White Collar Report*, Vol. 54 (August 26, 1983), p. 179.

decertification elections were held in all nineteen of the company's struck facilities which continued in operation. Certification of the results of those elections was delayed by the union challenges of ballots and charges of election misconduct, as also was the case at Phelps Dodge, but to little avail.

The NLRB's involvement in the campaign by Local P-9 of the UFCW against Hormel is an equally complex question of interpretation of labor law. The case arose out of a decision by Local P-9 to picket the offices and branches of a bank with which Hormel does business in two states, Minnesota and Iowa, where it has plants. That decision and resulting action led to a complaint by the NLRB regional director in Minneapolis in 1985[13] that the union engaged in unlawful secondary boycott activity designed to coerce the bank to cease doing business with Hormel. Late in that year a hearing was held before an administrative law judge on that charge, in the course of which the union defended its actions primarily on the grounds of the close business ties between the bank and Hormel which, in its view, made the two allies, if not a single employer, under board policy regarding secondary boycotts. The administrative law judge, finding little or no evidence of direct bank stock ownership or policy control in Hormel, was unpersuaded and upheld the charge of unlawful secondary boycotting against Local P-9 early in 1986.[14] In the fall of 1986, the NLRB sustained and extended the administrative law judge's finding of unlawful conduct.[15]

The general counsel of the NLRB more recently has been called upon by BASF to rule "on the validity under Section 8(b)(3) of an anti-employer campaign as virulent and extensive as this one."[16] In its charge filed with the NLRB regional director in New Orleans, the company stated that, "the course of conduct followed by OCAW in furtherance of its coordinated campaign, taken as a whole, far transcends the withholding of labor or other legitimate means to bring economic pressure to bear on BASF in support of its bargaining position in the labor dispute, and is inconsistent with good faith bargaining."[17] The company requested that a "complaint should be

[13]"UFCW's Continued Picketing at Bank Results in Second ULP Complaint," *Daily Labor Report*, No. 206 (October 24, 1985), p. A-5.

[14]"UFCW Local Unlawfully Picketed Banks in Dispute with Hormel, NLRB ALJ Rules," *Daily Labor Report*, No. 53 (March 19, 1986), pp. A-2–A-4.

[15]Local P-9 United Food and Commercial Workers, 281 N.L.R.B. No. 135 (1986).

[16]Letter from Mr. William R. D'Armond of the firm of Kean, Miller, Hawthorne, D'Armond, McCowan and Jarman, attorneys at law, to Mr. Hugh Frank Malone, Regional Director, National Labor Relations Board Region 15, New Orleans, Louisiana, dated May 17, 1986, Appendix I. p. 134.

[17]*Ibid.*

issued so the Board can resolve this important question."[18] On September 19, 1986, the general counsel of the NLRB informed the company by letter that "use of a corporate campaign by a union to assist in meeting its goals at the bargaining table does not violate the Act."[19]

The Department of State

If the NLRB is the first executive branch agency expected to be drawn into a labor dispute, the Department of State has to be the last. Nonetheless, that is where that department has been thrust as a result of the OCAW-IUD coordinated campaign against BASF. The international dimensions of that campaign were described by the company in its unfair labor practice charge in the following terms:

> OCAW has attempted to circumvent American Law and to cause different international legal standards to be imposed upon the negotiations, and to publicly embarrass BASF in international forums, by filing and processing a complaint with the organization for economic and Cooperative Development [sic] (OECD—a multi-national organization) through the U.S. State Department, and by that means has also sought to publicly embarrass BASF on an international basis.[20]

The internationalization of OCAW's campaign against BASF began in late 1984 when the union scheduled a meeting with German embassy officials in Washington. Those officials heard the union's case and subsequently that of the company. The embassy officials were in no position to act on the matter other than to submit a report to the German government outlining the nature and international character of the dispute.

The second step in the internationalization of the BASF campaign came in the spring of 1985 when the union filed a complaint against the company for violation of the guidelines of the Organization for Economic Cooperation and Development (OECD) on international business conduct. That complaint was made in a letter from the union to the Office of Investment Affairs of the Department of State which is the U.S. National Contact Point of the OECD. In that letter the union cited four cases of NLRB charges against the company which it argued constituted evidence of a pattern of anti-union activity by the company. Thus, the BASF dispute appears to concern

---

[18]*Ibid.*
[19]"NLRB General Counsel Dismisses Charges Stemming from Union Campaign Against BASF." *Daily Labor Report,* No. 195 (October 8, 1986), p. A-8.
[20]Letter from Mr. Willaim R. D'Armond, Appendix I. p. 133.

Paragraph 1 of the OECD guidelines, which reads:

> Enterprises should: respect the right of their employees to be repre-
> sented by trade unions and other bona fide organisations of employ-
> ees, and engage in constructive negotiations, either individually or
> through employers' associations, with such employee organisations
> with a view to reaching agreements on employment conditions, which
> should include provisions for dealing with disputes arising over the
> interpretation of such agreements, and for ensuring mutually
> respected rights and responsibilities.[21]

The Anglo-American tradition pertaining to recognition, bargaining
rights, strikes and lockouts, etc. is considerably more adversarial
than many continental European systems, and this fact has caused
problems with unions that wish Anglo-American practice were
otherwise.

The company was compelled by its particular circumstances to
take this matter quite seriously. The OECD has no power to discipline or sanction a company which violates its guidelines. Nonetheless, any OECD action implying that such a violation had occurred
could result in a substantial amount of bad press both in the United
States and, more importantly, in Germany and the European Economic Community where the OECD is a more imposing presence
than in the U.S. Thus, the company expended considerable energy in
preparing to defend itself at the hearing on the union's complaint
which was held on May 31, 1985, in Washington. The result of that
hearing was a decision by the National Contact Point to table the
issue while it studied its charter to determine whether it had jurisdiction in the matter.

In December 1985, a reconstituted U.S. National Contact Point
submitted to its German counterpart a selection of union and company materials pertaining to the BASF situation at Geismar, Louisiana, but without taking any position with respect to that situation.
The German National Contact Point responded regarding the matter
in early 1986, when it held a meeting with company representatives.
In that meeting the company took the position that it does not influence the decisions of the management of its subsidiaries in questions
of labor relations and that disputes concerning labor relations had to
be settled through the competent national disputes mechanisms.
That position was an obvious reference to the fact that the nine
employment and industrial relations guidelines are preceded by the

---

[21]Duncan C. Campbell and Richard L. Rowan, *Multinational Enterprises and the
OECD Industrial Relations Guidelines*, (Philadelphia: Industrial Research Unit,
Wharton School, University of Pennsylvania, 1983) pp. 35–54.

following language: "Enterprises should, within the framework of
law, regulations and prevailing labour relations and employment
practices, in each of the countries in which they operate..."[22] This
language has come to be known as the "chapeau clause" as it "tops
off" as would a hat the specific guidelines that follow it. Of greater
significance is the interpretation of the clause. Business/employer
interests say that at the very least the chapeau clause means that
what we are to make of the *specific meaning* of each individual
guideline can only be suggested by the national context in which the
subsidiary operates—not by some supranational standard implied, if
not imposed by the (voluntary!) guidelines.

The Alphabet Soup

The IUD treatise on coordinated campaigns states, quite cor-
rectly, that "businesses are regulated by a virtual alphabet soup of
federal, state, and local agencies..." and points out that, as a result
of complaints to such agencies, "an intransigent employer may find
that in addition to labor troubles, there are suddenly government
problems as well."[23] In the sample of campaigns studied, there was
frequent mention of such regulatory agencies and/or the types of
business behavior they are supposed to regulate. The actual involvement of those agencies as a salient element in those campaigns was,
with the exception of the BASF and Litton campaigns, remarkably
limited, perhaps because either the unions or agencies involved
heeded the IUD's admonition that "it is important to make sure that
any complaints the union makes are valid."[24]

The regulatory issue raised most frequently in the campaigns
studied was occupational safety and health. That issue was central
in the Hanes campaign and became an issue in the General
Dynamics campaign. Allegations of "unsafe operation" were made
in four other campaigns (BASF, Hormel, Louisiana-Pacific, and
Phelps Dodge), all of which were products of company decisions to
operate during a strike/lockout. The only serious involvement of regulatory agencies was in the first two cases and in both of those it
came independent of rather than as a result of the coordinated campaign. In the Hanes case the company and the Occupational Safety
and Health Administration (OSHA) had agreed that a problem
existed and agreed on a corrective action program before the campaign even began—a fact which was ignored throughout the course

[22]*Ibid.*, pp. 238–241.
[23]Industrial Union Department, AFL-CIO, *Developing New Tactics*, p. 6.
[24]*Ibid.*

of that campaign. In the General Dynamics case, the death of a worker engaged in an operation in which other workers had previously been overcome by toxic fumes provided the union with an opportunity to charge not only the company but the Michigan Safety and Health Administration with "criminal negligence"—a charge which may or may not have influenced a subsequent decision by the state to charge the company with involuntary manslaughter and willful violation of state safety standards.

A second point of potential regulatory vulnerability probed in a few of the campaigns studied is that of environmental pollution. The union's allusion to the possibility of a Bhopal-type disaster at BASF's Geismar facility might be placed in this category, although neither this community safety issue nor its related occupational safety issue became a matter for serious regulatory attention. Of greater regulatory importance to the company, as indicated in its unfair labor practice charge, was that:

> OCAW has repeatedly sought to injure the ability of BASF to properly conduct its business by seeking to cause government agencies to deny to BASF needed environmental permits, bond issue authorization and other governmental approvals.[25]

Two other target companies reported problems or delays in securing federal or state environmental licensing to commence or continue operation of a facility. In early 1984, the United Brotherhood of Carpenters (UBC) claimed that in its campaign against Louisiana-Pacific, "an air permit challenge by the Colorado State Council of Carpenters and environmental [challenges] have slowed the progress of the Montrose, Colorado, [waferboard] facility."[26] In May of that year, the UBC was able to enlist the aid of the Sierra Club in opposing a company request for a variance from the EPA requirement for secondary treatment of wastewater at its Samoa, California, pulp mill.[27] Phelps Dodge was the second company to report an unusual delay in approval of its application for an environmental operating permit from the state for one of its existing facilities. Both firms reported other delays and difficulties in dealing with state regulatory/licensing agencies above and beyond the bureaucratic norm after they became targets of corporate campaigns, but neither

---

[25]Letter from Mr. William R. D'Armond, Appendix I, p. 133.

[26]"Carpenter's L-P Strike Campaign," handout distributed at a Wall Street rally, March 22, 1984, p. 3.

[27]Letter from Ms. Judith Kunofsky, National Conservation Representative, Sierra Club to Mr. Harry A. Merlo, Chairman, Louisiana-Pacific Corporation, May 9, 1984, copy to Mr. Ed. Durkin, Industrial Union Department, AFL-CIO.

indicated that such delays or difficulties, per se, had altered their operations or plans.

A third point of potential regulatory vulnerability for a target company is its shareholder relations—the province of the Securities and Exchange Commission (SEC) and related state agencies. The SEC was involved in a number of the campaigns studied by virtue of its regulatory authority to rule on shareholder resolutions and to require the provision of shareholder lists to those making such resolutions. Beyond that "mundane" involvement, the SEC was drawn into the Beverly Enterprises campaign by a union complaint that the company may have failed to notify the public of the campaign against it and of the potential impact of that campaign as part of its offering of $70 million of debt in March, 1984.[28] If there is a state analogy to the SEC in the context of corporate campaigns it has to be the New York State system of insurance company regulation, as was proven in the case of the campaign against J. P. Stevens. Under the New York State law, a vote of all policy holders is required in the event of a contested election for seats on the board of directors of a mutual insurance company. In the Stevens case, the union threatened to cost the Metropolitan Life Insurance Company several millions of dollars in such "election expenses" by proposing two alternative candidates for that company's board of directors to protest the membership of Metropolitan's chairman on the board of J. P. Stevens, which reportedly led him to act "behind the scenes to persuade or encourage Stevens managers to reach a prompt settlement with the union."[29]

There are numerous other points of vulnerability to financial regulation. The BASF unfair labor practice charge cited denial of bond issue authorization. Two other firms reported similar difficulties— Louisiana-Pacific, with respect to an Urban Development Action Grant in Mississippi, and Beverly Enterprises, with respect to state industrial development bond funding in Massachusetts. In addition, BASF also charged that "OCAW sought to block the acquisition by BASF of another company... by making complaint to the U.S. Justice Department alleging that the acquisition would violate antitrust laws, and by filing a complaint on the subject with the OECD."[30]

---

[28]"Unions Net One of Ten Votes at Beverly Annual Meeting," *White Collar Report*, Vol. 53, No. 17 (April 29, 1983), p. 430.

[29]Neil W. Chamberlain and James W. Kuhn, *Collective Bargaining* (New York: McGraw-Hill Book Company, 1986), p. 35.

[30]Letter from Mr. William R. D'Armond, Appendix I, p. 133.

THE LEGISLATIVE BRANCH

The possibility of a legislated solution to the problems which give rise to a coordinated campaign was tried and almost came to pass in the J. P. Stevens case in the form of the AFL-CIO's campaign for "Labor Law Reform." The near success and ultimate failure of labor law reform point out both the promise and pitfalls of turning to the legislative branch of government for support in a labor-management dispute. The IUD has recognized both in pointing out:

> While the legislative route may appear to be a roundabout means of pressuring a corporation, the detour may prove worthwhile, if congress, a state legislature, a city council, a public utility commission or a revenue bond authority takes up the union's cause.[31]

The sample of campaigns studied provides few, if any, examples of legislative bodies or general publics living up to the hopes of the IUD. In the course of its campaign, Louisiana-Pacific was the subject of unfavorable city council resolutions in two of the almost twenty communities in which it operated struck facilities. The Campbell Soup Company suffered similar setbacks in four of seven referendums on its corporate behavior held on college campuses including Michigan and Notre Dame. The fact that Congress has not proven particularly helpful in the campaigns studied, however, does not mean that individual members of committees of Congress have not been involved in the form of inquiries, investigations, or hearings regarding issues raised in the course of those campaigns.

Legislative Initiatives

The corporate campaign against Litton Industries paralleled that against J. P. Stevens not only with respect to the involvement of the NLRB but also with respect to the involvement of Congress in an effort to bar the target company from receiving government contracts. In the case of Litton that legislative initiative began with a letter from Representative Burton (D-Cal.) to the company requesting its response to charges levelled against it by the UE. The company did respond, as requested, with a fairly detailed denial of the union's charges. That response, in turn, produced a letter from Representative (now Senator) Simon (D-Ill.) who took up the union's cause after the sudden death of Representative Burton in the summer of 1982. In that letter, Representative Simon conveyed to the company the UE's rebuttal of the company's denial of the union's

---

[31]Industrial Union Department, *Developing New Tactics*, p. 6.

charges and his own view that there was strong and growing sentiment in Washington that labor law violators should not be rewarded
with government contracts.

Representative Simon gave substance to his view when, on March
1, 1983, he introduced HR 1743 to debar repeated labor law violators
from holding government contracts—contracts which accounted for
more than a quarter of Litton's sales. Ten days later the general
counsel of the NLRB issued his instruction to regional offices to
search their files for all Litton cases for a special study of the corporation's labor law record. Approximately one month after that action
was taken, subcommittee hearings were held on HR 1743 at which
the unions involved in the campaign testified basically more against
Litton than in support of the bill. It was at those hearings that the
corporation was first formally given "the dubious distinction of having displaced J. P. Stevens as America's No. 1 labor law violator."[32]

The company was invited to testify at the hearing on HR 1743 but
declined that invitation. Its public position on the debarment initiative was that it was unjustified and would "not get off the ground."[33]
That view ultimately proved accurate as HR 1743 never reached the
floor of the House. It was, however, voted out of subcommittee on
October 31, 1983—the same day the general counsel of the NLRB
instituted the special procedures to monitor Litton cases. Neither of
these two political aspects of the campaign against Litton produced
concrete results. Whatever else they may have achieved remains an
open question.

The campaign against Beverly Enterprises involved a legislative
initiative akin to debarment at the state level. In the "profiteering
on public money" section of the unions' study of Beverly Enterprises in Michigan,[34] it was reported that Beverly's profits per
patient per day were nearly 30 percent above the industry average
and its facility costs were 22 percent above the state Medicaid average, with much of that 22 percent differential attributed to a high
level of interest expense. In addition, the report indicated that the
firm's administrative expenses were high and had risen by 26 percent in 1982, with most of that increase attributable to increases in
overhead charges for Beverly's (out-of-state) home office expense. On

[32]Tamar Lewin, "Litton's Angry Labor Conglomerate," *New York Times*, April 24,
1983, p. F-1.

[33]"Testing a New Weapon Against Litton," *Business Week*, December 27, 1982,
p. 32.

[34]Food and Beverage Trades Department, AFL-CIO, "Beverly Enterprises in
Michigan: A Case Study of Corporate Take-over of Health Care Resources," released
September 26, 1983, pp. 2.1–2.15.

the basis of those findings the unions put forth the following regulatory proposals: 1) a provision for yearly audits of home office and patient care expenses and other financial records; 2) a 10 percent cap on administrative expenses similar to that imposed in Minnesota; and 3) a regulation, similar to one adopted in New York, which effectively precludes out-of-state corporations from operating nursing homes.[35] While none of these proposals were adopted prior to the end of the Beverly campaign, it is not possible to conclude that they had no effect on the outcome of that campaign.

Legislative Investigations

It is unnecessary to put forth specific legislative proposals to involve the legislative branch in a corporate campaign. All that may be required to secure such involvement is the ability to arouse sufficient interest on the part of a congressman or congressional committee in a potential problem which might require legislative redress to lead them to make inquiry, launch investigation, or hold hearings to determine the nature and magnitude of the alleged problem. Any of those "oversight" actions provides a union with a public forum in which to state its case against a target company independent of the ultimate outcome, or lack thereof, of the action in question. For example, when the unions involved in the Beverly campaign utilized the release of the study of the firm's patient care record to issue a public call for an investigation of health care chains by the House Energy and Commerce Committee, that request was reported in the media—the outcome or, more accurately, non-outcome of that request was not.

The campaign against BASF, like that against Litton, has involved legislative as well as regulatory actions against the company. In addition to its international regulatory thrust, the campaign against BASF has also entailed a determined effort to secure a congressional investigation of union charges that the company was "gambling with human lives" in its Geismar operations as evidenced by the company's charge that "OCAW caused a congressional investigation of BASF's safety record and practices during the lockout (when no union-represented employees were at work) for the purpose of harassing BASF and injuring its reputation."[36]

---

[35]Statement by John J. Sweeny, President, Service Employees International Union, Lansing, Michigan, September 9, 1983, p. 3.

[36]Letter from Mr. William R. D'Armond, Appendix I. p. 133.

The safety issue first emerged in early 1985 when the union alleged that the Geismar facility was an unsafe facility containing many inherent workplace hazards which were compounded by the fact that, since the lockout, the company was operating with "people off the streets" who were inexperienced in chemical processes and operations.[37] The union's allegations were not well served by the announcement one week later that the plant had won BASF's highest award for safety by operating without a lost time accident in 1984—the second consecutive year in which it recorded no such accidents. Undaunted, the union claimed that the plant had achieved its good safety record by misrepresenting accident data and concealing such misrepresentations from the government in violation of the Occupational Safety and Health Act.[38] It was on the basis of this alleged violation of federal statute law that the union appealed to Congress to take an interest in the Geismar situation.

The union's charges reportedly led some members of Congress to make public their intention to punish companies which misreport or conceal safety and health problems with fines and prison sentences. One of those congressmen was Representative John Conyers (D-Mich.) who formally demanded from the company an answer to allegations of wanton disregard for safety, contained in a 150-page report submitted to him by OCAW, and scheduled a House subcommittee hearing on that subject. The company did respond to Representative Conyers' demand with a report just as detailed as that submitted by OCAW. Beyond that the company also briefed the leadership of the Senate Labor Committee and the entire Louisiana legislative delegation and all the minority members of Representative Conyers' subcommittee. All the members of the Louisiana delegation and the subcommittee were given copies of the company's response which was also presented to and discussed with the press at a Washington press conference.

The Labor and Education Committee of the House of Representatives provided the UAW with a forum to ask the Congress to "require more acceptable behavior by General Dynamics" as part of the UAW's campaign against that company. In June of 1984, UAW President Owen Bieber appeared before a subcommittee of that committee where he stated:

> When a company can charge outrageous prices, when it pays no income tax while making more than 30 percent return on equity, when

---

[37]"BASF Wyandotte a Hazard, Says Striking Union, *The Baton Rouge Morning Advocate,* February 19, 1985.

[38]"Union Sees Hazards at Louisiana Plant," *New York Times,* December 20, 1985, p. A-26.

it has a cozy relationship with its main customer, and when it can pass along as a reimbursable expense the cost of opposing improved working conditions, then the deck is stacked against the worker and they must look beyond the bargaining table to correct the situation.[39]

The fact that the U.S. House of Representatives has been the focal point of the game of politics on the legislative side is hardly surprising given its political composition and public visibility. It is not, however, the only possible source of legislative involvement in corporate campaigns as was demonstrated by the ability of the Carpenters to seek and secure legislative assistance at the local, state, and federal levels in their campaign against Louisiana-Pacific. At the local level, the union was the beneficiary of city council resolutions in two of the company's locations in support of the strike. At the state level it was able to link a Wall Street rally to a hearing by the New York State Assembly Labor Committee on the "Plight of the Collective Bargaining System" to gain an added measure of exposure and sympathy for its cause. Finally, it was also successful in getting the Labor-Management Subcommittee of the House Education and Labor Committee to launch a "preliminary investigation of the company's use of Urban Development Action grants from the U.S. Department of Housing and Urban Development to help finance its waferboard . . . facilities in the states of Minnesota, Michigan and Mississippi."[40]

---

[39]"House Digs At GD Sins," *UAW Washington Report*, Vol. 24, No. 25 (June 22, 1984), p. 1.
[40]"Carpenter's L-P Strike Campaign," handout at rally, p. 3.

CHAPTER IV

The Game of Protest

A third tactic identified by the IUD in its treatise on coordinated corporate campaigns is "stockholder actions."[1] Such actions generally are part of a broader strategy of "confrontation with owners/management."[2] The goal of this strategy is to draw higher levels of corporate governance of the target company into the dispute and into the public view. The game of politics is one designed to expand conflict horizontally by securing government involvement. The game of protest, by contrast, is one designed to expand conflict vertically by securing managerial/ownership intervention in the dispute. As such, it is a game whose success depends on the vulnerabilities of various levels of the organizational control structure.

The process of appealing to higher corporate authority, as observed in the campaigns studied, may take any or all of three forms: 1) an appeal to corporate management over the heads of division management; 2) an appeal to corporate directors, collectively or individually, over the heads of corporate operating management; and 3) an appeal to company shareholders over the heads of both managers and directors. Such appeals may be made sequentially or simultaneously as well as in any combination. The ultimate play in the game, however, typically is the threat or actual submission of a shareholder resolution for action at the annual meeting—a tactic long favored and utilized by the Interfaith Center on Corporate Responsibility.

There are a number of means which have been used to appeal to higher authority including letter writing campaigns directed at the corporate chief executive officer, designed to force both public acknowledgment of and responsibility for a problem, and protest marches, rallies, and other demonstrations designed to focus public and media attention on the same matters. There is one event which affords unions an opportunity to do both simultaneously—the

---

[1]Industrial Union Department, AFL-CIO, *Developing New Tactics: Winning With Coordinated Corporate Campaigns* (Washington, D.C.: Industrial Union Department, AFL-CIO, 1985), p. 9.

[2]James A. Craft and Marian M. Extejt, "New Strategies In Union Organizing," *Journal of Labor Research*, Vol. IV, No. 1 (Winter 1983), p. 22.

annual shareholder meeting. Such meetings provide an excellent forum, both inside and outside the meeting itself, to assert the existence of a problem, assign alleged responsibility for it, and ask for action to correct it.

THE CORPORATION

The quest for corporate involvement/intervention in a "local" labor dispute is predicated on the assumption that "corporate" management will or can be made to view that dispute differently than "local" management. Such a divergence in views might be a product of differences in managerial values or goals based on corporate management's responsibility for the long-run well being of the entire corporate entity as opposed to the short-run survival of any one of its constituent elements. It is also possible that such a divergence of views might be a product not so much of differences in basic long-run values as basic short-run vulnerability to the costs of continued disagreement with the union—one of the traditional elements in the determination of union bargaining power. In that context, the campaigns studied revealed two types of such incremental vulnerability at the corporate level: political and economic.

Political Vulnerability

The three campaigns in which unions sought to exploit the greater political vulnerability of the corporate parent than of its recalcitrant child were those against Litton Industries, General Dynamics, and BASF. The principle and political dimensions of those campaigns have been discussed in some detail, but deserve additional attention with respect to the question of corporate as opposed to divisional political costs of continued disagreement. Each of these cases offers a slightly different perspective on the how and why of corporate involvement in a local dispute.

The campaign against Litton Industries, which was launched in early 1982, began with a postcard campaign in which the union asked members of its locals across the country to send preprinted postcards to the chairman and chief executive officer of the corporation urging the company to adopt a more conciliatory stance in its negotiations with the union in Sioux Falls. That was followed by demonstrations by members at appliance dealers conducted for the purpose of encouraging the dealers to write to the company regarding its labor relations policies and practices, particularly at Sioux Falls. Finally, the union solicited letters to the company from political figures urging a quick conclusion to negotiations.

When those actions (coupled with a protest rally by the Coalition of Labor Union Women (CLUW) at the company's headquarters over the Sioux Falls situation during the CLUW convention in Los Angeles in the Spring of 1982) produced no corporate admission of responsibility for, control over, or interest in that situation, the union began its efforts to expand and escalate its offensive against the company. Those efforts, as has been indicated, involved enlisting the support of other unions and the NLRB in accusing the corporation of exercising centralized control over the labor relations of its subsidiaries and utilizing that control to pursue a corporation-wide "policy of flagrant, systematic and calculated lawlessness . . ."[3] In addition, the union also enlisted the support of other unions and sympathetic congressmen in an effort to exploit the political-economic vulnerability of the corporation to debarment—an action which would have had no discernible impact at Sioux Falls had it come to pass.

Whatever else the Litton campaign may have done or not done, it did strip away some of the political and perhaps public anonymity surrounding the company's operation of numerous, diverse subsidiaries, most of which did not bear the Litton name. The result was the potential for closer political and possibly public corporate accountability for the conduct of those subsidiaries, even if managerial responsibility for those subsidiary operations was decentralized. A similar phenomenon was observed in the campaign against General Dynamics in which the union was able, by virtue of its ability to shift the focus of attention from the local to the national corporate level, to link its charge of "grossly irresponsible conduct in collective bargaining . . . at its electric boat subsidiary" to a host of other alleged irresponsible corporate acts at other times and/or in other subsidiaries.[4] That expanded public/political vulnerability was at the heart of a rally and march on the corporation's headquarters in the spring of 1984, in which the union claimed that 1,000 General Dynamics workers from twelve different unions participated with supporters from church, women's, anti-war, and community groups carrying signs with such messages as: "Stop Killing People"; "I'm a Taxpayer and I'm Mad"; and "GD's Scabs at Groton Must Go."[5]

The campaign against BASF provides the most dramatic examples of the use of corporate escalation to accumulate and attempt to

---

[3]Charles Craypo, "Litton Industries as a Repeat Violator of the National Labor Relations Act," paper submitted to the Subcommittee on Labor-Management Relations of the U.S. House Committee on Labor, February 19, 1976 and published in *Oversight Hearing on the National Labor Relations Act* (Washington, D.C.: Government Printing Office, 1976), pp. 125–139.

[4]"News from UAW," February 1, 1984, p. 1.

[5]Jeff Stansbury, "Company Without a Conscience," *Solidarity*, March 1984, p. 13.

exploit irresponsible corporate acts committed at different times and in different places to exploit potential political vulnerability. In the United States that attempt involved an effort to taint BASF with the war crimes of the predecessor of its German parent corporation committed during World War II. In Germany, it involved an effort to taint the parent corporation with the alleged anti-union activities of its American subsidiary committed in Geismar, Louisiana, in claimed violation of international guidelines on acceptable behavior in union-management relations. This latter effort began in mid-summer 1984 in the form of a cable from the AFL-CIO Industrial Union Department (IUD) to BASF A.G. (the parent company) threatening a corporate campaign against that company unless it ceased its union-busting campaign. Some six months later, union representatives travelled to Germany to discuss the matter with officials of the parent company and the union members of its board of supervisors. They were unable to meet with the full board and reportedly received only a lukewarm reception from its union members, possibly because of their U.S. "Nazi" campaign. Two months after that largely unproductive visit, the union filed its complaint against the company under the OECD guidelines.

The BASF campaign clearly stands apart from the others studied in terms of the temporal and geographical reach of its efforts to exploit the potential for public/political corporate guilt by association. The fact that it alone among the campaigns studied transcended national and cultural boundaries makes it a clear deviant from the norm, but one which is not without value in defining the outer limits of the possible intracorporate differences in public/political vulnerabilities open to union exploitation in the game of protest. The BASF campaign also suggests that the game of protest, by raising the curtain of anonymity on corporate heredity and familial relationships, may prove embarrassing or uncomfortable for both parent and child, however far they may be geographically or organizationally separated.

Economic Vulnerability

The corporate campaign in which the union most obviously sought to exploit the greater economic vulnerability of the "parent" than of its target was that against Campbell Soup. The tomato and cucumber growers who were the true focus of the dispute were largely immune from economic pressure in either the product or the labor market. Their position as contract growers in effect made them producer rather than consumer goods producers. The fact that the Farm Labor Organizing Committee (FLOC) had been on strike against those growers for almost a decade when the campaign ended in 1986 provides ample testimony of the similarly insulated labor market position of the true targets of the union. Against that background, it is hardly surprising that the union chose to make Campbell the target of a campaign which included a call for a consumer boycott of all Campbell products—a call which was not well received by the United Food and Commercial Workers (UFCW) and other unions representing Campbell employees. The Campbell case of corporate escalation from producer goods "child" to consumer goods "parent" represents exactly the opposite tactic from that chosen by the United Electrical, Radio and Machine Workers (UE) in the Litton case. In both cases, however, the unions chose to wage their campaign on grounds most favorable to them.

The campaign conducted by Local P-9 of the UFCW against Hormel parallels quite closely that of FLOC against Campbell. The strike of Local P-9 against Hormel's Austin, Minnesota, plant did not prevent the company from continuing production at its other facilities or from resuming production at its Austin facility. Although the products produced at the Austin plant were consumer goods, their origin was not easily traced or distinguished from other company plants. In that context, it is hardly surprising that the local union pursued the course of corporate escalation by attempting to foment "sympathy strikes" at other company facilities through the use of roving pickets and by calling for a boycott of all Hormel products. In this case, as in the Campbell case, those actions were not well received by the UFCW which represented workers at other Hormel plants.

The campaign against Consolidated Foods provides an example of corporate escalation within a strictly consumer goods organization in which, as in the case of BASF, corporate cultures and values came into play. The campaign came as something of a surprise to the corporation which had only relatively recently acquired the Hanes operations which were the focus of the problem. The first clue that something might be about to happen came just before the company's annual shareholder meeting in October 1982 in the form of a letter to its CEO, John Bryan, from one of the Bennettsville Sisters, Sister Imelda Maurer, requesting a meeting to discuss "problems relating to tendinitis and other industrially related illnesses, the rights of women employees, the rights of workers to organize, the issue of Consolidated Foods Corporation food prices and CFC food consumer's concerns related to health and nutrition."[6]

---

[6]Letter from Sister Imelda Maurer, Connective Ministry Across the South, to Mr. John H. Bryan, Jr., Consolidated Foods Corporation, dated October 19, 1982, p. 1.

The corporation did not respond to that letter prior to its shareholder meeting—a meeting attended by, among others, Sister Maurer and Father Dahm of the Interfaith Center on Corporate Responsibility. At that meeting Father Dahm spoke against the reelection of Robert Elbersod, who had been the CEO of Hanes prior to its acquisition by Consolidated Foods, to the board of directors of the corporation. Sister Maurer then introduced some Hanes employees to provide testimony on the terrors of tendinitis and spoke herself about discrimination against women in the direct store delivery operations at Hanes. The response of the CEO at the meeting was that "there was no problem." That position was reiterated formally one week later in a letter to Sister Maurer from Mr. Bryan in which he responded to questions she had raised at the meeting and concluded, "that there is simply no basis in fact to the charges made by you and your associates at our annual meeting,"[7] a conclusion based on a hastily ordered corporate staff investigation of conditions at the Hanes subsidiary.

The letter from Mr. Bryan to Sister Maurer produced a response by wire within the week and by letter in early 1983. In that letter, Sister Maurer indicated that "it is your unwillingness to meet with us that compels us to pursue other measures for redress of this problem."[8] Those other measures actually had begun before the annual meeting. The "Hanes problem" had been aired at an October 1982 meeting of the Catholic Committee of the South. As a result of that meeting, the corporation received a large number of complaining letters from a host of Catholic orders and several other religious and civic groups. The company responded to each of those letters with an individualized acknowledgment accompanied by a copy of Mr. Bryan's original written rebuttal of Sister Maurer's charges sent after the shareholder meeting. The war of the written word went on for almost five months from November 1982 through March 1983 with neither side making any discernible progress. By March, the corporation was blessed by a diminishing stream of protest letters and an encouraging number of supportive letters from Hanes employees. At the same time, however, it was beset by an increasingly "nervous" board of directors, particularly its outside directors many of whom had been approached directly on the Hanes issue.

---

[7]Letter from John H. Bryan, Jr., Consolidated Foods Corporation, to Sister Imelda Maurer, Connective Ministry Across the South, dated November 4, 1982, p. 3.

[8]Letter from Sister Imelda Maurer, Connective Ministry Across the South, to Mr. John H. Bryan, Jr., Consolidated Foods Corporation, dated January 13, 1983, p. 2.

THE DIRECTORS

Once "the corporation" has become the focus of a campaign, the next intraorganizational step in the quest for "redress of grievances" is to appeal over the heads of operating management to those responsible for operating policy—the board of directors and its individual members. In fact, that means appealing to the "outside" members of the board who have no direct managerial link to the dispute in question, but who have indirect managerial authority to resolve the dispute. The appeal to such members of the board may be made either in their role as board members, e.g., as members of the committee on executive compensation or social responsibility, or in their role outside the boardroom, i.e., their basic professional activity. While the set of campaigns studied provides some examples of involvement of outside board members simply in that role, it provides far more numerous examples of such involvement based on outside affiliation. These latter examples suggest, once again, two types of vulnerability—political and economic—within the structure of corporate governance.

Personal Politics

Clearly, any outside board member is vulnerable to any number of forms of personal and/or professional harassment/embarrassment. In the campaigns studied, there were few examples of personal attacks and none of personal harassment. There were, however, several examples of attempts to embarrass individual board members professionally, designed either to force those board members to resign or to exert their influence on the board to force a reevaluation of existing policy and practice. The former goal was a salient part of the union's protest game in the J. P. Stevens campaign; the latter goal seemingly has become the focus of more recent campaign efforts to enlighten outside board members.

One of the symbolic victories claimed by the union in its campaign against J. P. Stevens was its success in forcing the CEO of New York Life Insurance Company to resign his membership on the Stevens board of directors. His resignation was attributed to his desire to avoid the need for a mail ballot of all policyholders, as required by state law, in the case of a contested election for membership on the board of New York Life—a possibility which the union threatened to make a reality, at an estimated cost of more than $1 million to New York Life. The sample of campaigns studied produced no examples of a similar tactical coup, although it did produce a few examples of opposition to the reelection of a specific member of the board of a target corporation (Consolidated Foods) and nomination of alternative candidates for positions on such boards (Beverly Enterprises). The sample of campaigns studied, however, did produce several examples of efforts to otherwise persuade outside board members to use their influence to effectuate a change in corporate labor policies and/or practices.

In the course of the campaign against Litton Industries, that corporation's two voting directors and one non-voting advisory director with academic affiliations were favored with protest rallies on their campuses. The first of those rallies took place on the campus of George Washington University in Washington, D.C. on April 10, 1983, the same day that House subcommittee hearings were held on HR 1743—the debarment bill. The stated purpose of that rally was to persuade Litton director Professor Jayne Spain to use her position on the Litton Board to effect change in corporate labor policy. Similar rallies were subsequently held at Stanford University and the University of Southern California. The purpose of those rallies, in the words of the union, was to demonstrate "the potential to unite trade unions . . . and other activist forces in a struggle against the unchecked exercise of corporate power."[9] The result of those rallies in terms of impact on the directors in question was, in the words of the company, nil.

The campaign against Campbell Soup involved protest rallies at the shareholder meetings of CoreStates Bank in Philadelphia on more than one occasion. The purpose of those rallies was to publicize the fact that the CEO of that corporation was a member of the Board of Directors of Campbell and to pressure him into supporting the union's cause, which he did not do, despite talk of a possible boycott against the bank.

The BASF campaign provides an interesting, if atypical, example of the political vulnerability of board members. The board of supervisors of BASF A.G., the parent West German company, includes among its members representatives of its union, IG Chemie. At the June 1985 shareholder meeting of BASF A.G., an IG Chemie member of the board of supervisors was reported to have spoken at length regarding his displeasure with the Geismar situation. After listening for some time, another board member reportedly inquired as to why the IG representative supported those who called them Nazis, after which the issue was dropped. Since then, IG Chemie has given only nominal support to OCAW in its corporate campaign and

---

[9]Lance Compa, "How To Fight a Unionbusting Conglomerate," *The Nation*, July 16, 1983, p. 41.

has been further alienated by alleged contacts by OCAW representatives with the "Greens," the German left wing political party.

The BASF case may be unusual but it is not unique in a world in which unions are gaining representation on corporate boards of directors by any of a number of means ranging from collective bargaining to collective ownership. There were no cases in the set of campaigns studied in which a union was in a position to name a director, but there was one case in which unions did nominate candidates for election to a board of directors. On two occasions the unions involved in the campaign against Beverly Enterprises nominated alternative candidates for board membership—Jacob Clayman, former U.S. Commissioner on the Aging (and also a former President of the IUD), in 1981 and Arthur Flemming, U.S. Secretary of Health, Education and Welfare under President Eisenhower, in 1982—neither of whom was elected.[10]

Professional Economics

The J. P. Stevens campaign also produced the model of the use of economic vulnerability to exert pressure on board members not to change corporate policy but to resign. The union's threat to force a policyholder election for board members at New York Life forced the chairmen of that company and of Stevens to resign from each other's boards. In addition, the threat of the withdrawal of some $1 billion in union funds from Manufacturers Hanover Bank led to the resignation of both the CEO of Stevens and an outside member of the Stevens board from the board of Manufacturers Hanover. That outside board member was the chairman of Avon Products who, two weeks later, also resigned from the Stevens board rather than "permit Avon to be subjected to the pressures which the union is exerting as a result of my Stevens board membership."[11]

Something akin to the Stevens scenario was played out in the campaign against Phelps Dodge. In February 1985, it was reported that, "as part of a United Steelworkers corporate campaign against Phelps Dodge Corporation, American Federation of Teachers President Albert Shanker announces that the New York State Teachers Retirement System is removing Manufacturers Hanover Trust Company as the investment manager for more than one-third of the

---

[10]"Union Pressure Grows in Advance of Beverly Enterprises Annual Meeting," *White Collar Report*, Vol. 53, No. 16 (April 22, 1983), pp. 392–393.

[11]Jack Egan, "Stevens Director Resigns: Avon Chairman Resigns From Stevens Board," *Washington Post*, March 22, 1978, p. 131.

fund's $1.5 billion in assets."[12] Shanker was reported to have attributed that action by the fund trustees both to the bank's alleged poor
performance in handling the fund's assets and to concern "that
Phelps Dodge chairman George Munroe was on the board of Manufacturers Hanover Trust, and that the bank had made substantial
loans to Phelps Dodge throughout the year-and-a-half-old strike
against the company, which is still continuing."[13] Further, Shanker
was quoted as saying "the financial judgment of George Munroe is
not the sort which Manufacturers Hanover Trust Company needs if
it is to return to an area of profitability to inspire confidence among
investors."[14] Two days later, it was reported that:

> At just about every turn the other day, Albert Shanker, the presi
> dent of the American Federation of Teachers, was seen apologizing for
> a pension fund deal that never existed, and hinting darkly that some
> one had taken advantage of him.[15]

THE SHAREHOLDERS

The ultimate control of corporate policy and practice rests with its
shareholders just as the ultimate control of union policies and practices rests with its members. In the case of unions, that control typically is exercised through the institution of the "convention." In the
case of corporations, that control typically is exercised through the
"annual shareholder meeting." Given that parallel in governance
structure, it is hardly surprising that unions have consistently utilized the annual shareholder meeting of target companies to seek the
sympathy and support of stockholders in the unions' quest to correct the malevolent or misguided policies of their agents—the managers and directors of their corporation.

The set of campaigns studied revealed two types of approaches to
shareholders in conjunction with their annual meeting. The first was
that of an "informal appearance" in the form of a protest rally at the
site of the meeting and/or distribution of literature to those attending the meeting and/or attendance at the meeting to question management and address the owners about the situation underlying the
campaign. The second was that of a "formal appeal" in the form of a
nomination of alternative candidates for the board of directors and/

---

[12]"Teachers Union Removes $450 Million from Pension Fund to Support Phelps
Dodge Campaign," *Daily Labor Report*, No. 34 (February 20, 1985), p. A-2.

[13]*Ibid.*, p. A-3.

[14]*Ibid.*

[15]Kenneth B. Noble, "Reporter's Notebook: Shanker 'Clarification,'" *New York
Times*, February 23, 1985, p. 8.

or submissions of shareholder resolutions for a formal vote by all represented shareholders. The former approach was utilized in every one of the campaigns studied and, therefore, would seem to be standard operating procedure in such undertakings. The latter approach was not as commonly used, but was observed in the majority of the campaigns studied.

The shareholder actions utilized in the campaigns studied produced few or no visible favorable results in terms of mandated changes in corporate policy or practice. Despite that fact, it appears that they did cause a certain amount of managerial discomfort, particularly in two cases where management went to great lengths to evade an "appearance" or to avoid an "appeal." In that context, it appears that the power of the shareholder approach rests more on its threat to management's aversion to internal controversy and desire for internal solidarity than on its threat of censure—a situation not unfamiliar to unions and their leaders at convention time.

Informal Appearances

The informal appearances of representatives of corporate campaigners at the shareholder meeting of Consolidated Foods, in the persons of Sister Maurer and Father Dahm, has already been discussed. Representatives of Local P-9 of the UFCW were much in evidence around and inside the Hormel Annual Meeting in 1986 as were representatives of what is now Local 1182 of the UFCW at the 1980 annual meeting of Seattle First National Bank. In that case, the union staged a demonstration march through downtown Seattle to the site of the meeting to protest the bank's labor policies and then succeeded, in the view of management, in "disrupting" the conduct of that meeting. A similar scenario was played out in conjunction with the 1983 annual meeting of Litton Industries which was the subject of a protest rally whose theme was "Litton Makes Misery—We Can Make A Difference" and whose program called for speeches by Howard Samuel of the IUD, Msgr. Higgins of Catholic University and Joyce Miller of the Coalition of Labor Union Women as well as two "Litton Victims," interspersed among an invocation by the pastor of a local African Methodist Episcopal church, an Old Testament reading by a local rabbi, a Littany for Justice by the executive director of the Southern California Ecumenical Council, a magnificat by the president of the Church of Women United, a Littany for Directors by the director of the Church and Society Network, West, and a benediction by a local Catholic priest.[16]

---

[16]"Litton Makes Misery," rally December 10, 1983.

There is no way to estimate the extent to which the unknown number of participants in the Litton rally, inspired as they must have been by those addressing them, were able to awe the shareholders attending the corporation's annual meeting at the Beverly Hills, California, high school or to antagonize the residents of that community which is far from being a likely location for a union-management confrontation. Clearly, however, one must suspect that the whole affair had to be something of an embarrassment to the community's local corporate citizen, Litton Industries. That probably also was the case for Campbell Soup when the *New York Times* reported that some 200 supporters of FLOC appeared at the company's 1984 annual meeting at which, "about 700 stockholders met under heavy security at a hotel as the farm workers from New Jersey, Ohio, Michigan, Pennsylvania, and Florida chanted 'Boycott Campbell' and sang union songs outside."[17]

One of the first steps in the campaign against Phelps Dodge was to confront the corporation's shareholders at their annual meeting in May 1984 with a warning that, "claims from those running Phelps Dodge that everything is rosy and mines and plants are running full swing are not correct" and an admonition to "return to the bargaining table so that this needless, costly conflict can be ended."[18] The union then asserted:

> The corporation not only has a responsibility to its shareholders, it must now also share in the responsibility of rebuilding the community spirit that was once taken for granted, so that the people who care about the community can once again work and live in harmony.[19]

The attendees at the annual meeting of Beverly Enterprises in April 1983 were confronted with a similar set of allegations and challenges in the form of a union survey of Beverly employees which purported to show that the company, "pays its employees poorly, understaffs its homes, and, in many homes, overmedicates patients to keep them 'quiet and immobile.'"[20] In that survey, 1,000 employees distributed 20,000 questionnaires at 475 homes in February 1983, of which 421 were returned in time to be tabulated prior to the annual meeting in April. Of those 421 respondents, 80 percent cited low pay and 60 percent cited lack of staff as their most critical problems with Beverly. In addition, 24 percent said that patients were

---

17"Farm Group Boycotting Campbell Puts Focus on Financial Concerns," *New York Times*, November 27, 1984, p. A 15.
18"USWA Confronts PD Stockholders," *Steelabor*, May 1984, p. 11.
19*Ibid.*
20"Union Pressure Grows . . ." p. 393.

"frequently" under large doses of medication.[21] The results of this survey were used to support the union contention that "it's immoral that the largest and most profitable nursing home in the country so neglects its employees as well as its patients."[22]

The chairman and CEO of the corporation openly criticized the survey, saying he was surprised that its sponsors had "the audacity to release the results of a survey of 20,000 people when only two percent of the people receiving it even bothered to return it."[23] In addition, the company sent a letter to all employees urging them to refer problems of the type covered in the survey to the corporate ombudsman. Those employees who did not respond to the survey were credited with "realizing the survey was just another organizing ploy."[24]

Louisiana-Pacific rotates the site of its shareholder meeting among the communities in which it has production facilities. In 1984, the community chosen was Rocky Mount, North Carolina—a place described by the union as "one of the most unlikely and inaccessible spots ever picked for a major corporate annual meeting."[25] The union characterized the choice of Rocky Mount "as part of a strategy to hide from the public, the media, its own shareholders and the family of organized labor."[26] In order to counter that strategy, the union conducted a "Reckoning at Rocky Mount" for which it "recruited some 400 participants from a variety of community, union, church and civil rights organizations, among them Rev. Joe Lowery, president of the Atlanta-based Southern Christian Leadership Conference"[27] (SCLC). The reckoning began with a pre-meeting rally and trial of Louisiana-Pacific as a first step "in bringing this billion-dollar corporate outlaw to justice." It then proceeded to the shareholder meeting which the SCLC had packed with its supporters and where Rev. Lowrey was joined by representatives of the IUD, the National Council of Churches, and environmental and senior citizen groups in speaking on behalf of union-initiated shareholder resolutions. The union and its supporters were successful in disrupting the meeting, but not in securing passage of any of their resolutions.

---

[21]*Ibid.*, p. 394.

[22]*Ibid.*

[23]"Unions Net One of Ten Votes at Beverly Annual Meeting," *White Collar Report*, Vol. 53 (April 29, 1983), p. 430.

[24]*Ibid.*

[25]"News From the UBC," May 9, 1984, p. 1.

[26]"It's Showdown Time for the Louisiana-Pacific Corporation," flyer distributed at the annual shareholder meeting, May 14, 1984, p. 2.

[27]"News From the UBC," May 9, 1984, p. 1.

The site issue also arose in the campaign against General
Dynamics. The United Automobile Workers (UAW) planned to bring
the IUD's "Coalition to Clean Up GD" to the company's 1984 annual
meeting in order to "greet the shareholders with a list of embarrassing demands from workers, taxpayers, women, and others."[28] When
the company learned of the union's plan, it changed the site of its
annual meeting, forcing the union to settle for a "Concerned Shareholders Meeting" in Clayton, Missouri, at which a number of its supporters reiterated the charges against the company. Despite the last
minute change in location for the annual meeting a few union supporters managed to attend the meeting including one who asked the
assembled shareholders to "rise in a moment of silence for Harvey
Lee"[29] (the General Dynamics' worker who was killed by the fumes
from the solvent used to clean M-1 tanks at the company's Center
Line, Michigan plant). Of the 200 people present, only the protesters
rose.[30]

Formal Appeals

Shareholder resolutions have been used to state the campaigner's
case in most of the campaigns studied. At Seattle First National
Bank, management reported that, after the union's initial success in
disrupting the 1980 annual meeting, demonstrations and shareholder resolutions calling for recognition of the union became annual
events but to no avail. At their 1984 meeting, the 700 Campbell Soup
Company shareholders who "met under heavy security at a hotel"
were asked to vote on a resolution calling for the company's board of
directors to "adopt as a policy the recognition of F.L.O.C. and support the three-way negotiations between Campbell, growers and
F.L.O.C."—a resolution which was "rejected by proxy vote of 27.3
million shares to 263,906."[31] On quite a different note, a shareholder
proclamation in 1986 was submitted to BASF A.G. in Ludwigshafen
recommending that the company set up a trust fund of 60 million
Deutsch Marks (about $30 million) to be placed at the disposal of the
families of locked out workers in Geismar, Louisiana. It was over-
whelmingly defeated.

The focal point of the "Reckoning at Rocky Mount" in the campaign against Louisiana-Pacific was three shareholder resolutions

---

[28]Jeff Stansbury, "Catching Up With General Dynamics," *Solidarity*, June 1984,
p. 9.
[29]*Ibid.*
[30]*Ibid.*
[31]"Farm Group Boycotting Campbell ... ," p. A-15.

proposed by the "L-P Workers for Justice Committee" (L-PWJC). That organization was comprised of striking L-P workers who were also, thanks to the company's stock purchase plan, shareholders, and was housed at the headquarters of the United Brotherhood of Carpenters in Washington, D.C. The stated purpose of the organization was to communicate with other Louisiana-Pacific shareholders on issues relating to company operations. In 1984 it did raise three issues in the form of the following proposals to the company's shareholder meeting at Rocky Mount:

1) Strike Impact Accounting: The proposal requested that L-P quantify for shareholders the cost of the strike to the company in terms of increased production costs, and decreased sales and profits related to the strike . . .

2) Independent Board of Directors: The second proposal concerned the composition of the L-P board, a majority of which is composed of individuals with past or present employment, business or financial relationships with the company . . .

3) Compensation Committee: The third proposal sought to reconstitute the board's executive compensation committee of which Mr. Harry Merlo, L-P's chairman and CEO is chairman . . . [32]

In search of support for those proposals, the L-PWJC provided "solicitation material to the holders of 26 of the company's 33 million outstanding shares."[33] That material indicated that "financial analysts have identified multi-million dollar cost for L-P related to the strike," suggested there had been "numerous costly legal infractions involving L-P which were attributed to the lack of a strong independent board," and pointed to "repeated instances where Mr. Merlo has benefitted handsomely from decisions of the compensation committee." The shareholder response to that solicitation was, in the view of the union, "very positive, with the L-PWJC representing over 2 million shares at the May 14 annual meeting in Rocky Mount, North Carolina."[34] Those two million shares were far from enough to carry the day or the proposals at Rocky Mount. Undaunted, the union indicated that:

The L-PWJC will continue to communicate with L-P shareholders, with the focus on L-P's continuing difficulties. Special emphasis will be given in the communication process to large institutional shareholders which hold significant positions in L-P stock and which handle union pension funds.[35]

---

[32]"Carpenter's L-P Strike Campaign," handout distributed at a Wall Street rally, March 22, 1984, pp. 2–3.

[33]*Ibid.*, p. 2.

[34]*Ibid.*

[35]*Ibid.*, p. 3.

Institutional investors were the target of two resolutions put before the shareholders of Beverly Enterprises in 1983 which were, in the words of the union, "designed to give the institutional investor a clear opportunity to stand up and be counted on quality of care."[36] One of those resolutions called for the appointment of an additional company director "with health care experience [who] would bring new expertise to Beverly's Board of Directors" and resolved that " ... the company's shareholders hereby request that the company establish a special search committee to include, but not be limited to, institutional shareholders to select an individual with a) national reputation in the long term health care field, and b) management experience, preferably as a corporate director, to serve as an additional director on Beverly's Board."[37] One resolution dealt with company's Quality Assurance Program in the following terms:

> **WHEREAS:** The health and well-being of those who utilize the services of Beverly Enterprises is of paramount importance, and
>
> **WHEREAS:** Significant competitive factors for the Company are reputation and quality of care, and
>
> **WHEREAS:** In 1982 and years past the Company has experienced a number of serious problems in delivering quality of care to its residents, and
>
> **WHEREAS:** These problems indicate deficiencies in the Company's current Quality Assurance Program (the "Program"), therefore be it
>
> **RESOLVED:** That the Company's Shareholders hereby request that the Company promptly establish an independent group of five nationally recognized experts in longterm care of its own choosing to: 1) Establish criteria to measure the quality of care in Company managed facilities, and the effectiveness of the Company's Quality Assurance Program; 2) Measure the quality of care in Company managed facilities and the Program's effectiveness; and 3) Prepare a detailed report of their findings and recommendations to the Board and Shareholders by the Company's next annual meeting, including an assessment of the quality of care in the Company's facilities, and be it further
>
> **RESOLVED:** That the independent experts chosen select their own staff to conduct the study and the Company allocate a minimum of $750,000 for this project.[38]

---

[36]"Union Pressure Grows ... ," p. 393.

[37]Food and Beverage Trades Department, AFL-CIO, "Independent Shareholders Solicitation, 1983 Annual Meeting of Shareholders, Beverly Enterprises, April 22, 1983," p. 6.

[38]*Ibid.*

The management of Beverly took the position that neither proposal was justified nor necessary in light of the company's "vigorous" Quality Assurance Program. The company's senior vice president for administration characterized the union's quality assurance
resolution as follows:

> On the surface, the proposal seems to have an entirely positive pur-
> pose. [But there is a] dangerous undertow... to discredit this com-
> pany, to discredit the work of our employees, and to discredit the ser-
> vice we provide to the elderly. As we would recognize a wolf in sheep's
> clothing, so let us be aware of what the union's real motive is in this
> resolution.[39]

Most of the shareholders represented at the meeting seemingly
did discern the union's real motive as the resolution was defeated by
a margin of 14.5 million shares to 1 million shares (as was the other
union resolution).[40] Among the 1 million shares voted for the union's
resolution were 482,900 held by the Chase Manhattan Bank which
"believed that it was in the best interest of all concerned to determine the degree of excellence, or lack of it," but also stated that
investment considerations were paramount and its shares were not
voted "to make the world a better place."[41]

The Litton campaign produced shareholder resolutions in both
1982 and 1983. In 1982, the resolution called for an accounting of
money spent by the corporation defending itself against unfair labor
practice charges—a resolution which was endorsed by only 1.9 percent of the shares voted. Undaunted, the union and its allies prepared to return to the shareholders with another resolution in 1983,
in which a stated goal of 3 percent of the vote would constitute a
moral victory. In pursuit of that self-set definition of success, the
following resolution was submitted for shareholder action at Litton's
1983 annual meeting where it won endorsement by 2.45 percent of
the shares voted:

> Whereas the right of employees to organize and bargain with their
> employer in good faith has long been recognized in our country and
> has been part of the ethical foundation of our religious life as
> expressed, for example, by the Social Principles of the United Method-
> ist Church, which state: "We support the right of the public and pri-
> vate... employees and employers to organize for collective bargain-
> ing into unions and other groups of their own choosing. Further, we
> support the right of both parties to protection in so doing, and their

---

[39]"Unions Net One of Ten...," p. 430.
[40]"Final Vote Count in Beverly Proxy Vote: Beverly 14 Million; Unions 1 Million,"
White Collar Report, Vol. 53, No. 19 (May 13, 1983), p. 481.
[41]"Unions Net One of Ten...," pp. 429–430.

responsibility to bargain in good faith within the framework of the public interest."

Whereas we believe shareholders as part owners of the corporation should be mindful of the statement of John Paul II (On Human Work): "They (the means of production) cannot be possessed against labor, they cannot even be possessed for possession's sake, because the only legitimate title to their possession is that they serve labor, and thus ... that they should make possible ... the universal destination of goods and the right to common use of them." In order to better serve the common good of shareholders and employees alike:

Be it resolved that the shareholders request the Board of Directors of Litton Industries form a Board Committee to develop a corporate code of conduct guaranteeing the right of employees to organize and maintain unions and affirming the principles of collective bargaining in good faith. This Committee shall seek outside counsel including from community, religious, business and labor leaders and shall submit the code for Board approval by December 1984. The code shall be printed in the next quarterly report and copies shall be sent simultaneously to all employees. Costs shall be limited to amount deemed reasonable by the Board.[42]

The chairman of the corporation characterized the union's proposal as "unworkable and unnecessary" and "counterproductive for both parties." After the proposal was voted down, he suggested the creation of a five-member study group, composed of two company and two union representatives and a neutral chairman, which would report on "the allegations of unions and others against the company, how collective bargaining and industrial relations between the company and its unions can be improved, and how productivity can be improved through our joint efforts."[43] Three representatives of the National Litton Campaign addressed the meeting after the chairman made his proposal—Howard Samuel, Joyce Miller and Msgr. Higgins—all of whom reportedly "condensed their planned remarks and welcomed [the] offer."[44] One unofficial ally of the campaign, Rev. George Ogle, Director of the Department of Economic and Social Justice of Church and Society of the United Methodist Churches, however, reportedly "expressed some caution about Litton's offer and said he hopes the resolution of the dispute will be more than a pledge to obey the law."[45]

The corporate campaign against Consolidated Foods, which began at its 1982 annual meeting, ultimately was resolved through

---

[42]Litton Industries, Inc., Notice of Annual Meeting of Shareholders to be held December 10, 1983, shareholder proposal No. II, pp. 20–21.

[43]"Litton Chairman Suggests Labor-Management Study on Charges of Labor Law Violations," *Daily Labor Report*, No. 239 (December 12, 1983), p. A-4.

[44]*Ibid.*, p. A-5.

[45]*Ibid.*

discussions/negotiations between the corporation and its religious adversaries. The first major development in that process was a meeting in San Antonio in mid-May to address the concerns of the Sisters of Divine Providence as stated in Sister Billeaud's letter of March 28. The order was represented at that meeting by an interesting array of individuals from three distinct constituencies: 1) the Sisters of Divine Providence (Sister Billeaud), 2) the Connective Ministry (Sister Maurer), and 3) the Interfaith Center on Corporate Responsibility (Ms. Dara Demmings). The appearance of Ms. Demmings suggested to the company that it faced the possibility of a classic ICCR campaign in which shareholder resolutions play a central role, as indeed proved to be the case. The agenda for the meeting suggested that any such campaign likely would be focused on two issues—the incidence and impact of tendinitis and related disorders and equal pay and opportunity.

The corporation's perception that it might be the target of an ICCR campaign led it to establish an independent dialogue with that organization through Ms. Demmings during the summer of 1983. By the end of August, that dialogue made it clear that ICCR's real interest was EEO data and that it was preparing to press that interest through a shareholder resolution. At the same time, it became clear through the on-going dialogue with the Sisters of Divine Providence that release of the report of the medical task force to the order and other shareholders would also be a potential subject of a shareholder resolution. Finally, Sister Maurer's constituency was also heard from in the form of a proposed resolution from the Women Against Pornography condemning Hanes' hosiery advertisements.

The company's response to these potential shareholder initiatives was a determined effort to head them off at the pass. It was prepared to fight the pornography resolution before the SEC on grounds of relevance, but nonetheless agreed to meet with representatives of Women Against Pornography to hear their complaints and to convince them to withdraw their proposed resolution, which they ultimately did. The company felt it could not profitably fight the other two initiatives and so it turned to negotiations in an effort to avert those initiatives. By the end of September, the corporation had succeeded in reaching agreements with Sister Billeaud and Ms. Demmings under which both agreed to withdraw their organization's proposed shareholder resolution. In exchange, the corporation agreed to provide a copy of the TRD study to any shareholder who requested one and to publish its basic EEO data in its annual report. With those two issues settled, the 1983 shareholder meeting was remarkably quiet, as was that in 1984.

CHAPTER V

The Game of Pressure

One potentially painful point of vulnerability for any firm is at the point of sale of its products or services. Efforts to exploit such vulnerability through "consumer actions," traditionally known as boycotts, represent another approach involving horizontal conflict expansion. In that respect, the game of pressure is like the game of politics. Indeed, when the government is a major purchaser of a firm's goods or services, the two games may become one in at least some respects, as will be seen in the cases of Litton Industries and Beverly Enterprises.

Boycotts have long been part of labor's arsenal of weapons in dealing with recalcitrant employers and are frequently used independent of formal corporate campaigns. Thus the fact that they have been adopted as a tactical option in a corporate campaign is not surprising. There are, however, two potential drawbacks to that tactical option from the union standpoint which may limit its use or usefulness. The first is that a successful boycott can be a double-edged sword which hurts unionized workers as much or more than it helps them, which is a problem that makes boycotts most suitable in scorched earth campaigns against firms like Louisiana-Pacific and Phelps Dodge which have broken strikes and unions. The second is the limited vulnerability of producer goods companies such as Louisiana-Pacific and Phelps Dodge to consumer actions in contrast to producers of consumer goods or services such as Campbell Soup and Seattle First National Bank (SeaFirst).

The potential drawbacks to boycotts did not prevent their relatively widespread use in the sample of campaigns studied. One or more forms of "consumer action" or threat thereof appeared in all of the campaigns except those against General Dynamics and Phelps Dodge. The remaining three producer goods targets—BASF, Litton, and Louisiana-Pacific—were subjected to forms of boycott pressure but, as expected, with limited effect. Two of the consumer goods services targets—Beverly and Consolidated—had to contend with real or implied boycott threats; the other three—Campbell, Hormel, and SeaFirst—confronted actual boycotts. It may or may not be coincidental, but the Campbell, Hormel, and SeaFirst campaigns were conducted by local unions with the advice and counsel of Ray

Rogers of Corporate Campaign Inc.

PRODUCER GOODS TARGETS

The two producer goods companies which were the targets of the most extensive boycott activity were Litton Industries and Louisiana-Pacific. Both of those companies had some direct consumer exposure, Litton through its production and sale of microwave ovens, and Louisiana-Pacific through its sales to do-it-yourself carpenters, but both were far more economically dependent on nonretail sales. In the case of Litton, the union sought to deprive the company of one source of such sales through debarment. In the Louisiana-Pacific case the union sought to do the same through appeals to building contractors. The BASF campaign produced a similar appeal in the form of an attempt to publicly discredit a company product.

Debarment

The threat of debarment utilized by the United Electrical, Radio and Machine Workers (UE) in its Litton Campaign did not originate with that union or campaign. There was a clear precedent for such an approach to consumer action in the J. P. Stevens campaign and the proposals for the AFL-CIO's "Labor Law Reform" for which it became a symbol. The impact of debarment on Litton would have been substantial since defense contracts accounted for about one quarter of its revenues at that time. Its impact on unionized Litton workers would have been even more dramatic because almost one-half of its 21,000 such workers were employed in building ships for the U.S. Navy at Litton's Ingalls Shipbuilding in Pascagoula, Mississippi.

The prospect of sacrificing the jobs of some 10,000 AFL-CIO members for those of 1,000 UE non-AFL-CIO members had to tax the spirit of brotherhood and solidarity of even the most ardent unionist to the breaking point. That trade-off had to be a consideration in the decision of the AFL-CIO to assume command of the campaign two weeks after HR 1743 was voted out of House subcommittee, as it undoubtedly was in the remarkable absence of any mention of debarment in the United Automobile Workers' (UAW) campaign against General Dynamics on behalf of 2,000 of that company's 90,000 employees. In the Litton case, an additional consideration may have been a growing realization that the UE's only goal was to force a settlement for its members at Sioux Falls, whose jobs were not at risk in the event of debarment, as evidenced by its admission in late 1982 that if such a settlement were reached, "the question of us playing a leading role [in the campaign] would have to be reviewed."[1]

The fact that Congress had twice failed to enact union initiated debarment legislation aimed at repeated labor law violators did not deter the states of Wisconsin, Connecticut, Maryland, Michigan, and Ohio from enacting just such legislation. In that context, it is important to note again the regulatory proposals made to the governor of the state of Michigan in conjunction with the release of the unions' study of "Beverly Enterprises in Michigan," including one which would have effectively prohibited out-of-state corporations from operating nursing homes. Although that proposal was not implemented and the Wisconsin debarment law was struck down on constitutional grounds,[2] the possibility of effective debarment by one means or another at the state level deserves attention.

Dissuasion

The corporate campaign against Louisiana-Pacific formally began in December 1983 when the AFL-CIO and United Brotherhood of Carpenters (UBC) launched a nationwide boycott of Louisiana-Pacific's wood products. In order to effectuate its announced boycott, the UBC established "Louisiana-Pacific Support Committees" in each of its 1,800 locals with "the responsibility of coordinating and conducting regular boycott activities" at retail lumber yards.[3] Such activities typically began with a letter to a retail outlet from the union informing it of the existence of the labor dispute and of the possibility that it could be subject to "lawful noncoercive boycott activities" in conjunction with that dispute. The outlet would then be subject to picketing and consumer handbilling.

By March of 1984 the union reported that such committees in conjunction with other labor organizations were conducting "boycott activity on an ongoing basis at over four hundred outlets throughout the country."[4] At that time, the UBC claimed that "boycott activity has produced a very positive response from the consuming public"

---

[1]"Testing a New Weapon Against Litton," *Business Week*, December 27, 1982, p. 33.

[2]Wisconsin Department of Industry, Labor and Human Relations et al. v. Gould, Inc., U.S. Sup. Ct. No. 84-1484, February 26, 1986.

[3]"Carpenter's L-P Strike Campaign," handout distributed at a Wall Street rally March 22, 1984, p. 1.

[4]*Ibid.*, p. 2.

and that "responding to the expressions of consumer support for the boycott, retailers at many locations have ceased selling Louisiana-Pacific wood products."[5] The company denied publicly and privately that this retail boycott had any appreciable impact on sales and the *Wall Street Journal* seemingly agreed when it reported in June 1984 that the boycott "has apparently had little effect."[6]

A special focus for boycott activity was Louisiana-Pacific's new waferboard product which "is promoted as a plywood substitute and is a high margin profit product for L-P."[7] At that time, the company was "embarked on an ambitious waferboard expansion, with the hopes of doubling its present waferboard capacity by 1985."[8] In its effort to undo the company's hopes, the union "identified the present distribution system for L-P's existing waferboard facilities" and intensified its boycott activities in "cities such as Houston, Minneapolis, Chicago, New York, Indianapolis and major New England cities."[9] Special attention was paid therefore to informing building contractors of the union's labor dispute with Louisiana-Pacific. The company privately admits that this latter effort had some effect on sales in the form of at least temporarily slowing the growth of sales as construction activity expanded in 1985 and 1986. Despite that effect, the expansion in construction activity has resulted in record company sales.

BASF is fundamentally a producer goods manufacturer. In 1986, however, the company introduced a new diet supplement into the market. The action created a consumer action opportunity for OCAW not associated with most other company products. In its unfair labor practice charge filed against the union, the company stated:

> OCAW has threatened to publish a message intended to dissuade consumers from purchasing a new beta carotene diet supplement being introduced into the market by BASF, to arouse public distrust, suspicion, fear and hatred of BASF, and to injure the sales and reputation of BASF by assertions that BASF is attempting to "cash in" on the fear of cancer by selling an "unproven untested food supplement," that in truth consumers have a great deal to fear from BASF, that BASF is one of the world's largest producers of cancer-causing chemi-

---

[5]*Ibid.*

[6]Patricia A. Bellew, "Lumber Firm Wins Big Fight With Strikers," *Wall Street Journal*, June 26, 1984, p. 37.

[7]"News From the UBC," June 26, 1984, p. 2.

[8]"Carpenter's L-P Strike Campaign," handout p. 2.

[9]*Ibid.*

cal substances and toxic wastes and is attempting to "cash in on cancer, not once but twice. . . . Once on the cause, once on the cure." . . . [10]

The only other case of such a sweeping attempt to discredit a target company in the eyes of its actual or potential consuming public would be the union report on "Beverly Enterprises Patient Care Record" cited earlier. In questioning that record, the unions clearly raised some similar issues of life and death, albeit not on quite the scale of the union's charges against BASF. That difference in scale could hardly have been of comfort to Beverly Enterprises given its position as a provider of consumer services which must sell those services not only to individuals but to third party payers.

CONSUMER GOODS TARGETS

Consumer actions played a significant role in only two of the campaigns against consumer goods/services companies—those against Campbell Soup and SeaFirst. The possibility of a call for a boycott was never mentioned in the campaign against Beverly Enterprises, although the union challenges to the company's quality of care and operating characteristics might have provided the basis for such a call. At the other extreme, the call for a boycott was loudly and repeatedly made in the course of the campaign against Hormel, but with virtually no effect. The failure of that call was the product not of a lack of potential company market vulnerability to consumer action but to the lack of the activist network required to generate such on the part of Local P-9. Lacking the support of its international union for a boycott, Local P-9 could not do what the Carpenters could and did do to give force to their call for a boycott of Louisiana-Pacific wood products—establish a physical presence in the company's major markets.

The case of Consolidated Foods provides an interesting contrast to the cases of both Beverly Enterprises and Hormel. The corporation had a high degree of potential market vulnerability to consumer action, particularly if that action extended beyond its Hanes subsidiary to its other consumer products. At the same time, the ability of the religious sponsors of the campaign to mount an effective consumer action, as opposed to letter writing action, through their network was somewhat suspect. That ability was not put to the test

---

[10]Letter from Mr. William R. D'Armond of the firm of Kean, Miller, Hawthorne, D'Armond, McCowen & Jarman, attorneys at law, to Mr. Hugh Frank Malone, Regional Director National Labor Relations Board. Region 15, New Orleans, Louisiana, dated May 17, 1986, Appendix I, p. 132.

because the religious sponsors of that campaign never even mentioned the possibility of a product boycott. The fact that they did not
do so may be a result of the corporation's decision to pursue an open
and responsive strategy in dealing with the issues in the campaign.

There was one mention of a possible boycott of Hanes products in
the course of the Consolidated Foods campaign, but it came from the
labor movement, not the religious community. In July 1983, Joyce
Miller of the Coalition of Labor Union Women (CLUW) was reported
to have made a "comment about a boycott" by women's groups after
a "July 14 Washington hearing."[11] That comment produced further
evidence of the double-edged sword phenomenon in the form of an
influx of protest letters from Hanes' largely female workforce to
women's groups such as the National Organization for Women
(NOW). That comment also opened another potential battle front or
avenue for dialogue for the corporation which it pursued in an
August 1983 meeting with the president of NOW in which the company presented its side of the story on the tendinitis and equal pay
issues. No commitments were sought or made by either side at that
meeting, but NOW and other such groups did not undertake a boycott of Hanes' products or otherwise join in the campaign against
Consolidated Foods, quite possibly because they had never seriously
considered doing so, Ms. Miller's comment notwithstanding.

The two campaigns in which boycotts played a major role—
Campbell Soup and SeaFirst—are noteworthy primarily for what
they reveal about the nature and extent of market vulnerability. In
neither of those two cases did consumer action appear to have a significant adverse impact on company sales or profits or to cause serious customer relations problems. Despite that fact, in the final analysis consumer action was successful in "coercing" one of those
companies, Campbell Soup, although not the other. That difference
can be traced only to differences in the nature of their market vulnerabilities and sensitivities thereto, differences possibly reflected
in the fact that the campaign against Campbell was treated as a
matter to be handled by public relations rather than employee relations as was the case at SeaFirst.

The Campbell Soup Boycott

The Campbell campaign began with a strike of some 900 farm
workers employed by growers under contract to Campbell Soup in

---

[11]Letter from Mr. Leo Contois, Consolidated Foods Corporation, to Ms. Judy Gold-
smith, President of the National Organization for Women, dated August 22, 1983, p. 1.

1978. The campaign was escalated in 1979 to include a call for a consumer boycott of Campbell Soup products. That call went largely unheard by the consuming public until 1983. In that year, in the words of the *Wall Street Journal*:

> Now the long-simmering fight is coming to a boil. To promote their boycott, the farmworkers have begun a media campaign against the company. Some 70 of them recently began a month-long march from FLOC's Toledo, Ohio, base to Campbell's Camden, N.J., headquarters, spreading the word through the flatlands of Ohio and the mountains of Pennsylvania.[12]

The culmination of that march was timed to coincide with Campbell's shareholder meeting in August of 1983 which was to be visited with the protest activities previously described. Upon their arrival in the Philadelphia area, the marchers were greeted by expressions of sympathy and support from the area's labor movement. Such sympathy and support, however, did not include endorsement of the boycott, largely because the United Food and Commercial Workers (UFCW) which represented some 10,000 Campbell employees nationwide, including more than 1,000 in the company's Camden plant, was one of "Campbell's Unions . . . which are furious at FLOC for calling a boycott."[13] Indeed, throughout what proved to be the seven-year term of the boycott, the UFCW and other Campbell unions opposed the boycott and neutralized most other union support for that action.

The next major media event involving the boycott came in July 1984 at the Democratic National Convention. The Rev. Jesse Jackson gave what the *Daily Labor Report* described as a "dramatic speech" in which he was reported to have said, "The Rainbow Coalition is making room for . . . workers in Ohio who are fighting the Campbell Soup Company with a boycott to achieve legitimate worker rights."[14] When Rev. Jackson made that statement,

> . . . delegates on the floor unfurled a huge banner urging millions of viewers to "boycott Campbell." Scores of FLOC supporters on the floor also waved signs, painted to look like the familiar red-and-white soup can, that carried the same message. The signs were visible during much of Jackson's 50-minute speech.[15]

---

[12]Paul A. Engelmayer, "Campbell Soup Image on Line in Union Fight," *Wall Street Journal*, July 21, 1983, p. 29.

[13]*Ibid.*, p. 37.

[14]"Campbell Soup Boycotters Welcomed by Jesse Jackson," *Daily Labor Report*, No. 139 (July 19, 1984), p. A-10.

[15]Tom Torok, "Campbell Gets Little Reaction to Televised Call For Boycott," *Philadelphia Inquirer*, July 19, 1984, p. 10-C.

The company was forewarned that "something would happen" during Rev. Jackson's address and its public-relations personnel "were braced for the worst as they sat in corporate headquarters and waited for the phones to ring."[16] A Campbell spokesman admitted, "I thought we would get a lot of media calls" and added, "but we got nothing."[17] There was, in the words of the company "no giant swell of public reaction—or any reaction, for that matter."[18] The company, however, did report a reaction from a Republican from Virginia who was quoted as saying "I'd like to know where I can buy a case of Campbell's soup so I can put a stop to this kind of thing."[19]

The company consistently has maintained that the boycott which was to continue for another two years after Rev. Jackson's speech had "little effect" on company sales and profits. Three months after Rev. Jackson's speech a company spokesman was reported to have said "profits have continued to increase every year since the boycott, and in fiscal 1983 Campbell reported a 16 percent increase in earnings and an 11 percent jump in sales, to $13.6 billion."[20] In a private interview almost two years later that same company spokesman indicated that, while the figures were not the same, the basic trends were, and that while some sales undoubtedly had been lost such loses were trivial compared to overall corporate financial results.

In the fall of 1984, the leaders of the boycott, Baldemar Velasquez of FLOC and Rogers of Corporate Campaign Inc., were reported to agree that their boycott "has not hurt Campbell financially," but to disagree "that it has had no effect."[21] In the reported words of Velasquez, "They moved from giving no response to being the only company talking about farm-worker issues" and of Rogers, "If it weren't successful, they wouldn't respond at all."[22] The obvious question is, "Why would a profitable and growing company which felt no discernible economic effect from a boycott respond to it?" The obvious answer is "customer relations," but that also lacks plausibility in a company with an annual volume of consumer inquiries of between 125,000 and 130,000 of which, at most, 350–400 were ever related to FLOC or its boycott. Given that fact, it would seem that the campaign and boycott did not even create a "public relations" problem for the company.

---

[16]*Ibid.*

[17]*Ibid.*

[18]*Ibid.*

[19]*Ibid.*

[20]Pat Winters, "Union To Step Up Attack On Campbell," *Advertising Age*, October 29, 1984, p. 67E.

[21]*Ibid.*

[22]*Ibid.*

The answer to the question as to how an obviously ineffective boycott can be effective in forcing its target to respond is to be found in a headline of a 1983 *Wall Street Journal* article on the dispute which declared, "Campbell Soup Image on Line In Union Fight."[23] That article, written at the outset of the 1983 protest march, reported that, "the company, uncharacteristically worried, has responded by belittling the union in a media blitz of its own" and that "Campbell has recently taken the offensive, preparing pamphlets and sending anti-FLOC broadsides to new organizations along the march's route."[24] In the view of the *Wall Street Journal* the reason for such uncharacteristic corporate behavior was the fact that:

> At stake for Campbell is the company's squeaky-clean public image, cultivated in its "soup is good food" commercials and in its corporate-giving record. Officials consider that all-American reputation a priceless asset, and they display an almost filial protectiveness toward the company. "How would you like to have your mother criticized unjustly?" says Raymond S. Paige, vice president for corporate relations.[25]

One year later, the *Philadelphia Inquirer*, in describing the Rev. Jackson speech crisis, touched on the same theme in more succinct and more colorful terms when it reported that, "what happened had all the ingredients for being mmmm-mmmm bad for Campbell's public relations."[26] In that context, the company must have been stung by the boycott symbol of the familiar red and white can labeled "Cream of Exploitation Soup."

The one underpinning of Campbell's "squeaky-clean" public image which proved most vulnerable to boycott pressure was its "corporate-giving record," in general, and its "Labels for Education Program," in particular. That program offers schools the opportunity to exchange Campbell Soup labels for needed educational equipment on terms like those of the now largely nonexistent trading stamps. In the early 1980s, approximately 28,000 schools participated in the program, redeeming some 300 million labels annually. The *Business and Society Review*, in an article highly critical of virtually all of Campbell's corporate policies and practices, described that program in the following terms:

> One charitable program that has been most instrumental in spreading Campbell's benevolent corporate image nationally in the past dec-

---

[23]Englemeyer, "Campbell Soup Image . . ." pp. 29 & 37.
[24]*Ibid.*, p. 29.
[25]*Ibid.*
[26]Torok, "Campbell Gets Little Reaction . . ." p. 10-C.

ade is the Labels for Education Program. Initiated in 1974, the program provides audio-visual and sports equipment to elementary schools throughout the country in exchange for labels from Campbell Soup cans. . . . the Labels program is an effective and cheap promotional scheme. School children not only aid in advertising but promote sales urging their families and neighbors to buy Campbell Soup to support the schools. Campbell, in effect, exploits the lack of resources of schools. The Labels program has become institutionalized in many schools; the schools come to depend on the Labels program to supplement their meager resources to purchase needed equipment. Moreover, Campbell is able to polish its image of performing community service.[27]

That critical article closed the circle on Campbell's image by stigmatizing both its product and program with the brand of "exploitation." The fact that neither stigma came from a particularly objective source might have given some intellectual solace, but little emotional solace, to a management with an "almost filial protectiveness toward the company."

The Labels for Education Program, by its very nature, provided a measure of the possible adverse effects of the boycott on the company's image. Beginning in the early 1980s, after the involvement of the Archdiocese of Boston in the dispute, the company became aware of some changes in patterns of participation by Catholic schools. Those changes become more evident after the involvement of the National Council of Churches in the dispute in 1983. In some cases, the change seemed to involve withholding labels for one year for submission in the next year. In other cases, however, the change appeared to involve total withdrawal from the program. Whatever the nature and magnitude of those changes, they were a source of concern to Campbell management long before the June 17, 1985 announcement by the Roman Catholic Bishops in Ohio that "they [would] support the right of farm workers to collective bargaining by urging Catholic schools and hospitals in Ohio to join the union boycott of Campbell Soup Co. products" and that "they [would] urge Catholic Elementary Schools to refrain from taking part in the company's label-redemption, fund-raising programs."[28] Interestingly, that announcement came a month after an understanding had been reached between the company and the union which created a commission to resolve the question of worker representation.

---

[27]Jim Terry, "Campbell Soup in Hot Water with Organized Labor," *Business and Society Review*, Summer 1983, pp. 38–39.

[28]"Discussions May Bring End to Farm Workers Boycott of Campbell Soup," *Daily Labor Report*, No. 120 (June 21, 1985), pp. A-5–A-6.

The Seattle First Boycott

The refusal of SeaFirst to recognize and bargain with Local 1182 of the Retail Clerks International Union (RCIU) following the First-bank Independent Employees Association's affiliation vote was met by a call from the local union for an "in house" boycott of the bank. Members of the union and the bargaining unit were asked to with-draw funds, to close accounts, to return bank charge cards cut in half, and to pay bills with numerous small checks in order to disrupt the check-clearing process during the spring and summer of 1978. This effort produced little in the way of concrete results, providing instead the first evidence that the union did not hold the hearts and minds of most bank employees.

The union's next step was to broaden the scope of its boycott appeal to the Seattle labor community. Unions in the area were con-tacted and asked to write to the chairman of the board of SeaFirst threatening to cease doing business with the bank and to urge union members to do the same if the bank did not begin bargaining in good faith. Individual members of RCIU locals and other unions in the area were asked to send forms to the chairman of the board which read as follows:

> As a depositor at Seattle First National Bank and a union member, I am appalled at the hostile attitude your bank has taken during the course of labor negotiations with the employees of Seattle First National Bank.
>
> It is extremely upsetting to me when I realize that my money, deposited at your bank, is being used to deny bank employees the rights and protection that any working person deserves.
>
> Therefore, if Seattle-First National Bank does not begin to bargain in good faith in the very near future, your actions will force me to withdraw all funds from my personal accounts.[29]

The union also sought to widen its boycott appeal both within the labor community and among religious and other interest groups by questioning some of SeaFirst's business relationships. The union urged the bank to call in its loans to and to cease doing business with Wien Air Alaska, which was then operating during a strike by the Air Line Pilots Association. When the bank declined to do so, the union accused it of supporting the company in its labor dispute. The union also challenged the bank's policy of providing loans to compa-nies doing business in South Africa or other countries with socially

---

[29]"Management Memo," Seattle First National Bank, No. 59 (December 4, 1978) Attachment 1.

unacceptable national policies. These allegations laid the ground-
work for a drive to deluge bank board members with postcards carrying the following message:

> I am aware of the hostile and illegal attitude your bank has taken
> during the labor negotiations with your employees.
>
> It is upsetting to me when profits made off of my money, deposited
> at your bank, are being used to deny bank employees the rights and
> protection working people deserve, to fund companies during strikes
> (such as Wien Air Alaska), to lobby against the best interests of work-
> ing people, and to make substantial loans to countries, or companies
> doing business in countries such as South Africa and Chile which have
> little or no regard for human rights. These facts, as they become more
> widely publicized, certainly will not enhance the image of Seattle
> First National Bank in the eyes of the public nor with labor unions and
> concerned religious and community groups.
>
> This card is to inform you that if in the very near future you do not
> begin to bargain in good faith with your employees and also begin to
> fulfill a moral obligation to the citizens of Washington, your actions
> will force me to withdraw all funds from my personal accounts or
> to refrain from using Seattle-First National Bank for any future
> business.[30]

The union's fundamental operating assumption during the period
when its petition for an amended certification was pending before
the NLRB was that the prospect of a possible large-scale withdrawal
of funds would lead the bank to rethink its refusal to recognize the
union. The fact that a mass withdrawal of funds might affect the
jobs of bank employees did not go unnoticed by either the bank,
which reportedly was "warning its workers that any substantial success in the AFL-CIO campaign to pull money out of Sea-First would
jeopardize their own jobs," or the union, which reportedly admitted
that it "hopes its pressure will cause the bank to negotiate a contract before any workers are knocked out of their jobs."[31]

If, as reported by *Forbes*, "the knowledge that mass withdrawals
could operate as a double-edged sword, hurting the unionized workers as much as they did the bank, worries the campaign strategists,"
it did not worry the reported "master planner of the whole effort,"
Ray Rogers, who, also as reported by *Forbes*, "is convinced that the
bank will chicken out before the ax falls on employees."[32] This conviction was based on his view that "banks and insurance companies
are the most vulnerable of all businesses, . . . because what they con-

---

[30]*Ibid.*
[31]A. H. Raskin, "Show 'Em the Clenched Fist!" *Forbes*, October 2, 1978, p. 32.
[32]*Ibid.*

trol they don't own. They are totally dependent on the support of their depositors and policyholders."[33]

The expectations of the union and of Rogers were not fulfilled. The threat of a withdrawal of funds did not force the bank to back down in its confrontation on the recognition issue either before or after the NLRB's initial favorable (to the union) ruling on affiliation and certification. What the union and Rogers apparently failed to anticipate was that the bank was convinced it could not afford to "buckle" under a threat of deposit withdrawals or promise of new deposits without forever making itself a potential hostage to the union movement, its future causes, and its allies. What the union also failed to anticipate was that it would be blamed as much as, if not more than the bank, for any loss of jobs as a result of the threatened boycott, thereby further weakening its already limited support within its claimed bargaining unit.

The decision of the bank to challenge the NLRB's certification ruling by refusing to bargain with the RCIU forced the union's hand. In the spring of 1979, the union was compelled to implement its long-threatened boycott against the bank. It formally designated April 23 as "withdrawal day" and called upon unions, social action and community groups, and the general public to withdraw funds from SeaFirst in a show of support for the union in its battle for recognition by the bank—support which the union claimed totalled over $2 billion in withdrawal pledges from unions and other organizations.

The April 23 "withdrawal day" came and passed with relatively little abnormal withdrawal activity. The union publicly claimed its boycott had cost the bank from $20 million to $70 million in business. The bank, however, privately estimated the amount of funds actually withdrawn as a result of the boycott to have been less than $2 million as of the end of June 1979.[34]

The boycott effort did not end with "withdrawal day." By July 1979, the RCIU had published an article in its own newspaper again urging its members to boycott SeaFirst and providing detailed instructions as to how to do so at minimum personal cost and inconvenience. In addition, it conducted public demonstrations protesting the bank's labor and lending policies, hired pickets to walk in front of at least one branch on a daily basis, and launched a "Boycott SeaFirst" bumper sticker campaign. These activities produced little

---

[33]*Ibid.*
[34]Data supplied by the bank.

additional withdrawal activity, and by the end of September the bank estimated that only slightly more than $3 million in deposits had been lost because of the boycott.

In the fall of 1979, the union further escalated its "Boycott SeaFirst" campaign in an attempt to broaden its appeal to the general public. By October the union's efforts were expanded to the renting of billboard space in Spokane, the passing out of "Boycott SeaFirst" balloons in Seattle, and the posting of two picket lines rotating from branch to branch. Finally, the union rented ad space on the side of transit authority buses to carry its "Boycott SeaFirst" plea. Ironically, many of those same buses also carried ads posted by the transit authority (not the bank) thanking SeaFirst for its support of public transit through a decision to institute a free bus transport system for its employees as part of its benefit program. This system induced more employees to ride the buses on which the union was advertising its boycott message—a message which did little to enhance their affection for the union, whose campaign threatened their jobs.

The bank's response to the union's campaign, by design, was low key. It did respond to all letters which it received, explaining its position and asking the individuals or organizations in question to maintain their accounts. It also placed leaflets carrying the same messages in all of its branches. It did not, however, undertake any special mass media marketing efforts either to rebut the union's allegations or to recruit new clientele.

The bank's most aggressive response to the boycott was in the area of internal communications. In dealing with its own employees it took great care to explain the basis for and process of its legal challenge to the recognition of the RCIU, focusing attention on the "freedom of choice" issue. In addition, the bank pointed out the potential effects of a successful boycott on existing employees. On the issues of free choice and job security, the institutional interests of the union clearly conflicted with the individual interests of employees and consequently constituted obvious points of vulnerability for the union in gaining the loyalty of employees. In this context, the fact that the union was on the "wrong side" of the "free choice" issue may have been key in that, in the view of one observer, "if the union had allowed all employees to vote and the bank was resisting recognition on purely technical grounds, the story might have been different."

By the end of 1979, the RCIU claimed that its "Boycott SeaFirst" campaign had cost the bank more than $200 million—about 10 percent of its original $2 billion withdrawal threat. The bank, for its part, estimated its total loss of deposits at no more than $5 million. Beyond that relatively minor loss, the bank suffered little additional damage as a result of the boycott. A survey of its depositors conducted in late 1979 reportedly disclosed that only one-third were aware of the boycott and that 80 percent of those disapproved of it.[35] Thus, it appears that the union had expended considerable energy and money to mount a boycott which did little to affect adversely the bank's customer relations or to affect positively its own relations with either the bank's customers or employees.

---

[35]Data supplied by the bank.

CHAPTER VI

The Game Of Principal

The final point of potential corporate vulnerability open to exploitation in a coordinated campaign is access to capital, both debt and equity. In the words of the AFL-CIO Industrial Union Department (IUD): "A campaign should take advantage of vulnerabilities in the relationship between the target company and its financial backers."[1] Inevitably, that entails exerting pressure on the financial institutions and institutional investors which are an integral part of most corporate financial families in what amounts to another form of vertical conflict expansion akin to that of the game of protest. The game of principal, like that of protest, is based on the exploitation of some political and/or economic sensitivity of, in this case, financial backers. Again in the words of the IUD:

> Unfortunately, prohibition of secondary boycotts limits the campaign in this respect. Even so, there is still considerable room for lawful action, especially from reason rather than threats. The union should demonstrate to members of the financial community that it understands the economics of the situation and is sensitive to their concerns.[2]

Beyond reason and sensitivity, "the union should consider taking concrete actions against creditors and lenders that will impose costs—whether financial or in terms of public image—for their backing of the target company."[3] Such concrete actions could include an assault on a financial backer on any of five fronts—public relations, government relations, stockholder relations, customer relations, investor relations—on which any coordinated campaign may be waged. In the area of customer relations, the IUD specifically suggests:

> The union should also make known to the financial powers that it is aware of the potential monetary leverage it can bring to bear. Unions

---

[1] Industrial Union Department, AFL-CIO, *Developing New Tactics: Winning With Coordinated Corporate Campaigns* (Washington, D.C.: Industrial Union Department, AFL-CIO, 1985), p. 7.
[2] *Ibid.*, pp. 7–8.
[3] *Ibid.*, p. 8.

often are large commercial clients in their own right and union trustees of pensions can, within the limits of their obligations to benefi-
ciaries, exert considerable influence over how pension funds are
invested.[4]

The game of principal, more than any other, directly involves not
only the primary target, but possibly also secondary targets. In
light of that fact, it is hardly surprising that the IUD, in discussing
the tactic of "Pressuring Lenders and Creditors," states that "it is
essential that legal counsel be contacted before any action is implemented," and later reiterates, "again it is important that legal counsel be consulted before any action is taken in this regard."[5] The sample of campaigns studied revealed two cases in which that advice
apparently went unheeded resulting in ill-advised if not illegal secondary activity (Phelps Dodge and Hormel). The sample of campaigns studied also revealed several instances of apparently ineffective primary activity on the financial front (Phelps Dodge and
Louisiana-Pacific).

PRIMARY ACTIVITY

The union movement enjoys a measure of influence, if not control,
over the investment of billions of dollars of various types of "fund
assets." The IUD, in its primer on coordinated corporate campaigns,
discusses the possibility of "Using Fund Assets," but exclusively in
the secondary activity context of its view that, "Pension fund management is an extremely profitable and competitive business and
investment firms do not want to antagonize unions any more than
necessary."[6] The possibility of using such "ownership leverage" to
threaten directly the stock price or credit rating of a target company
was not addressed by the IUD, but was raised at least implicitly in
the course of the campaign against Consolidated Foods—the only
one in which the company admitted that the sale of blocks of its
stock was possibly attributable to the campaign against it.

The first four or five months of the campaign against Consolidated Foods which began in October 1982 were spent in a war of
written correspondence. In the course of that war, the corporation
received two types of financially interesting letters. The first was
typified by the first of what was to prove a long series of letters from
Sister Theresa Billeaud of the Sisters of Divine Providence to the

---

[4]*Ibid.*
[5]*Ibid.*
[6]*Ibid.*

company which began:

> I am writing in the name of the Central Administration of the Sisters of Divine Providence. As Director of the Social Justice Office of our Congregation, I work closely with our treasurer in monitoring our investments for social responsibility so that they might provide us with financial security as well as make a contribution to the betterment of humankind. We own 1000 shares of stock in Consolidated Foods.[7]

The second was typified by a letter from an individual who identified himself as "a trustee of the California Public Employee Retirement System, which currently holds 427,461 shares of Consolidated Foods Corporations stock in its portfolio," and who wrote:

> ... as an individual trustee who wishes to obtain from you a more complete understanding of what your corporation's labor relations posture is regarding its Hanes Division and how this may affect our Fund's investments in Consolidated Foods.[8]

The Consolidated Foods campaign was not the only one to generate such correspondence. It did, however, generate the largest quantity of such correspondence and in doing so provided the clearest evidence of a pattern to such correspondence. That pattern is one in which the threat and possible reality of disinvestment is the one most quickly and easily exercised by religious groups, individual trustees, or other individuals responsible for the investment of public sector retirement funds. Noticeably absent among the correspondents in the Consolidated and other campaigns were "union trustees of pensions" in the private sector or from those responsible for the management of, in the words of the IUD, "the assets of general funds [which] also constitute a large pool of funds which can be moved in a corporate campaign."[9]

The sample of campaigns studied produced a few other examples of what may be termed "primary financial boycott activity." In both the Phelps Dodge and Louisiana-Pacific cases, the unions took their case from Main Street to Wall Street, probably for lack of a viable alternative focus for a campaign. In the case of Beverly Enterprises and perhaps Louisiana-Pacific, the union carried its case beyond Wall Street public relations to back street government relations in the form of industrial development funds. The unions in question

---

[7]Letter from Sister Theresa Billeaud, Sisters of Divine Providence, to Mr. John H. Bryan, Jr. Consolidated Foods Corporation, dated March 28, 1983.

[8]Letter from Mr. Wilson Riles, Jr., Councilman, City of Oakland, to Mr. John Bryant, President, Consolidated Foods Corporation, dated December 13, 1982.

[9]Industrial Union Department, AFL-CIO, *Developing New Tactics*, p. 8.

appeared to have fared far better in the latter than in the former
arena of financial combat.

Public Relations

In the spring of 1984, the United Brotherhood of Carpenters
(UBC) took its campaign against Louisiana-Pacific to Wall Street in
the form of a noon rally at the New York Stock Exchange (NYSE)
following a morning of publicity leafletting in the financial district.
In announcing that action, the union indicated that it was designed
to "show Louisiana-Pacific we will be taking action from Main
Street to Wall Street" in "making our case against Louisiana-
Pacific not just to the consuming public, but also to the investing public, shareholders, government officials and regulatory
agencies."[10]
Prior to that rally, the UBC had written to a major insurance company which was Louisiana-Pacific's largest shareholder to inform it
of the existence of the campaign and to suggest that it was in a
unique position "to exercise informed discretion and independent
judgment as to how the present dispute might best be resolved."[11]
The union also wrote to a major bank which was signatory to a
credit agreement with Louisiana-Pacific to inform it of the campaign, citing a section of the credit agreement providing that the
bank was to be promptly apprised of any strike involving 1,000 or
more Louisiana-Pacific employees which continues for more than
thirty days. Neither of those financial institutions responded to such
invitations to involve itself in the dispute.

The union's efforts produced only one positive response known to
the company. One small San Francisco money fund, Working
Assets, wrote to Louisiana-Pacific to indicate that it would "not purchase prime commercial paper of Louisiana-Pacific Corp. because
your company has been placed on the national AFL-CIO 'Do Not
Patronize' list."[12] Further, the fund indicated that it would "notify
our shareholders of your company's violation of our social and
economic investment criteria, and ask that they not purchase your
products."[13]

[10]UBC Press Release, March 20, 1984.

[11]Letter from Mr. Patrick J. Campbell, General President, United Brotherhood of
Carpenters, to Mr. Edward B. Rust, President and Chief Executive Officer, State
Farm Mutual, dated February 6, 1984, p. 2.

[12]Letter from Mr. John C. Harrington, Vice President, Working Assets, to Mr.
H. A. Merlo, Chairman and President, Louisiana-Pacific Corp., dated March 30, 1984,
p. 1.

[13]*Ibid.*

The Steelworkers also took their campaign against Phelps Dodge from Main Street to Wall Street on the stated assumption that the "Wall Street creditors are the company's only hope of survival."[14] The first step in that effort was a charge in August 1984 that the company's recently released form 10Q report to the Securities and Exchange Commission (SEC) showed that Phelps Dodge "has failed to act in a prudent manner" towards its stockholders and investors.[15] The next step was the creation of a task force to question the company's creditors who have union clients "about the credit worthiness of Phelps Dodge, while we of the Labor Movement question our continued relationships with those institutions."[16] According to *Business Week*:

> The USW is mounting a "corporate campaign" by trying to enlist the help of large creditors, such as Chase Manhattan Bank, Metropolitan Life Insurance Co., and Citibank. Arguing that the company has hurt itself by continuing to operate its Arizona mines despite depressed demand for copper, the USW hopes to persuade these institutions to press Phelps Dodge—which is already in shaky financial condition— to change its position toward the union. If creditors refuse, the Steelworkers and other sympathetic unions are threatening to withdraw $250 million in strike and pension funds from these institutions.[17]

The fact that Phelps Dodge was, in the words of one financial analyst, "in a survival mode" clearly made the corporation vulnerable to pressure from its creditors. Despite that fact, "Even with these serious problems, financial experts are skeptical about the impact of the USW's corporate campaign."[18] One such expert, a vice-president of Chase Manhattan who met with representatives of the union was quoted as saying, "I certainly think the union is serious. But I have never seen this kind of campaign before, and I just don't know whether it will have any effect."[19] Whatever effect it did have was not sufficient to change the company's economic viability until it could return to profitable operation as it did in 1985.

---

[14]"Phelps Dodge Corporate Ties Targeted," *AFL-CIO News*, Vol. 29, No. 35 September 1, 1984, p. 3.

[15]"Steelworkers, On Strike 14 Months At Phelps Dodge, Announces Corporate Campaign Against Copper Firm," *Daily Labor Report*, No. 163 (August 22, 1984) p. A-13.

[16]*Ibid.*

[17]"A Final Union Onslaught At Phelps Dodge," *Business Week*, September 24, 1984, pp. 43–44.

[18]*Ibid.*, p. 44.

[19]*Ibid.*

Financial Relations

The sample of campaigns studied provides little evidence to suggest that unions have been able to alter substantially established financial relationships involving target companies or to impede the access of those companies to equity or debt capital. That does not mean that unions have not been able to complicate financial relations and access to funds, particularly where such relations and access involve government.

In the Beverly campaign, the union challenged the company's offering of $70 million of convertible, subordinated debt before the SEC on the grounds that the company may have failed adequately to notify the public of the existence of the campaign and its potential impact on the corporation. Although the company termed the union's challenge "too ridiculous for comment," it could hardly have welcomed that challenge given its ongoing need for capital to sustain its rapid growth. In that context, the ability of the union to block company access to $15 million in Massachusetts Industrial Revenue Bonds was even more disquieting because of the company's reliance on such funding in the past for some of its modernization efforts in newly acquired operations.

A somewhat similar set of events occurred in the Louisiana-Pacific campaign. There the union was able to convince the Labor-Management Subcommittee of the House Education and Labor Committee to undertake a "preliminary investigation of the company's use of Urban Development Action Grants from the U.S. Department of Housing and Urban Development to help finance its waferboard...facilities."[20] Further, the union claimed it had been instrumental in forcing the company to withdraw one application for such a grant. The company claimed that its grant application was withdrawn for other reasons—a change in proposed plant site—and that it was little bothered by the preliminary investigation which never went beyond that stage.

SECONDARY ACTIVITY

The basic goal of secondary activity is to convince a financial institution(s) to cease doing business with the target company rather than use its influence to counsel the target company to change its policy or position. That effort may be undertaken either through per-

---

[20]"Carpenter's L-P Strike Campaign," handout distributed at a noon rally on Wall Street, March 22, 1984, p. 3.

suasion (embarrassment) or coercion (harassment). Although it is often difficult to draw a precise boundary between the two, the former usually involves a public relations campaign against the secondary target while the latter entails a financial relations campaign against the secondary target.

The premier case of such secondary activity came in the campaign against J.P. Stevens. That campaign involved "successful pressure by unions, led by the Amalgamated [Clothing and Textile Workers], upon Manufacturers Hanover, to sever boardroom ties with J.P. Stevens on threat of removing union pension funds from the bank."[21] At that time, "the assets of the unions, union members, and union pension funds on deposit with the bank were estimated at approximately $1 billion."[22] The right of unions to select pension trust managers for the trusts they control is subject only to limited constraint under ERISA. The exercise of that right in the context of a corporate campaign, however, has prompted the following question: "But if banks or other financial institutions yield to the kind of pressure under which Manufacturers Hanover folded, what is to prevent corporations with far more economic muscle from applying counter pressure?"[23]

Public Relations

The Campbell Soup campaign involved three financial concerns as secondary targets—Prudential Insurance, Equitable Life Assurance and Philadelphia National Bank. Those three companies were chosen because "Prudential's chairman and chief executive officer, Robert Beck, is a member of Campbell's board of directors as is Andrew Lewis, an Equitable director. R. Gordon McGovern, the president of Campbell, serves on the boards of the Philadelphia National Bank and its parent company, the CoreStates Financial Corporation."[24] The purpose to be served in involving those companies in the campaign was, in words attributed to Ray Rogers:

---

[21]James P. Northrup and Herbert R. Northrup, "Union Divergent Investing of Pensions: A Power, Non-Employee Issue," *Journal of Labor Research*, Vol. II, No. 2 (Fall 1981), p. 203.

[22]Terry W. Mullins and Paul Luebke, "Symbolic Victory and Political Reality in the Southern Textile Industry: The Meaning of the J. P. Stevens Settlement for Southern Labor Relations," *Journal of Labor Research*, Vol. II, No. 1 (Winter 1982), p. 84.

[23]James P. Northrup and Herbert R. Northrup, "Union Divergent Investing of Pensions . . . ," p. 203.

[24]"Farm Group Boycotting Campbell Puts Focus on Financial Concerns," *New York Times*, November 27, 1984, p. A-15.

... to draw these big financial institutions into the conflict so that the general public and the policyholders of these companies, and the administrators of these companies, are well aware of their role in the treatment of farm workers. It's using divide-and-conquer strategy against the corporate power structure.[25]

The only one of the three financial institutions to receive substantial attention during the course of the campaign was CoreStates which is headquartered in Philadelphia just across the Delaware River from Campbell's headquarters in Camden. The CoreStates annual meeting was visited by Farm Labor Organizing Committee (FLOC) supporters both in 1984 and 1985. At the 1985 meeting, those supporters "spoke before the meeting and passed out copies of a 'FLOC Annual Report' that asked shareholders to dismiss McGovern from the board."[26] Further, "As about 100 demonstrators marched outside the bank, local FLOC director Mike Casey said that within 10 days FLOC would decide whether to begin the boycott of PNB that it had threatened at last year's annual meeting."[27]

The chairman of CoreStates told the company's shareholders at their 1985 meeting that the corporation would "continue to refrain from intervening in a dispute between a farm labor union and Campbell Soup Co. despite a threatened boycott." At the same meeting Mr. McGovern was re-elected to the CoreStates board. The threatened boycott of Philadelphia National Bank never came to pass, although there were instances of protests at PNB branches, including one on Philadelphia's Main Line some four months after the CoreStates annual meeting. A local paper reported that incident as follows:

> Handing out leaflets with a large picture of a can of "Cream of Exploitation" Campbell's Soup drawn upon them, supporters of the Farm Labor Organizing Committee gathered with picket signs in front of the PNB Bank in St. Davids Friday afternoon to protest what they feel are unfair working conditions for migrant workers on midwestern farms ...
>
> Petitions drawing 400 signatures had been circulated throughout the Main Line area by Farm Labor Organizing Committee members and were presented to PNB officials at the time of the small demonstration. Coordinator Mike Casey said the committee wants to see PNB withdraw its financial obligations to Campbell Soup Co. and remove Gordon McGovern from his position on the bank's board.[28]

---

[25] *Ibid.*

[26] Alexis Moore Love, "CoreStates Will Stay Out of Dispute Between Campbell and Farm Workers," *Philadelphia Inquirer*, April 17, 1985, p. 13-D.

[27] *Ibid.*

[28] Susan Greenspoon, "Pickets Protest PNB, Campbell Soup Co.," *Main Line Times*, August 29, 1985, p. 5.

The corporate campaign against Phelps Dodge paralleled that against Campbell Soup in that a bank, Manufacturers Hanover Trust Company, became a target of union attention by virtue of the fact that "Phelps Dodge Chairman George Munroe was on the board of MHT, and that the bank had made substantial loans to Phelps Dodge throughout the year-and-half-old strike against the company."[29] The major difference between the two campaigns was the report that "as part of a United Steelworkers corporate campaign against Phelps Dodge Corporation, American Federation of Teachers President Albert Shanker announces that the New York State Teachers Retirement System is removing Manufacturers Hanover Trust Company as the investment manager for more than one-third of the fund's $1.5 billion in assets."[30] A spokesman for the bank was subsequently reported to have responded to that announcement as follows: "The facts were wrong, the dates were wrong, the figures were wrong and the reasons were wrong."[31] Apparently, the bank was right and Mr. Shanker was wrong as indicated in the latter's subsequent "clarification" of his original announcement.[32]

The Steelworkers' assault on "banks that lend money to Phelps Dodge Corporation" began auspiciously enough in October 1984 when it was reported that the "USW says it will withdraw $10.8 million from Chase Manhattan Bank and will terminate its custodial arrangement with the bank. In addition $750,000 in securities which the union held in the name of Manufacturers Hanover Trust Company are being terminated."[33] For the next almost four months there was no other significant activity reported on this campaign front, lending credence to an earlier observation by *Business Week* that, "It is unclear whether the USW can attract enough support from other unions to mount a credible threat against financial institutions."[34] In retrospect, it is clear that the USW, like the union at SeaFirst, could not gain such support which would explain the why if not the how of Mr. Shanker's, in his own words, "being sucked in" to a "publicity stunt" in announcing the withdrawal of pension funds

---

[29]"Teacher Union Removes $450 Million from Pension Fund to Support Phelps Dodge Campaign," *Daily Labor Report*, No. 34 (February 20, 1985), p. A-3.

[30]*Ibid.*, p. A-2.

[31]"Editors' Note," *New York Times*, February 23, 1985, p. .

[32]Kenneth B. Noble, "Reporter's Notebook: Shanker 'Clarification,'" *New York Times*, February 23, 1985, p. 8.

[33]"Steelworkers Begin Withdrawing Funds from Banks that Lent to Phelps Dodge," *Daily Labor Report*, No. 195 (October 9, 1984), p. A-3.

[34]"A Final Onslaught At Phelps Dodge," p. 44.

from Manufacturers Hanover in February 1985.[35] In the same article that quoted Mr. Shanker as using those words, the *New York Times* reported that:

> Officials of the A.F.L.-C.I.O. said that despite Mr. Shanker's effort to justify the withdrawal of funds as a business judgment, it was clearly a move to protest loans the bank made to the Phelps Dodge Corporation, which has been involved in a bitter strike led by the steelworkers union since July 1983.
>
> The officials predicted that the move against Phelps Dodge would serve as a showcase of labor's potential strength.[36]

Financial Relations

Unions, individually and collectively, are substantial direct and indirect consumers of financial services—a fact which has not gone unnoticed in the financial community. The sample of campaigns studied suggests that, thus far, unions and the union movement have been unable or unwilling to utilize their "consumer power" in the game of principal. The Chase Manhattan Bank was not rocked by the Steelworkers' withdrawal of $10.5 million of union funds nor was SeaFirst by the response of Seattle-area unions and their members to what is now the United Food and Commercial Workers' (UFCW) call for consumer boycott. Furthermore, the sample yields no evidence of the effective use of the role of unions as administrators of, trustees of, or signatories to pension and insurance programs to secure the aid of a financial institution in a corporate campaign. That does not mean that unions cannot utilize their role as indirect consumers of financial services (on behalf of their members) to influence financial institutions, but it does suggest that the limits of fiduciary responsibility and limits on secondary boycotts have imposed real constraints on the exercise of the potential leverage.

In only one of the ten campaigns studied did the game of principal become a game of hardball rather than softball—the campaign of Local P-9 of the UFCW against Hormel. In that campaign, the local union and its outside "consultant-strategist," Ray Rogers, decided to encourage a consumer boycott by the general public, not just the union or its members, of a bank which had financial ties to the company—the First Bank System, headquartered in Minneapolis. In conjunction with that effort the local union, in addition to withdrawing its own funds from First Bank, picketed not only the bank's

---

[35]Noble, "Reporter's Notebook," p. 8.
[36]*Ibid.*

Minneapolis headquarters but several of its branches in Minnesota, Wisconsin, and Iowa in what the President of Local P-9 was to admit was an attempt "to break consumer loyalty to First Bank and break the bank's ties to Hormel."[37] Those ties were a product of the fact that:

> First Bank Chairman DeWalt Ankeny, Jr. sits on the Hormel board of directors, and Hormel Chairman Richard Knowlton sits on the First Bank board. In addition, First Bank Minneapolis holds about 14 percent of Hormel stock in four pension and profitsharing trusts and occasionally provides short-term loans to Hormel.[38]

The union's actions prompted Hormel to ask "the NLRB to halt picketting and pamphleteering aimed at customers of First Bank System . . . " despite the fact that both Hormel and First Bank "have said the corporate campaign has cost them little business."[39] As a result of that request, the Minneapolis regional director of the NLRB on two occasions in the fall of 1985 issued complaints charging Local P-9 with "engaging in unlawful secondary boycott activity in picketing a bank to bring pressure on the primary employer to settle the labor dispute."[40] Those complaints led to a hearing before an administrative law judge in December 1985—a hearing whose outcome "could set a precedent at a time when labor unions are turning to novel tactics to bring consumer and financial pressure on employers."[41]

It is still too early to determine what precedent will be set by the Hormel/Local P-9 case. At the hearing, the union, as already indicated, admitted its goal of breaking the bank's "ties to Hormel but defended that goal on the grounds that the bank's ties to Hormel make it a major ally with the power to influence Hormel's labor policies."[42] The administrative law judge was not impressed by the union's defense and upheld the charges against it in a decision issued in March of 1986.[43] On September 30, 1986, the NLRB upheld that finding of a violation of Section 8(b)(4)(ii)(B) of the Taft-Hartley Act.[44]

---

[37]David Hage, "Hormel Monitored Bank Pickets," *Minneapolis Star and Tribune*, December 4, 1985, p. 2M.

[38]*Ibid.*, p. 1M.

[39]*Ibid.*, pp. 1M & 2M.

[40]"UFCW's Continued Picketing at Bank Results in Second ULP Complaint," *Daily Labor Report*, No. 206 (October 24, 1985), p. A-5.

[41]Hage, "Hormel Monitored Bank Pickets," p. 1M.

[42]*Ibid.*

[43]"UFCW Local Unlawfully Picketed Banks In Dispute With Hormel, NLRB ALJ Rules," *Daily Labor Report*, No. 53 (March 19, 1986), p. A-2.

[44]Local P-9 United Food and Commercial Workers, 281 N.L.R.B. No. 135 (1986).

The legal questions raised but not yet finally resolved in the Hormel case clearly are of more than passing interest to unions, managements, and particularly to financial institutions. Of equal significance to all of those interested parties is the related practical question of the degree of vulnerability of financial institutions to consumer boycotts, whether primary or secondary in character. The experience at SeaFirst and apparently at First Bank suggests that although the impact of consumer boycott activity is not trivial it is far less significant than might be expected based on the claims of the proponents of such action. Thus far, the impact of such action seems to have been felt primarily in some loss of new as opposed to established business and/or customers judging by developments at SeaFirst and First Bank and also at Equitable Assurance during its tenure on the AFL-CIO's boycott list.

CHAPTER VII

The Outcome of the Game

It has now been more than six years since "one of the longest and most bitter labor-management struggles in recent times culminated in a signed contract between J.P. Stevens & Company and the Amalgamated Clothing and Textile Workers Union (ACTWU)" in October 1980.[1] That contract constituted a clear symbolic victory for the union given Stevens' vow "never" to sign a union contract, but it also was "widely heralded as a historic breakthrough in a decades-old attempt to organize Southern industry."[2] That latter prospect apparently has not materialized as, "Southern industry is less than 15 percent unionized, no more than it was five years ago,"[3] giving credence to the view that:

> Thus, the ACTWU-Stevens settlement, far from a "labor break-through," is almost limited in its impact to the single case. The contract was a great symbolic victory for ACTWU since Stevens had said "never," but substantively the union-management battle will be fought individually at each plant in the South, within the context of the particular industrial sector and management attitudes at each company.[4]

The problem of distinguishing symbol and substance in the results of a corporate campaign exists even where no claim is made for impact beyond the target company. The problem arises because assessment of results requires more than a description of the terms on which a campaign ended. It also requires a determination of the longer-run implications of those terms for union-management relations and perhaps for the relations of the company to other interested parties such as the religious, community, government, and activist groups. Those longer-run implications are no less

---

[1]Terry W. Mullins and Paul Luebke, "Symbolic Victory and Political Reality in the Southern Textile Industry: The Meaning of the J.P. Stevens Settlement for Southern Labor Relations," *Journal of Labor Research*, Vol. III, No. 1 (Winter 1982), p. 81.

[2]William Serrin, "Union At Stevens, Yes; Upheaval No," *New York Times*, December 5, 1985, p. A 18.

[3]*Ibid.*

[4]Mullins and Luebke, "Symbolic Victory..." p. 88.

significant than short-run impact in defining the record of corporate campaigns.

THE RESULTS

The corporate campaign against BASF is still very much actively in progress and its outcome still very much in doubt. The remaining nine campaigns are, for all intents and purposes, over and done with. Five of those campaigns ended with a negotiated settlement of one sort or another which, as in the Stevens' case, could be grounds for a claim of at least symbolic victory on the part of those conducting the campaign. The other four campaigns ended without any formal settlement, which presumably might make them candidates for claims of at least symbolic victory by the target of the campaign.

The Settlement Campaigns

The five campaigns which concluded with some form of negotiated settlement were those against Beverly Enterprises, Campbell Soup, Consolidated Foods, General Dynamics, and Litton Industries. The first three are consumer goods/services producers. The latter two are producer goods manufacturers and defense contractors.

The campaign against Beverly Enterprises began in January 1983 and ended in March 1984 when the company and the Service Employees International Union (SEIU) and the United Food and Commercial Workers International Union (UFCW) "reached an understanding that provides the basis for a more positive relationship between the company and the unions."[5] The details or text of that understanding were not and have not been made public, and efforts to secure a copy of the agreement from the parties were unsuccessful. Thus, what is known of the character of the agreement which ended the campaign comes largely from what the parties said jointly in announcing that agreement and what they have subsequently said individually about it.

At the heart of the understanding was, in the words of a company representative who does not want to be identified, "an agreement by both sides to stop calling the other names." It was in that context that the unions agreed to end their corporate campaign in exchange for the company's commitment to make "every effort to ensure a noncoercive atmosphere during election campaigns."[6] The parties

---

[5]"Beverly Enterprises, UFCW, and SEIU Announce Accord Aimed At Cooperation," *Daily Labor Report*, No. 43 (March 5, 1984), P. A–5.
[6]*Ibid.*

jointly characterized that commitment as a reaffirmation of "the principles of employee freedom of choice on union representation" at the time their agreement was announced. Since then the company has consistently denied that it agreed to neutrality and the unions have carefully avoided characterizing the agreement as a neutrality pact, stating only that the agreement "will make it substantially easier for workers to organize."[7]

A second aspect of the understanding was an agreement to establish a national labor/management task force to resolve disputes and problems. One of those problems was the fact that the unions reportedly were experiencing considerable difficulty "in securing collective bargaining agreements, both following a successful NLRB election or when Beverly Enterprises acquired a health care facility that had been previously organized by one of the two unions."[8] In an effort to alleviate that problem, one of the first tasks undertaken by the national task force was the development of contract language on certain noneconomic matters such as grievance procedures for the benefit of those negotiating contracts at the local level. Two years later, the UFCW indicated that "recently, SEIU and the UFCW negotiated an addendum to the agreement that includes a pledge from the company to bargain contracts in newly unionized facilities within three months" and company agreement "to honor union contracts at existing homes it purchases."[9]

At the time the understanding was announced, the SEIU/UFCW effort to organize Beverly Enterprises had been underway for fifteen months. During that time the unions claimed to have won twenty-eight of forty-one NLRB elections in Beverly Enterprises facilities for a victory rate of 70 percent.[10] One year later, in 1985, the total number of election victories since the inception of the campaign had risen to a reported sixty-three which still represented about 70 percent.[11] The lack of change in the union election victory rate would seem to indicate that the understanding did not make it easier to organize Beverly Enterprises facilities. The SEIU, however, claimed that its win rate "since the accord has increased to 91 percent" based on victories in twenty of twenty-four elections with

---

[7]*Ibid.*, p. A–6.

[8]Ibid.

[9]United Food and Commercial Workers International Union, "Beverly Workers Nationwide Voting to Join UFCW," *UFCW Action*, Vol. 8, No. 4, July–August 1986, p. 6.

[10]"Beverly Enterprises, UFCW, and SEIU Announce Accord . . ." p. A–5.

[11]"Unions Targeting Beverly Enterprises Say Election Win Rate is 71 Percent," *White Collar Report*, Vol. 57, No. 10 (March 13, 1985), p. 251.

the results of two of the union losses having been set aside and new elections scheduled.[12] The company characterized the union election figures as "reasonably accurate" but also indicated that it was "very, very clear" that the unions had not achieved their goal of organizing Beverly Enterprises as only about sixty of the company's 908 long-term care facilities were under union contract.[13] By 1986, 145 of the company's 1,025 facilities reportedly were under contract as a result of the fact that:

> Since the joint Service Employees-UFCW Organizing Program began nearly three years ago, the UFCW has won representation elections in 58 Homes. SEIU has conducted 51 successful organizing programs. An additional three dozen union nursing homes remained under union contract after being purchased by Beverly.[14]

In March 1985, "both company and union representatives noted that the parties are heavily involved in collective bargaining negotiations for contracts in homes where the unions have gained representation rights."[15] In discussing those negotiations one union spokesman was reported to have indicated that "while bargaining is going fairly well," Beverly Enterprises does not "give up easily." Despite that fact, the UFCW and SEIU were able to report in June 1985 that, between them, they had seventy-eight Beverly Enterprises homes under contract (43—SEIU, 35—UFCW).[16] In announcing the "wave" of first contract settlements negotiated since the beginning of 1985, the president of the UFCW was quoted as stating "the winning of the contracts means we've really put down some roots in this company. The UFCW is escalating our organizing in Beverly Enterprises to a great extent this year because of our success in negotiating decent first contracts."[17] There is no way to determine the extent to which that success was the by-product of the corporate campaign and/or the work of the task force it spawned, but it seems clear that one of the problems which led to the creation of that task force has been substantially diminished since its formation.

The corporate campaign against Campbell Soup, which began with the announcement of a boycott in 1979, ended on February 21, 1986 when Farm Labor Organizing Committee (FLOC) announced

---

[12]*Ibid.*

[13]*Ibid.*

[14]*UFCW Action*, p. 6.

[15]"Unions Targeting Beverly Enterprises . . . ," p. 251.

[16]"Improved Patient Care, Modest Wage Hikes Highlight New Beverly Nursing Home Pacts," *Daily Labor Report*, No. 120 (June 21, 1985) p. A–3.

[17]*Ibid.*

to the press, "We are here today to announce the suspension of our 7 year old boycott of Campbell's products. We feel that the collective bargaining agreements just signed are unprecedented in content and as multi-party agreements, and for the first time give the farmworkers a voice over their own affairs."[18] The first concrete step in the process which produced those agreements came on May 6, 1985 in the form of an "Understanding Between Campbell Soup Company and the Farm Labor Organizing Committee" which established a commission to resolve the question of representation of workers employed by growers under contract to Campbell Soup Company. The growers in question were not party to that "understanding" which necessitated a second agreement reportedly signed by the company on May 13, 1985 under which it agreed "to urge the growers to participate on a commission set up to establish guidelines for the elections, which could make FLOC the collective bargaining agent for some of the 6,000 to 7,000 farm workers employed by the growers."[19] The union stance at that point was that "an end to the boycott is contingent on the *outcome* of the elections and on negotiations over wages and working conditions."[20] (Emphasis added.)

Pursuant to its mandate and perhaps mindful of the union's conditions, the "Commission . . . held representation proceedings in northwest Ohio during the last week of August 1985 on the farms of 13 tomato growers (members of the Campbell Tomato Growers Association) and on the farms of 7 cucumber growers."[21] The union was declared the victor in those proceedings when a majority of migrant workers voted in favor of representation by FLOC. On the basis of that questionable victory, FLOC was made the bargaining agent for approximately 150 workers employed by sixteen (not thirteen) farms belonging to the Campbell Tomato Growers Association in Ohio and for approximately 400 independent contractors employed in the harvesting of cucumbers for twelve (not seven) growers in Michigan.[22]

After five months of negotiations, the "Commission [was] pleased to announce that two collective bargaining agreements have been

---

[18]Farm Labor Organizing Committee, "Press Statement," issued February 21, 1986, p. 1.

[19]"Discussions May Bring End to Farm Workers Boycott of Campbell Soup," *Daily Labor Report*, No. 120 (June 21, 1985), p. A–5.

[20]*Ibid.*

[21]"Report of Commission and Agreements Between Campbell Soup Company and Farm Labor Organization Committee," reproduced in *Daily Labor Report*, No. 38 (February 26, 1986), p. D–1.

[22]*Ibid.*

agreed upon and signed"—one for tomato and one for cucumber growers.[23] The tomato agreement was to run until January 31, 1989 and the cucumber agreement until December 31, 1989, "although both agreements may be reviewed annually in the light of experience with the assistance of the Commission."[24] The preamble to each of these trilateral agreements states:

> The following agreement is entered into to resolve long-standing disputes, to establish viable and constructive working relations, and to effectuate the Understanding between Campbell Soup Company and FLOC dated May 6, 1985, developed in accordance with the procedures established by the Commission thereunder.[25]

The president of FLOC characterized the union's achievements at Campbell Soup Company as "an approach that is the future of Farm-Labor organizing." The first step in that future was to come in the summer of 1986 when "the growers of cucumbers in Ohio have agreed to representation elections on all farms, growing cucumbers for Vlasic . . . under the aegis of the Commission."[26] (Vlasic is a subsidiary of Campbell Soup) Beyond that FLOC looked to the agreements to help organize workers on farms under contract to other major food processors, "particularly the Beatrice Grocery Group . . . and the H. J. Heinz Company."[27] The union's hopes for a triumphal representational march through the large and labor-intensive cucumber fields of the major food processors in Ohio and Michigan encountered a problem in the emergence of a determination on the part of Campbell's Ohio cucumber growers to campaign against the union in the representation elections they agreed to in 1985. Those same hopes, however, were bolstered by an agreement by the Heinz USA Division of H. J. Heinz to "enter into three way labor talks" similar to those which preceded FLOC's "victory" at Campbell Soup.[28]

The corporate campaign against Consolidated Foods, which began at its 1982 shareholder meeting, was largely, but not completely, over by the time of its 1983 shareholder meeting. The negotiated settlements reached with the Sisters of Divine Providence and the Inter-

[23]*Ibid.*

[24]*Ibid.*, pp. D-1 and D-2.

[25]*Ibid.*

[26]*Ibid.*, D-1.

[27]Keith Schneider, "Campbell Soup Accord Ends a Decade of Strife," *New York Times*, February 24, 1986, p. B-7.

[28]Huntly Collins, "Heinz, Farm Workers to Open Labor Talks," *Philadelphia Inquirer*, August 19, 1986, p. 3B.

faith Center on Corporate Responsibility in September 1983, which led to the withdrawal of their respective shareholder resolutions, effectively ended their active role in the campaign and thereby effectively ended the campaign. The last step in ending the campaign came with the release of the final report of the medical task force in November 1983. That report generally confirmed that the incidence of tendinitis and related disorders (TRD) was limited, but that the problem was real. As a result of the study, which was made available to shareholders, the company expanded its ergonomics program, instituted a physical conditioning program and experimented with mandatory work breaks.

The results of the study and subsequent company action were acceptable to Sister Billeaud and the Sisters of Divine Providence, but not to Sister Maurer of the Bennettsville Sisters. With the aid of ACTWU's occupational safety and health staff she prepared a report challenging the integrity of the members of the task force and one challenging the validity of their methodology, findings, and conclusions.[29] That "Counter-Report" was issued in March 1984, but received little public attention. Undaunted, the Bennettsville Sisters continued to leaflet Hanes plants urging workers to write to the CEO of the parent company detailing their health problems. In addition, they accused the company of fighting workers compensation claims for TRD. That accusation attracted the attention of Sister Billeaud who, in turn, attracted the attention of the corporation which, in turn, found that their insurance carrier was dragging its feet in dealing with such claims. That situation was corrected and by the fall of 1984 the processing of such claims had been expedited to the point where the corporation was receiving congratulatory letters from the religious community.

The conclusion of the campaign against Consolidated Foods left unanswered the question of whether the ACTWU, which quietly encouraged and assisted the Bennettsville Sisters' role in the campaign, would benefit from the campaign. The first test of the possible effects of the campaign on the ACTWU's organizing prospects at Hanes' plants came on November 11, 1984 in a representation election held at the Galax, Virginia, Plant—the same plant in which the union won an election in 1979, only to have that victory invalidated by the U.S. Court of Appeals, Fourth Circuit in 1982.[30] The union

---

[29]These two reports were titled, respectively, "Hanes Group Medical Task Force Report, 1984" and "We All Know What's Making Us Sick: Corrective Ministry Across the South's Response to Hanes Medical Task Force Report, 1984."

[30]Hanes Corp. V. N.L.R.B., 677 F. 2d 1008 (1982) 4th Circuit.

lost the 1984 election by a vote of 669 to 359. Since then, there have been no other representation elections at Hanes plants involving the ACTWU.

The corporate campaign against General Dynamics which began in February 1984 was ended six months later by a collective bargaining agreement which ended a fifteen-month strike by UAW-represented Draftsmen, Designers and Clerical Workers against the company's Electric Boat Division. That agreement was not described by either party as an agreement to end anything more or different than a normal, if prolonged, labor dispute as opposed to a corporate campaign. Nonetheless, there does appear to have been something unusual about the settlement. Specifically, after announcing in February 1984 that it had only 500 openings for any returning strikers and reducing that number to 200 in March of that year, the company agreed in August 1984 to rehire 700 still striking workers at the expense of replacements hired during the strike.[31] It is not clear, however, as to the extent to which that "unusual" settlement might have been prompted not by the campaign, but by the fact that as early as March 1984, the UAW was "already predicting a stormy confrontation next year, when its contract expires for 5,600 workers who assemble the M-1 tank, one of GD's largest government projects."[32]

The corporate campaign against Litton Industries, which began at its December 1981 shareholder meeting, ended quite abruptly two years later after its 1983 shareholder meeting which took place only one month after the IUD assumed control and leadership of the National Litton Campaign from the United Electrical, Radio and Machine Workers (UE). Depending on one's perspective, that makes the Litton campaign either one of the longer or shorter campaigns among those concluded by agreement. The agreement in this case came in response to the suggestion, made at the shareholder meeting by the company's chairman, that a union/management study group chaired by a neutral party approved by him be constituted to look into labor relations at Litton. After the shareholders' meeting, the attending representatives of the National Litton Campaign met and decided to make "a positive" recommendation "to accept the proposal" to the presidents of the participating unions, on the grounds that they were "confident that this is a sincere offer" to be treated

[31]"News From the UAW," August 24, 1984, p. 1 Appendix.
[32]"A Harder Push on General Dynamics," *Business Week*, March 26, 1984, p. 36.

"very seriously."[33] By December 12, the participating unions were reported to have placed a "moratorium" on campaign activities but not to have dismantled the campaign structure.[34] Thereafter, they quietly accepted the proposal and equally quietly dismantled their campaign structure.

The "Joint IUD-Litton Committee" was formally constituted on December 21, 1983 and began its work in January 1984. In November of 1984, after the "Chairman and/or the members of the committee [had] spent 52 days in meetings, travel and consultation," the committee issued a report which stated, "the committee's effort has produced some significant successes, has identified areas of continuing friction and has suggested a variety of continuing activities aimed at diminishing the potential for future problems."[35] Foremost among the areas of continuing friction was that of "the allegations of the union against the company" which had been the focal point of the Litton campaign. In that area, the report of the committee, in part, stated:

> It is clear that the parties view the nature of their problems from very different perspectives. The unions maintain that Litton's labor relations policies constitute a centrally directed plan to deny them their rights . . .
> Litton states categorically that it operates on a decentralized basis, with its divisions preferring to operate without unions. The company notes that this preference for a non-union atmosphere is legal . . . [36]

The report of the committee also indicated that "perhaps the greatest success the committee had was in encouraging the conclusion of negotiations at the microwave facility in Sioux Falls, South Dakota."[37] The committee may have had considerable help in that process from an NLRB administrative law judge who found both parties had violated their obligation to bargain in good faith. In any event, the committee reported that:

> the talks that led to this agreement were intense and arduous. Final agreement might have been achieved earlier, but when a preliminary announcement about the unit's sale was issued, the committee determined that contract negotiations should be suspended in favor of bargaining directed to the effect of the sale. After the sale fell through,

---

[33]"Litton Chairman Suggests Labor-Management Study on Charges of Labor Law Violations," *Daily Labor Report*, No. 239 (December 12, 1983), p. A-4.

[34]*Ibid.*

[35]Report of Joint IUD-Litton Committee, *Daily Labor Report*, No. 228 (November 27, 1984), p. D-1.

[36]*Ibid.*

[37]*Ibid.*

the committee encouraged a series of negotiating sessions between the partis [*sic*] which culminated in an August 24, 1984 agreement.[38]

The Non-Settlement Campaigns

The four campaigns which "ended" without any formal agreement or settlement included those conducted by local unions with the assistance of Ray Rogers against Hormel and SeaFirst and those conducted by national unions with the assistance in at least one case of the Kamber Group against Louisiana-Pacific and Phelps Dodge. The former two targets clearly are consumer goods/services producers. The latter two basically are producer goods producers, but neither is a major defense or government contractor. The campaign conducted by Local P-9 of the UFCW effectively began in August 1985 when the union struck the company's Austin, Minnesota facility and ended in May 1986 when the national union placed Local P-9 in trusteeship. That latter action was taken only after a protracted public battle of words between the leaders of the national and local union over both the goals and tactics of the campaign which in the view of the national union were self-destructive. The action of the national union, which is under legal challenge by the local union, was taken in the hope of terminating that alleged self-destructive activity before it could cost the UFCW bargaining rights at Hormel's Austin facility. As of the anniversary date of the beginning of the strike in August 1985, striking workers were no longer assured the right to join their replacements in voting on a question of representation should one be raised. Thus, it is not surprising that the imposition of trusteeship was quickly followed by a return to negotiations by the union in search of agreement on a new contract. Such an agreement was reached in the fall of 1986, but it, unlike that reached at General Dynamics, did not provide for reinstatement of striking workers, only for their right of recall.

The Hormel campaign is better viewed as one in which the true target was not the company but the national union. The goal of the campaign was to break a company/industry wage pattern set by national union wage policy. The tactics of the campaign—a product boycott coupled with roving pickets to encourage sympathy strikes—if successful, could and, in the latter case, did cost other union members their jobs. To make matters still worse, the strike and campaign did not prevent the company from reporting record earnings for 1985 which were "more impressive when placed in per-

---

[38]*Ibid.*

spective of a closed Austin plant for most of the fourth quarter" and included fourth quarter results which were "an all-time record for both volume and profit."[39] Finally, the strike and campaign seemed destined to force a company which proclaimed "we are not a union busting company" to confront the need to violate that principle if it was to deliver on its promise that, "it is fully our intention to build that Austin plant back up. . . . The idea is not to do away with jobs but to have people returning."[40]

The corporate campaign against SeaFirst, which consisted primarily of the boycott activities of mid-1978 to mid-1979, quietly subsided by the end of 1979. The union's campaign ground thereafter shifted almost exclusively to the courts where it has won some major victories over both the bank and the NLRB. The most notable of those victories was a Supreme Court decision upholding a Ninth Circuit Court decision that invalidated the NLRB's Amoco IV policy requiring that nonunion members of bargaining units be allowed to vote in affiliation referenda.[41] Despite that legal setback, the bank continues to refuse to recognize the union and is pressing its case based on an alternative legal challenge to the union's claim to inherited bargaining rights. Essentially the bank claims that the union no longer represents a majority of its employees and seeks an NLRB election to settle the issue. If this second legal challenge takes as long as the first to be resolved, it will be 1994 before the outcome of this dispute is known.

The most significant result of the corporate, as opposed to the legal, campaign waged against SeaFirst has to be its failure to confirm Ray Rogers' hypothesis that "banks and insurance companies are the most vulnerable of all businesses . . . because what they control they don't own."[42] In the context of that hypothetical vulnerability, the SeaFirst campaign provides at least suggestive evidence that consumer actions (boycotts) are a campaign attack animal whose bark may be far worse than its bite in the world of financial institutions. The testing of that possibility, however, requires the kind of courage and determination with which SeaFirst entered into its game of boycott pressure with its union adversary.

---

[39]"Impact of Austin Strike Diminishing, Hormel President Tells Stockholders," *Daily Labor Report*, No. 20 (January 30, 1986), p. A–7.

[40]*Ibid.*

[41]"Justice Faults NLRB Meddling in Union Affairs; Approve Member Only Vote on Union Affiliation," *Daily Labor Report*, No. 39 (February 27, 1986), p. A–5.

[42]A. H. Raskin, "Show 'em the Clenched Fist!" *Forbes*, October 2, 1978, p. 32.

The final two campaigns, those against Louisiana-Pacific and Phelps Dodge, are so similar in both origin and outcome as to be considered identical twins. In both cases, the campaigns stemmed from a decision by the target company to refuse to follow an industry pattern set in 1983 negotiations and to insist, instead, on concessions. In both cases, the demand for concessions was met by a strike to which the company responded by hiring replacements to continue operations. In both cases, the unions were unable (by peaceful or, particularly in the case of Phelps Dodge, by violent means) to prevent the companies from hiring replacements and continuing operations, which led them to the recourse of a corporate campaign. In both cases, such campaigns involved carrying the cause from "Main Street to Wall Street."

The campaigns against Louisiana-Pacific and Phelps Dodge ended not with an agreement to rehire strikers, as in the case of General Dynamics, but with the retention of replacements and decertification of unions. The strike at Phelps Dodge involved thirty bargaining units represented by thirteen different unions—all of which were decertified by the summer of 1986. The strike at Louisiana-Pacific involved a total of twenty bargaining units of which nineteen were still in operation in the summer of 1986. Unions had been decertified in sixteen of those nineteen units at that time, with the results of decertification elections in two other units awaiting certification and a rerun election pending in the final unit. As impressive or depressing, depending on one's viewpoint, as those figures may be, it is equally impressive or depressing to note that those companies in both industries which followed the pattern in 1983 arrived at the bargaining table in 1986 demanding concessions—demands not well-received but reluctantly accommodated by their unions.

THE REASONS

There was considerable variability in the results of the nine campaigns studied which have run their course. Although it is somewhat imprudent to talk of victories and defeats in labor-management confrontations, it is also clear that in three campaigns—Beverly Enterprises, Campbell Soup, and Consolidated Foods—the campaigners were largely successful in achieving their immediate stated goals. On the other hand, it is clear that in four campaigns—Hormel, Louisiana-Pacific, Phelps Dodge, and SeaFirst—the campaigners came away empty handed. In the remaining two campaigns—General Dynamics and Litton—the campaigners achieved something less than they sought but more than nothing.

It is relatively simple to label campaigns as wins, losses, or ties. It is far more difficult to identify the forces and factors which explain the differences in results. That task involves an attempt to isolate the particular point or possibly combination of points of vulnerability which spelled the difference between victory and defeat for the campaigners. Unfortunately, that is easier said than done, because losers are not prone to honest and expansive analysis of their weaknesses and winners are prone to overlook theirs. Thus, in the final analysis, the reasons for the success of a campaign are more a matter of informed speculation than empirical specification, at least until the universe of such campaigns expands substantially.

The Beverly Enterprises Campaign

Despite the fact that the SEIU and UFCW are still far from their goal of organizing Beverly Enterprises' 1,025 long-term care facilities, their joint campaign against the company has to be credited with considerable success in changing the company's posture with respect to union organizing. That success contrasts dramatically with the failure of the corporate campaign against SeaFirst, the other consumer service target company studied. That raises the obvious question of what did the union do and do right in the Beverly Enterprises campaign which it didn't do or do right in the SeaFirst campaign.

The first and foremost difference between these two campaigns lies in the way the unions played the game of principle. In the Beverly Enterprises campaign, the unions succeeded in linking their cause to that of quality of patient care. In the SeaFirst campaign, the union was unable to link its cause to a higher purpose and was at the further disadvantage that the bank held the high ground vis-à-vis employees on the freedom of choice issue. In the Beverly Enterprises campaign, the company actively fought the unions for the high ground of quality patient care in the first half of 1983, before abandoning that battle as counterproductive in terms of its own reputation and ultimately embracing its adversary in that battle in an "understanding" based "upon a recognition that both labor and management are committed to providing quality health care for residents and dignity and decent standards for employees and that both should work together to achieve those ends."[43]

The quality of patient care issue struck an institutionally and eco-

---

[43]"Beverly Enterprises, UFCW, and SEIU Announce Accord . . ." p. A–5.

nomically sensitive corporate nerve. The emergence of the issue threatened the corporation's public and its own private self-image. It is difficult to assess the extent of image damage or its role in motivating the ultimate "understanding," but conversations with corporate executives suggest that it was an important source of the power of the campaign. The company also had to be sensitive about its public image, not so much for the benefit of its relations with the general public as for its relations with the federal and state governments which licensed and otherwise regulated its facilities. In addition, federal and state governments were reported to have provided much of the cash needed for the company's successful strategy of growth through the leveraged acquisition of existing facilities. These two highly practical aspects of its governmental relations undoubtedly also enhanced the company's sensitivity to union talk of the "corporatization of health care" and more mundane questioning of Beverly's charges for administrative and facility expense.

In the absence of both a public relations and governmental relations point of vulnerability, the union in the SeaFirst campaign was left with little more than customer relations as a basis for pressuring the bank. That approach failed the union twice, first as a threat and second as a reality. The union's appeal to the general public to engage in a consumer boycott of its target failed to generate a substantial response and left it no place to turn or return to but the courts. The failure of the union's call for a boycott by the general public was but the first of such setbacks suffered by unions in those campaigns studied in which this tactic was used.

The Campbell/Hormel/Consolidated Campaigns

The campaigns against Campbell Soup and Hormel were strikingly similar in many respects other than their results. Both campaigns were conducted by local unions without the encouragement or assistance of the larger labor movement. Both campaigns originated in largely ineffective strikes and relied heavily on product boycotts as the primary source of supplementary pressure on the target company. In theory, both target companies were vulnerable to such pressure as producers of clearly identified consumer goods. In practice, however, neither suffered noticeable losses of sales as a result of the boycott. Despite all those similarities, one campaign—that against Campbell Soup Company—resulted in a victory for the union while the other—that against Hormel—resulted in a union defeat.

The basic difference between the successful Campbell Soup Company campaign and unsuccessful Hormel campaign was "image." FLOC was successful in portraying itself as a champion of migrant and child labor victims of the greed of a distant corporate entity. Local P-9 was not able to cast itself in any such heroic role and was left with the image of a greedy local union seeking wages in excess of the pattern set by its own national union. FLOC's march from Toledo to Camden proved an effective way to focus attention on its cause, as did the picket line activities of Local P-9 which resulted in the calling out of the National Guard at one point and the arrest of Ray Rogers and the local union president at another point in the conflict. Local P-9 was far more successful than FLOC in attracting media and public attention, but in so doing it cast itself in the role of villain rather than hero as FLOC was able to do in its peaceful protest march.

The ability of FLOC to seize the high ground and cast itself in the role of good guy and the company in the role of bad guy was instrumental in the success of its campaign in two ways. First, it enabled FLOC to secure the support not so much of the general public as of the specific public of the religious community, in general, and the Catholic church, in particular—allies who were in a position to inflict tangible damage on Campbell's corporate self-image by withdrawing from its labels program. Second, it exposed the company's Achilles' heel, its priceless all-American, squeaky-clean public image and reputation. In the final analysis, it was probably that sensitivity to the bruising of the corporate ego which was the key to the union's success in its campaign against Campbell Soup. In that respect there is some parallel between the Campbell Soup Company and Beverly Enterprises campaigns, although Beverly Enterprises had far greater economic reason for its concern about its public image than did Campbell Soup, judging by the results of the consumer boycott against it.

The campaign against Consolidated Foods is similar to that against Campbell Soup in many ways including its outcome. Both campaigns involved corporate escalation by the campaigns, which was designed to hold the parent company responsible for and possibly hostage to the actions of one of its corporate children. Religious groups and organizations played important roles in both campaigns—a supporting role at Campbell Soup and a starring role at Consolidated. The campaign against Consolidated, unlike that against Campbell Soup, did not include a general consumer boycott of the company's products. It did, however, produce the suggestion of the possibility of a call for a boycott by the specific public of the women's movement which, had it come about, would have been analogous to the boycott of Campbell Soup by the religious community.

The most salient similarity between the Campbell Soup and Consolidated campaigns is the phenomenon of corporate escalation. In the Campbell Soup campaign, the company's public position from the outset was that the dispute was between the union and the growers and was beyond the control of the corporation. Privately, however, it undermined that position by meeting with representatives of the union as early as 1978 and continuing to do so sporadically throughout the course of the campaign. In retrospect, the company admits that its willingness to talk privately with the union may have been "a mistake." In the Consolidated campaign, the corporation's public position was stated in a letter from Mr. Bryan to Sister Maurer "responding to the issues she and Father Dahm raised during the [Annual] meeting." In the course of the war of correspondence which followed the annual meeting, the company responded to inquiries about the Hanes situation with a copy of that letter and a note which indicated, "we have advised Sister Maurer and Father Dahm that any further questions on this subject will be referred to our Hanes Company." When Sister Maurer refused to be relegated to dealing with Hanes, the corporation decided to attempt to open a private dialogue on the issues in dispute through the order to which she belonged. In retrospect, the corporation defends that decision as the "right thing to do."

The central question which emerges from these two campaigns is why the two targets privately acquiesced to corporate escalation while publicly undertaking corporate de-escalation. What led Campbell Soup into its private dialogue with FLOC? What led Consolidated to actively seek out such a dialogue with the Sisters of Divine Providence and later the Interfaith Center on Corporate Responsibility? What made that company so intent upon avoiding shareholder resolutions at its 1983 annual meeting? The companies themselves were unable and/or unwilling to provide cogent answers to these questions. In the Campbell case, its decision probably was a by-product of its corporate commitment to and record of good deeds for agricultural labor in Ohio and elsewhere. In the case of Consolidated it was the product of a "nervous" board of directors, which begs the question as to the source of its nervousness. In theory, the corporation was at risk on three fronts—public relations, customer relations, and stockholder relations. The extent of those risks was not known, but clearly was judged to be potentially great enough to warrant a pre-emptive strategy. In short, it appears that the company's strategy and the campaign's success were a product of corporate uncertainty (as to what a campaign would involve). That possibility raises the question of whether risk aversion is as much an integral part of the corporate character of Consolidated Foods as concern for corporate image is of the corporate character of Campbell Soup. Unfortunately, that question must go unanswered.

The General Dynamics/Litton Campaigns

The campaigns against General Dynamics and Litton Industries are ones from which the unions emerged with symbolic victories or, more appropriately in the case of Litton, symbolic non-defeats. Those outcomes raise some interesting questions regarding the reasons for the partial success of the unions involved in those campaigns. In the case of General Dynamics, the question centers on why the company, which in March of 1984 was reported to insist "that it will not be cowed into a settlement,"[44] signed an agreement less than six months later under which it agreed to fire replacements and rehire strikers. In the case of Litton Industries, the nature of its settlement with the labor movement and the process by which it was reached raise two questions. First, why would the company, after two years of stonewalling, suddenly make a conciliatory proposal in the midst of an annual meeting and protest rally? Second, why would the union movement, after two years of intense effort, so quickly accept the company's first conciliatory proposal?

The obvious answer to these questions is that the campaigns had become burdensome and/or embarrassing to those who compromised to end them. That answer raises the further question as to why those campaigns did so while those against Louisiana-Pacific and Phelps Dodge did not. The obvious answer to that question is that the former two target companies are defense contractors while the latter two are not. A more subtle but equally relevant answer, however, may be that the disputes at General Dynamics and Litton involved only a very small part of their total operations in marked contrast to the disputes at Louisiana-Pacific and Phelps Dodge which involved substantial segments of corporate production.

General Dynamics clearly had a political vulnerability growing out of the fact that almost 90 percent of its sales were made to the Pentagon. In June 1984, the union probed that vulnerability when, in an appearance before a subcommittee on the House Labor and Education Committee, UAW President Beiber asked Congress to "require more acceptable behavior by General Dynamics."[45] It is

---

[44]"A Harder Push on General Dynamics," p. 36.
[45]"House Digs at General Dynamics Sins," *UAW Washington Report*, Vol. 24, No. 25 (June 22, 1984), p. 1.

impossible to determine the extent to which this political initiative added momentum to the parties' search for a negotiated settlement—a search heavily driven on the side of the company by its operational vulnerability growing out of its other, more important bargaining relationships with the UAW. In comparison to that operational vulnerability, the union's public, governmental, and stockholder relations activities constituted little more than a nuisance.

Litton Industries also had a measure of political vulnerability arising out of the fact that about 25 percent of its sales were made to the government and out of the union's success in focusing NLRB attention on the possibility of centralized corporate control of labor relations. Although neither of the union's initiatives to exploit these vulnerabilities bore fruit, they did have a definite nuisance cost to the company. That cost, in the view of the company, was not sufficient to warrant any substantive change in the labor relations policies of its divisions or their bargaining positions in existing disputes. The cost was, however, sufficient to warrant buying out of the campaign on a procedural rather than substantive basis, as was done, in order to permit a return to corporate anonymity.

The unions involved in the national Litton campaign have given no public insight into their reasons for the rapid conclusion of that campaign, but it appears that the institutional costs of the campaign had come to outweigh any potential substantive gains likely to be won in pursuing the campaign to its intended conclusion. To the extent that any such substantive gains were dependent on government action, the prospects for success during the Reagan administration were hardly good. More importantly, continued pursuit of such gains through the campaign would be economically and ideologically divisive within the union movement. At the heart of the problem was the unwillingness of the Metal Trades Council to have its 10,000-worker unit in Pascagoula held economic hostage to the UE unit in Sioux Falls and the uneasiness of the moderate AFL-CIO in its alliance with the radical UE and its activist allies. These same problems confronted the UFCW at the national level as a result of Local P-9's campaign against Hormel—problems which eventually led the national to place the local in trusteeship and end the campaign.

The symbolic and substantive defeats experienced by the unions in the campaigns against Louisiana-Pacific and Phelps Dodge are not difficult to explain. Both of those campaigns arose out of high stakes economic disputes. In that context, the challenge facing the unions was that of generating sufficient economic pressure on the company to force a change in its economic benefit/cost ratio. The games of principle, politics, and protest were irrelevant in that effort as the target companies had, by virtue of the action taken which forced the campaign, indicated a lack of sensitivity with respect to corporate image and visibility. The games of pressure and principal involving consumer and investor boycotts were relevant and were played but, here as elsewhere, with little tangible economic effect. That will continue to be the case until unions and their allies are able to influence or control the actions of more than a very small minority of participants in product and capital markets.

CHAPTER VIII

Conclusions

The outcomes of the ten corporate campaigns studied suggest that this is a situation in which the whole may be greater than the sum of its parts. The myriad sub-games of principle, politics, protest, pressure, and principal played in the ten campaigns produced few, if any, "victories" for those conducting the campaigns. Despite that fact, several of the campaign games ended in victories for the campaigners. The campaigns against Beverly Enterprises, Campbell Soup, and Consolidated Foods clearly fall into this category. The campaign against BASF may also fall into this category by the time it is concluded, as one must suspect that the company's charge that the campaign against it constitutes an unfair labor practice is a last-ditch effort to keep its German parent corporation at arm's length and avert a repetition of the intervention which took place in 1970.

The most salient common characteristic of the four companies which were the targets of successful campaigns was a high degree of sensitivity to adverse publicity. It was an aversion to such publicity which drove BASF A.G. to intervene in the labor relations of its American subsidiary in 1970 and probably also drove that subsidiary to file its section 8(b)(3) charge with the National Labor Relations Board in 1986. The questions raised about quality of patient care at Beverly Enterprises homes clearly drove that company to its understanding with the Service Employees International Union (SEIU) and the United Food and Commercial Workers International Union (UFCW,) just as the allegations of exploitation of migrant and child labor drove Campbell Soup to its agreement with the Farm Labor Organizing Committee (FLOC). The desire of Consolidated Foods to avoid public confrontation which led it to pursue a private dialogue with the Sisters of Divine Providence and the Interfaith Center on Corporate Responsibility also drove it to negotiate a settlement of their proposed shareholder resolutions.

The four successful campaigns suggest that the game of principle, more than any other, has been the key to the effectiveness of corporate campaigns. In that context, the four campaigns indicated the existence of four types of vulnerability open to exploitation in that game. The first is corporate desire for anonymity in its operations—

all of the four companies. The second is corporate concern over consumer attitudes—Campbell, Consolidated, and, to a lesser extent, Beverly. The third is corporate exposure to governmental or quasigovernmental sanctions/regulations—BASF and Beverly. Finally, there is the matter of corporate image—Campbell and, to a lesser extent, Beverly.

The four unsuccessful campaigns—those against Hormel, Louisiana-Pacific, Phelps Dodge, and SeaFirst—like their successful counterparts, confirm the importance of the game of principle. In none of those four campaigns was the union successful in escalating the conflict beyond the level of a simple labor dispute or in enlisting the support of allies outside the labor movement. In none of the cases could the union charge that the target company was operating outside the law in its dispute with the union. Indeed, in all four cases the unions were the party operating outside the law by virtue of picket line violence at Hormel, Louisiana-Pacific, and Phelps Dodge, and at least in principle by disenfranchising non-members in the affiliation vote at SeaFirst. In that context, all the campaigners could do was charge the target company with being anti-union, a charge which was easily dismissed by Hormel and SeaFirst and which hardly worried Louisiana-Pacific, Phelps Dodge, and BASF (although it did worry its German parent company) given their economic stakes in the disputes in question.

The other sub-games—politics, protest, pressure, and principal—in the campaigns studied for the most part also have been games of public relations. The governmental initiatives and investigations prompted by unions as part of their campaigns have provided them with a public forum in which to raise questions and/or make accusations regarding target company behavior, but have produced no concrete results. The protest activities of unions at shareholder meetings have done the same, but have produced no resignations of board members since the Stevens' campaign, no election of a union candidate to the board in opposition to a management candidate, and no approval of a union-sponsored shareholder resolution. (The 6 percent of the vote garnered by the union at Beverly's 1983 annual meeting is the highest achieved in the campaigns studied.) The product and/or financial boycotts launched by some unions in games of pressure and principal with the target company often have received considerable publicity, but equally often have had little or no real impact on the target company.

The fact that the games of politics, protest, pressure, and principal in the campaigns studied proved to be more a matter of form than substance does not mean they were totally without effect. Target companies did experience regulatory challenges and delays in the conduct of their businesses. Similarly, they did have their annual meetings disrupted and did have to face the prospect of proxy battles. SeaFirst did lose some $5 million in deposits as a result of its boycott and Chase Manhattan $10 million in deposits as a result of the Steelworkers' campaign against Phelps Dodge. Consolidated Foods reported sales of blocks of its stock possibly attributable to the campaign against it and both Campbell and Louisiana-Pacific admitted that the boycotts of their products undoubtedly slowed the rate of growth of their sales.

The public relations results of the game of principle as supplemented by the public relations results and nuisance consequences of the games of politics, protest, pressure, and principal created a "no win" situation for a majority of the ten target companies studied. That majority included General Dynamics and Litton Industries as well as BASF among the producer goods targets, in addition to Beverly, Campbell, and Consolidated among the consumer goods/services targets. In each of those six cases, with as yet the exception of BASF, the target company, whether out of fear or frustration, elected to buy its way out of the situation with a negotiated settlement which constituted a "victory" for the campaigner(s) and a "non-defeat" for the target.

The fact that a majority of the ten campaigns were, in some sense, successful suggests this new development holds considerable promise for the union movement in its organizing and bargaining battles with management. The minority of the campaigns studied which were not or not yet successful suggest that campaigns may not hold great promise in union battles against managements willing and able to operate during strikes, as was demonstrated in the cases of Hormel, Louisiana-Pacific, and Phelps Dodge, unless, as in the case of General Dynamics and possibly BASF, those managements have larger fish to fry with the union movement. The Hormel, Louisiana-Pacific, and Phelps Dodge cases point out both the importance and impotence of primary and secondary boycott actions, particularly on the financial front, in mounting effective challenges to such management action. In that context, the ultimate outcome of the case against Local P-9 arising out of its picketing of First Bank may have great significance for the future both of operating during strikes and of corporate campaigns against companies pursuing that course of action.

In the final analysis, the most salient characteristic distinguishing the corporate winners from the corporate losers in the ten campaigns studied was the fact that the winners had openly announced that they would no longer play even the semblance of the role of "Mr. Nice Guy" vis-à-vis their unions. In so doing, they effectively removed themselves from the game of principle which thus far appears to be the key to a successful campaign. They did, however, remain vulnerable to the game of principal, but that game is the one in which unions are most severely restrained by the law of financial responsibility and secondary boycotts. There is no way to estimate how long or how far unions can go with corporate campaigns based primarily on the game of principle and public relations. When that game has been played out, they may well have to turn to the game of principal and financial relations and challenge the legal restrictions which handicap them in playing that game.

The other three sub-games—politics, protest, and pressure— appear to offer less substantial prospects for enhancing the costs of disagreement for recalcitrant employers. A change in the philosophical composition of the NLRB or the political character of its general counsel could enhance the power of the game of politics, as was evident in the campaigns against Litton and Louisiana-Pacific, but only within the limits suggested by the failure of the AFL-CIO's "Labor Law Reform" in a Democratic administration with a Democratic-controlled Congress. The game of protest, including that played against BASF, seems to be limited by the limited ability of unions to establish a common cause with directors and shareholders, other than those who are part of the union family of activist and religious groups. Similarly, the prospects for greater success in the game of pressure seem dependent upon the ability of a union to enlist the support of more than the union family in its consumer as well as its shareholder actions. In both cases it is important to note that union power is more dependent upon its ability to enlist the support of "special" publics of particular relevance to the target company than the support of the "general" public. The campaigns studied indicate that the union movement is not without its friends among such special publics, but they also indicate that those friends are, as yet, still too weak or disorganized in the stock market and/or product market to make a difference in the outcome of most corporate campaigns.

The experience of the ten target companies studied and the unions which conducted the campaigns against them may have been summarized in that section of the BASF unfair labor practice charge in which the company asserted:

The president of the Industrial Union Department, Howard D. Samuel, has told BASF it will be "the target of a comprehensive anti-BASF campaign" which "neither you nor we will consider a pleasant experience."[1]

---

[1]Letter from Mr. William R. D'Armond of the firm of Kean, Miller, Hawthorne, D'Armond, McCowan and Jarman, attorneys at law, to Mr. Hugh Frank Malone, Regional Director, National Labor Relations Board, Region 15, New Orleans, Louisiana, dated May 17, 1986, Appendix I, pp. 131–132.

Appendices

BASF Corporation

The following is the text of a letter from Mr. William R. D'Armond of the firm of Kean, Miller, Hawthorne, D'Armond, McCowan & Jarman, attorneys at law, to Mr. Hugh Frank Malone, Regional Director, National Labor Relations Board (NLRB), Region 15, New Orleans, Louisiana, dated May 17, 1986, a copy of which was provided by the corporation and is in the author's possession. On September 19, 1986, the general counsel of the NLRB informed the company by letter that "use of a corporate campaign by a union to assist in meeting its goals at the bargaining table does not violate the act."[1]

> We are enclosing for filing on behalf of BASF Corporation Chemicals Division a Section 8(b)(3) charge against Oil, Chemical and Atomic Workers International Union and its Local 4-620.
>
> Until June 15, 1984, the union and BASF (formerly BASF Wynadotte Corporation) were party to a collective bargaining agreement covering certain BASF employees at the Geismar, Louisiana, plant. The parties failed to reach agreement on a new collective bargaining contract to succeed the one that expired on June 15. Since that date BASF has locked out the employees represented by the union, and no collective bargaining agreement has been reached.
>
> Essentially, the grounds for the present charge are as follows:
>
> I. **Corporate Campaign**
>
> Since in or about June, 1984, and continuing to the present, OCAW has engaged in an intensive course of conduct maliciously intended to injure and interfere with BASF in its business, trade and reputation. This course of action has been described by OCAW as a "coordinated campaign" or "corporate campaign." Its express purpose, as stated by OCAW President Joseph W. Misbrener, is to make the consequences to BASF for the lockout "as unpleasant, disagreeable and expensive as possible." OCAW has stated its intent to precipitate "a crisis . . . in employee, customer, and public confidence—and loyalty." In mounting this coordinated campaign, OCAW has obtained the participation of the Industrial Union Department of the AFL-CIO. The president of the Industrial Union Department, Howard D. Samuel,

---

[1] "NLRB General Counsel Dismisses Charges Stemming from Union Campaign Against BASF," *Daily Labor Report*, No. 195 (October 8, 1986), p. A-8.

has told BASF it will be "the target of a comprehensive anti-BASF campaign" which "neither you nor we will consider a pleasant experience." The course of conduct followed by OCAW in furtherance of its coordinated campaign, taken as a whole, far transcends the withholding of labor or other legitimate means to bring economic pressure to bear on BASF in support of its bargaining position in the labor dispute, and is inconsistent with good faith bargaining.

The following means, among others, have been utilized by OCAW in furtherance of its coordinated campaign.

1.   OCAW has appealed to prejudice and sought to arouse the animosity of the community by publicly and repeatedly referring to the German ownership of BASF's parent corporation, alleging "foreign oppression," linking BASF with the Nazi party by the use of swastikas and other means, referring to BASF as "co-conspirators of the Third Reich," alleging that BASF "helped to bring you World War II," accusing BASF of "oppressing" the rights of "American Workers," and similar conduct.

2.   OCAW has threatened to publish a message intended to dissuade consumers from purchasing a new beta carotene diet supplement being introduced into the market by BASF, to arouse public distrust, suspicion, fear and hatred of BASF, and to injure the sales and reputation of BASF by assertions that BASF is attempting to "cash in" on the fear of cancer by selling an "unproven untested food supplement," that in truth consumers have a great deal to fear from BASF, that BASF is one of the world's largest producers of cancer-causing chemical substances and toxic wastes and is attempting to "cash in on cancer, not once but twice. . . . Once on the cause, once on the cure," that BASF is attempting "to make a fast buck on our fear" and similar assertions.

3.   OCAW has sought to arouse public animosity, distrust, fear and suspicion of BASF by repeatedly and publicly asserting that BASF is a safety hazard to the Geismar community and other communities. OCAW has charged both a) that BASF is operating its plant unsafely and with inadequately trained workers during the lockout, as a result of which the safety of the workers and the community is put in jeopardy, and b) that conditions which prevailed before the lockout and which will remain after the lockout ends (e.g., hazardous waste disposal practices, use of certain chemicals in plant operations) present great hazards. OCAW has sought to inflame the passions of the public against BASF by repeatedly comparing the Geismar operations to the disaster at Bhopal, India, by referring to the plant as a "ticking time bomb," and by other inflammatory statements.

4.   OCAW has sought to arouse public animosity, distrust, suspicion and fear of BASF both internationally and domestically by publicly and repeatedly asserting that BASF is engaging in an intentional and extensive course of anti-union conduct in violation of Federal law.

5.   OCAW has sought to arouse public animosity, distrust, suspicion and hatred of BASF by causing BASF to be listed on the so-called "Labor's Dishonor Role" by the Industrial Union Department of the AFL-CIO, and by causing the publication of such listing in the local and national news media, including the *Wall Street Journal*.

6. OCAW has repeatedly sought to injure the ability of BASF to properly conduct its business by seeking to cause governmental agencies to deny to BASF needed environmental permits, bond issue authorization and other governmental approvals.

7. OCAW has obtained and publicly disclosed confidential and proprietary financial data of BASF.

8. OCAW caused a congressional investigation of BASF's safety record and practices during the lockout (when no union-represented employees were at work) for the purpose of harassing BASF and injuring its reputation.

9. OCAW has acquired and threatened to disclose without the consent of BASF the formula for an antifreeze product manufactured by BASF under the name "Alluguard." The formula for Alluguard is a trade secret of BASF. The formula was acquired by the OCAW by improper means, specifically by breach of inducement of a breach of a duty to maintain secrecy.

10. OCAW has unlawfully and without consent of BASF accessed, communicated with, stored data in, retrieved data from or otherwise made use of the resources of BASF's computers, computer system or computer network.

11. OCAW has attempted to circumvent American law and to cause different international legal standards to be imposed upon the negotiations, and to publicly embarrass BASF in international forums, by filing and processing a complaint with the Organization for Economic and Cooperative Development (OECD—a multi-national organization) through the U.S. State Department, and by that means has also sought to publicly embarrass BASF on an international basis.

12. OCAW sought to block the acquisition by BASF of another company (American Inca) and thereby damage and interfere with business ventures of BASF unrelated to the Geismar plant by making complaint to the U.S. Justice Department alleging that the acquisition would violate anti-trust laws, and by filing a complaint on the subject with the OECD.

13. OCAW has engaged in malicious personal attacks against, publicly ridiculed, and published personal financial data of, executives of BASF.

Many of the accusations made and publicly disseminated by OCAW by press conferences, press releases, radio and TV appearances, and other means are erroneous or outright misrepresentations.

This course of conduct is intended to have a permanent and irreparable adverse effect on the business and reputation of BASF. It goes far beyond publicizing the union's legitimate positions in the negotiations, or the traditional withholding of labor. To a large extent, the attack is unrelated to any issue in negotiations or to the business of the Geismar plant. The means used are so extreme as to constitute disloyalty. Its effects will extend beyond the duration of the labor dispute. It has created an atmosphere that is not conducive to bargaining. Moreover, it has required both the company and the union to devote very substantial resources in time and money to these attacks which could better have been devoted to bargaining. The course of conduct, taken as a whole, is inconsistent with the union's duty to bargain in good faith.

As far as we can determine the Board has never ruled on the validity under Section 8(b)(3) of an anti-employer campaign as virulent and extensive as this one. Complaint should be issued so the Board can resolve this important question.

We will, of course, present during the course of the investigation extensive evidence of the union's corporate campaign.

II. By-Passing and Attempting to Intimidate Company Negotiating Committee

The union has by-passed and attempted to intimidate the company's negotiating committee. It has made a sustained effort to deal directly with top management of BASF Corporation (an American corporation) and its parent corporation in Germany. This attempt to by-pass and intimidate the company negotiating committee constitutes an independent Section 8(b)(3) violation.

APPENDIX II

Beverly Enterprises

Beverly Enterprises is the largest operator of nursing homes in the United States. In 1983, the year in which the campaign was launched, it controlled some 780 homes with 69,000 employees in 43 states and the District of Columbia, although its facilities were concentrated in eight states—Texas (10,800 beds), California (9,200 beds), Arkansas (5,100 beds), Michigan (5,000 beds), Georgia (4,100 beds), Florida (3,400 beds), Virginia (2,600 beds) and North Carolina (2,000 beds).[1] By 1985, the number of homes operated by the company had grown to over 900[2] and by 1986 exceeded 1,000[3], continuing a pattern of rapid growth which began in the late 1970s. According to a "Corporate Profile" of the company prepared by the Food and Beverage Trades Department (FBTD) of the AFL-CIO, much of the company's growth came through the leveraged acquisition of existing facilities with, in many cases, as much as two-thirds of the necessary cash for such transactions being provided by federal and state governments.[4] That same profile also noted that the company and its facilities are regulated by the Social Security Administration (Medicare), the Health Care Financing Administration (Medicaid), the Veterans Administration and various state agencies.[5]

The campaign against Beverly Enterprises was conducted by the Service Employees International Union (SEIU) and the United Food and Commercial Workers (UFCW), both of which were members of the FBTD, in conjunction with their joint organizing campaign aimed at Beverly's facilities. At the time the campaign was launched, the SEIU represented employees at twenty-one of those facilities in four states and the UFCW at ten facilities in five states.

[1]Beverly Enterprises, *1983 Annual Report*, p. 1.

[2]"Unions Targeting Beverly Enterprises Say Election Win Rate Is 71 Percent," *White Collar Report*, Vol. 57 (March 13, 1985), p. 251.

[3]United Food and Commercial Workers International Union, "Beverly Workers Nationwide Voting to Join UFCW," *UFCW Action*, Vol. 8, No. 4, July–August 1986, p. 6.

[4]Food and Beverage Trades Department, AFL-CIO, "Beverly Enterprises: A Corporate Review," released January 1983, p. 7.

[5]*Ibid.*, p. 19.

Some three years later, the UFCW reported that "approximately 12,000 workers at 145 Beverly facilities nationwide can speak first-hand about the difference having a union has made in their lives."[6] Those represented workers were the product of the fact that:

> Since the joint Service Employees-UFCW organizing program began nearly three years ago, the UFCW has won representation elections in 58 homes. SEIU has conducted 51 successful organizing programs. An additional three dozen union nursing homes remained under union contract after being purchased by Beverly.[7]

The goal of both the corporate and organizing campaigns was to overcome the company's policy of being opposed to unions because:

- We like to deal and communicate directly with our employees. We do not believe a third party organization should come between Beverly and its employees.
- Unions may force employees to strike, thereby causing a loss of income and benefits to employees.
- Unions charge each member anywhere from twelve to twenty dollars per month for dues.
- Unions cannot guarantee increased benefits to employees. A union can only promise such items.
- In general, Beverly employees represented by a union receive reduced benefits.[8]

That policy, in view of the unions, was supported by the best benefits package in the industry and a preventative labor relations program to teach administrators to detect early signs of organizing activity.[9] In addition to such efforts to resist unionization, the SEIU and UFCW reportedly also were experiencing difficulty "in securing collective bargaining agreements, both following a successful NLRB election or when Beverly Enterprises acquired a health care facility that had been previously organized by one of the two unions."[10]

The Launching of the Campaign

The national campaign against Beverly Enterprises was announced in January 1983 and was accompanied by the widespread

---

[6]*UFCW Action*, p. 6.

[7]*Ibid.*, p. 6.

[8]Food and Beverage Trades Department, AFL-CIO, "Beverly Enterprises: A Corporate Review," p. 11.

[9]*Ibid.*, p. 11.

[10]"Beverly Enterprises, UFCW and SEIU Announce Accord Aimed at Cooperation," *Daily Labor Report*, No. 43 (March 5, 1984), p. A-6.

leafletting of employees and the release of an FBTD study of "Beverly Enterprises Patient Care Record: Preliminary Findings."[11] In announcing the campaign, the president of the UFCW indicated that it was the product of the union's concern about the quality of patient care—the central theme of the entire campaign. Specifically, he stated:

> We have pleaded for the kinds of staffing ratios, equipment, and supplies which would allow our members to deliver decent patient care.
> Quality care is sometimes difficult to deliver in the best of circumstances. In the worst of circumstances, when discouraged workers are under-staffed, under-equipped and under-paid, it is impossible.[12]

That theme was repeated in the leaflets distributed at Beverly facilities which announced the formation of a Beverly Employees Cooperative Action and Reform Effort (CARE) which was to form an employee organization in every Beverly facility. The leaflet told workers "You are not alone," and then asked "Do you go home every night concerned because you know your patients may not be getting the care they deserve? Do you seem to be working harder and harder for less money?"[13] According to the leaflet, which included a mail-in coupon and a toll-free hot-line number, "Patient care and working conditions are bound together—when one suffers, the other suffers.[14]

The FBTD's forty-page report on Beverly's patient care record focused on homes in California, Texas, and Arkansas and concluded that Beverly's "spectacular corporate track record has not been matched by growth in quality of care in Beverly Homes."[15] The report was based on statements of deficiencies (inspection reports), Medicaid cost reports, civil court records and other government documents and dealt with expenditure patterns, patient care deficiencies and administrative fines and civil suits. In its first section, the report found that in all three states Beverly spent a smaller proportion of its per day expenditures on patient care than did the industry as a whole and that "Beverly allocated significantly more money to the combination of profit, administrative fees and facility charges than the rest of the industry."[16] In its patient care deficiencies sec-

---

[11]Food and Beverage Trades Department, AFL-CIO, "Beverly Enterprises Patient Care Record: Preliminary Findings January 27, 1983," released January 27, 1983.

[12]"SEIU, UFCW Launch Drive at Some 400 Beverly Nursing Homes," *Daily Labor Report*, No. 20 (January 28, 1983), pp. A-6–A-7.

[13]"Beverly Employees Cooperative Action and Reform Effort," leaflet distributed in January 1983.

[14]*Ibid.*

[15]Food and Beverage Trades Department, AFL-CIO, "Beverly Enterprises Patient Care Record . . . ," p. 1.

[16]*Ibid.*, p. 9.

tion, the report indicated that "significant problems" existed with insufficient staffing and outside professional services, drug administration, and food preparation.[17] In support of that finding, the report provided extensive and often lurid anecdotal evidence and some possibly misleading statistics which were only partially explained.

The findings of the report provided the basis for two union requests for greater government oversight of nursing homes. The Energy and Commerce Committee of the House of Representatives was asked to investigate the need for oversight of health care chains. The Securities and Exchange Commission was asked to require the industry to provide full disclosure of patient care records.[18] Nothing concrete came out of either request.

The company's response to the opening salvos in the unions' campaign was an effort to reduce the issue to a simple matter of organizing. The chief operating officer of the company publicly took the position that segments of the AFL-CIO "have spent millions of their members' dues dollars during the past several years in their overtures to the employees of Beverly" and "failing significant success, they desperately attempt to create a false portrait of Beverly in order to gather support from a public genuinely sympathetic to the plight of the Nation's elderly."[19] The company, however, was unwilling and/or unable to rest its case on that characterization of the union cause and chose to defend itself in the court of public opinion by asserting:

> Every resource available to Beverly is dedicated to providing the best possible health care and environment to elderly Americans. No other organization in the nation can boast a record of such consistent quality and innovation in health and nursing care.[20]

The Annual Meeting

The company's annual shareholder meeting in April of 1983 was the second point of highly visible activity in the unions' campaign. That annual meeting was the third such meeting at which the unions made their presence known. In 1981, they nominated Jacob Clayman, former U.S. Commissioner on the Aging, and former President of the AFL-CIO Industrial Union Department, for a position on the

[17]*Ibid.*, p. 20.
[18]"SEIU, UFCW Launch Organizing Drive at Some 400 Beverly Nursing Homes," *White Collar Report,* Vol. 53, No. 4 (January 28, 1983), p. 111.
[19]*Ibid.*
[20]*Ibid.*

board of directors. In 1982, Arthur Flemming, Secretary of Health, Education, and Welfare in the Eisenhower administration, was nominated for a position on the board and union activists staged a 37-hour sit-in to demand the release of patient care information.[21]

In early 1983, the unions conducted a survey of Beverly employees designed to show that the company "pays its employees poorly, understaffs its homes, and, in many homes, overmedicates patients to keep them 'quiet and immobile'."[22] One thousand employees distributed 20,000 questionnaires at 475 homes in February and the results were released just before the company's annual meeting in April 1983. A total of 421 employees completed the questionnaire which was designed to produce negative responses. When asked about their most critical problems with Beverly, 80 percent of the respondents said low pay and 60 percent said lack of staff. In response to a question regarding medication of patients, 24 percent of the respondents indicated that patients were "frequently" under large doses of medication.[23] The conclusion drawn from those responses was that "it's immoral that the largest and most profitable nursing home in the country so neglects its employees as well as its patients."[24] In support of that conclusion the unions noted that Beverly's stock price had risen 1000 percent over the past five years and that average hourly earnings of hospital and nursing home employees in 1981 was $7.31 while 56 percent of the employees responding to the survey earned less than $3.87 per hour.

The company openly criticized the survey, saying it was surprised that its sponsors had "the audacity to release the results of a survey of 20,000 people when only two percent of the people receiving it even bothered to return it."[25] In addition, the company sent a letter to all employees urging that problems be referred to the company's ombudsman. Those employees who did not respond to the survey were credited with "realizing the survey was just another ploy."[26]

The unions also used the annual meeting to propose two shareholder resolutions "designed to give the institutional investor a clear opportunity to stand up and be counted on quality of care."[27] Proxy

---

[21]"Union Pressure Grows in Advance of Beverly Enterprises Annual Meeting," *White Collar Report,* Vol. 53 (April 22, 1983), pp. 392–393.

[22]*Ibid.,* p. 393.

[23]*Ibid.,* p. 394.

[24]*Ibid.*

[25]"Unions Net One of Ten Votes at Beverly Annual Meeting," *White Collar Report,* Vol. 53 (April 29, 1983), p. 430.

[26]*Ibid.*

[27]"Union Pressure Grows . . . ," p. 393.

solicitations were mailed eleven days prior to the meeting and were followed by an advertisement in the *Wall Street Journal* obviously aimed at Beverly's institutional investors. Despite those efforts, both resolutions were defeated by a margin of 14.5 million shares to 1 million shares.[28] The unions, which garnered only 6 percent of the vote, claimed that the significance of the vote "goes far beyond the numbers" and maintained its position that it is "institutional investors who hold the key to assuring quality of care in Beverly homes."[29] At least one of those institutional investors, Chase Manhattan Bank, apparently agreed as it voted its almost 500,000 shares for the unions' proposal because it "believed that it was in the best interest of all concerned to determine the degree of excellence or lack of it."[30]

The first of the unions' shareholder resolutions dealt with the Quality Assurance Program in the following terms:

WHEREAS: The health and well-being of those who utilize the services of Beverly Enterprises is of paramount importance, and

WHEREAS: Significant competitive factors for the Company are reputation and quality of care, and

WHEREAS: In 1982 and years past the Company has experienced a number of serious problems in delivering quality of care to its residents, and

WHEREAS: These problems indicate deficiencies in the Company's current Quality Assurance Program (the "Program"), therefore be it

RESOLVED: That the Company's shareholders hereby request that the Company promptly establish an independent group of five nationally recognized experts in long-term care of its own choosing to: 1) Establish criteria to measure the quality of care in Company managed facilities, and the effectiveness of the Company's Quality Assurance Program; 2) Measure the quality of care in Company managed facilities and the Program's effectiveness; and 3) Prepare a detailed report of their findings and recommendations to the Board and Shareholders by the Company's next annual meeting, including an assessment of the quality of care in the Company's facilities, and be it further

---

[28]"Final Vote Count in Beverly Proxy Vote: Beverly 14 million; Unions 1 Million," *White Collar Report,* Vol. 53, No. 19 (May 13, 1983), p. 481.

[29]"Union Pressure Grows . . . ," p. 393.

[30]"Union Net One of Ten Votes . . . ," pp. 429–430.

RESOLVED: That the independent experts chosen select their own staff to conduct the study and the Company allocate a minimum of $750,000 for this project.[31]

The second union shareholder resolution called for the appointment of an additional corporate director as follows:

WHEREAS: The primary concern of Beverly Enterprises should be toward the patients the company has chosen to serve, and

WHEREAS: The Company's economic viability is based not only on investor confidence but also on public confidence, and the quality of care delivered, and

WHEREAS: An additional individual with health care experience would bring new expertise to Beverly's Board of Directors, and

WHEREAS: Company By-Laws permit expansion of the Board of Directors to a total of eight (8) persons, therefore, be it

RESOLVED: That the Company's shareholders hereby request that the Company establish a special search committee to include, but not be limited to, institutional shareholders to select an individual with a) national reputation in the long-term health care field, and b) management experience, preferably as a Corporate Director, to serve as an additional director on Beverly's Board.[32]

The management of Beverly took the position that neither proposal was justified nor necessary in light of the company's "vigorous" Quality Assurance Program. The company's senior vice president for administration characterized the union's quality assurance resolution as follows:

On the surface, the proposal seems to have an entirely positive purpose. [But there is a] dangerous undertow... to discredit this company, to discredit the work of our employees, and to discredit the service we provide to the elderly. As we would recognize a wolf in sheep's clothing, so let us be aware of what the union's real motive is in this resolution.[33]

The unions also mounted resistance to a management proposal to adjust the employee stock option plan to the previous year's three-for-two stock split. As with its other resolutions, the unions lost by a

---

[31]Food and Beverage Trades Department, AFL-CIO, "Independent Shareholder Solicitation, 1983 Annual Meeting of Shareholders, Beverly Enterprises, April 22, 1983," p. 6.
[32]*Ibid.*, p. 10.
[33]"Unions Net One of Ten Votes . . . ," p. 430.

wide margin. The company's financial dealings were also the target
of a union petition to the Securities and Exchange Commission concerning the company's March 1983 offering of $70 million of convert-
ible, subordinated debt. The unions claimed that Beverly may have
failed to notify the public of the existence of the corporate campaign
and of its potential impact, despite having communicated that information to its shareholders and employees. The company took the
position that investors had been informed of the campaign and characterized the unions' claim as "too ridiculous for comment."[34]

The Michigan Study

The next major event in the campaign against Beverly Enterprises came in September of 1983 when the unions released a study
of "Beverly Enterprises in Michigan—A Case Study of Corporate
Takeover of Health Care Resources."[35] That report was presented to
the governor of Michigan along with the following proposals for
changes in the state's licensing, certification, and reimbursement
policies for nursing homes:

1) Provision for yearly audits of home office patient care and financial
   records;
2) A 10 percent cap on administrative expenses, similar to that
   imposed in Minnesota;
3) Adoption of a regulation, similar to one in New York state, which
   effectively prohibits out-of-state corporations from operating nursing homes.[36]

The release of the report provided the president of the SEIU with
an opportunity to offer the following comment on Beverly's "threat"
to the public:

   In Michigan, as in four other states we have studied, we've docu-
   mented that Beverly Enterprises has perfected techniques of manipu-
   lating the state medicaid system and skimping on patient care in
   order to make obscene profits at taxpayer expense and to build vast
   personal fortunes for its officers.
   But this report tells far more than the story of one large company's
   continuing greed. It begins to tell the saga of the corporatization of
   health care in the country....
   The impact of the corporatization of health care will be as dramatic
   as if the State of Michigan sold its public schools to big business.[37]

[34]*Ibid.*
[35]Food and Beverage Trades Department, AFL-CIO, "Beverly Enterprises in
Michigan: A Case Study of Corporate Takeover of Health Care Resources," September 26, 1983.
[36]Statement by John J. Sweeny, President, Service Employees International Union,
Lansing, Michigan, September 9, 1983, p. 3.
[37]*Ibid.*, p. 1.

The introduction to the report stated the unions' warning of concentration in the nursing home industry. The first substantive section of the report then examined Beverly's "Monopoly Power" in Michigan. Noting that the firm controlled 75 percent or more of nursing home beds in ten counties, the report asserted that Beverly has "the ability to control access to care to the detriment of Michigan residents most in need of nursing home care."[38] The second section of the report examined the firm's "profiteering on public money" and found that Beverly's profits per patient day were nearly 30 percent above the state average.[39] Administrative costs were also found to be high and to have risen by 26 percent in 1982 with 72 percent of that increase attributable to Beverly's out-of-state, home office expense. This section of the report also indicated that the $2.5 million in state funds used by Beverly in acquiring a 26-home chain in the state would have paid for the state's 1981–1982 Medicaid cuts in hearing aid, fluoride treatment, and prescription drug benefits. In its section on patient care, the report indicated that state inspection citations for 1982 placed 23 percent of the company's homes below average, as compared with 16 percent of all homes in the state, and only 13 percent of its homes above average, as compared with 22 percent of all homes in the state.[40] As in the earlier report on patient care, extensive anecdotal evidence was also provided.

The Settlement

The campaign against Beverly Enterprises prior to the company's 1984 annual meeting ended when, in March 1984, the company and the SEIU and UFCW "reached an understanding that provides the basis for a more positive relationship between the company and the unions."[41] The details or text of that understanding were not and have not been made public and efforts to secure a copy of the agreement from the parties were unsuccessful. Thus, what is known of the character of the agreement which ended the campaign comes largely from what the parties said jointly in announcing that agreement and what they have subsequently said individually about it.

At the heart of the understanding was, in the off-the-record words of a company representative, "an agreement by both sides to stop calling the other names." It was in that context that the unions

---

[38]Food and Beverage Trades Department, AFL-CIO, "Beverly Enterprises in Michigan . . . ," p. 1.7.

[39]*Ibid.,* p. 2.4.

[40]*Ibid.,* pp. 3.1–3.7.

[41]"Beverly Enterprises, UFCW and SEIU . . . ," p. A-5.

agreed to end their corporate campaign in exchange for the company's commitment to make "every effort to ensure a noncoercive atmosphere during election campaigns."[42] The parties jointly characterized that commitment as a reaffirmation of "the principles of employee freedom of choice on union representation" at the time their agreement was announced. Since then the company has consistently denied that it agreed to a neutrality pact and the unions have carefully avoided characterizing the agreement as a neutrality pact, stating only that the agreement "will make it substantially easier for workers to organize."[43]

A second aspect of the understanding was an agreement to establish a national labor/management task force to resolve disputes and problems. One of those problems was the fact that the unions reportedly were experiencing considerable difficulty "in securing collective bargaining agreements, both following a successful NLRB election or when Beverly Enterprises acquired a health care facility that had been previously organized by one of the two unions."[44] In an effort to alleviate that problem, one of the first tasks undertaken by the national task force was the development of contract language on certain noneconomic matters such as grievance procedures for the benefit of those negotiating contracts at the local level. Subsequently, the company and the unions "negotiated an addendum to the agreement that includes a pledge from the company to bargain contracts in newly unionized facilities within three months" and "to honor union contracts at existing homes it purchases."[45]

---

[42]*Ibid.*
[43]*Ibid.*, p. A-6.
[44]*Ibid.*
[45]*UFCW Action*, p. 2.

APPENDIX III

General Dynamics

General Dynamics Corporation was the target of a somewhat limited corporate campaign waged by the United Auto Workers and the Industrial Union Department of the AFL-CIO in 1983 and 1984. The union pressure was confined to public relations and political forums, and was directed against "the nation's premier symbol of the arrogance of corporate power."[1]

The Company

As the nation's largest defense contractor, General Dynamics has been a major beneficiary of the government's recent arms build-up, and was enjoying its second straight year of record profitability. In 1983, a 16 percent increase in sales to $7.15 billion led to a 78 percent increase in earnings from continuous operations to $286.6 million. The firm's principal business segments are:

Government aerospace	50%
Government shipbuilding	20%
Land systems (military tanks)	18%
Other governmental	1%
Commercial	11%

Thus a total of 80 percent of all sales are to the Pentagon; the other 11 percent is divided between commercial shipbuilding, construction materials, coal mining and data processing equipment.[2] Nationwide, the company headquartered in St. Louis, Missouri, employs 94,000 people.

The Origins of the Campaign

The campaign grew out of the United Automobile Workers' (UAW) failing strike action against General Dynamics' Electric Boat Division in 1983. The union had gained bargaining rights for 2,200 draftsmen, designers, and clerical workers at the Groton, Connecti-

---

[1]"News From the UAW," press release dated February 1, 1984, p. 1.
[2]John Curley, "On the Defensive," *Wall Street Journal* (May 18, 1984), p. 21.

cut, nuclear submarine factory in 1982, when the Marine Draftsmen's Association (MDA) voted to affiliate by an 897–737 margin.
This election was the first to be held under the NLRB's Amoco Production Company ruling, which required that all bargaining unit
members be allowed to vote in affiliation elections, regardless of
their union membership status and approximately 225 nonmembers
were eligible to vote at the plant. The company chose to take a
"hands-off position" on the election, viewing it as an internal union
affair.[3]

One reason for the affiliation was probably a 1979–80 strike by the
MDA which split the workers. Hundreds of the members crossed
picket lines to work during the eight-month walkout, in part because
of the union's minimal strike benefits.[4]

The 1983 contract negotiations lasted from April to June. General
Dynamics made a final offer of an eighteen-month wage freeze and a
3 percent raise over the second eighteen months. The workers
rejected the proposal by a vote of 1247–265; the union's final offer
called for an 8 percent raise in year one and additional increases if
the company won a contract for the first attack submarine which
was due to become operational in the 1990s.[5]

On June 9, the union struck Electric Boat. UAW officials estimated that 2,100–2,200 employees walked out, but the number of
strikers dropped throughout the campaign, and considering the
1979–80 MDA strike, it is probably reasonable to assume that many
employees remained on the job. Both sides prepared for a long strike
almost immediately: the union promised benefits of $85 per week
plus health insurance, and the company hired 400 replacements to
help operate the plant.[6]

The UAW charged that the firm was paying replacements more
than the regular workers had been receiving, but the firm noted that
the difference was because the replacements were not receiving any
fringe benefits. On the political front, fourteen Democratic congressmen requested Defense Secretary Caspar Weinberger to ask General
Dynamics to curb its "belligerence" toward the union.[7] These tactics
were a harbinger of the rest of the campaign; but over time, the

[3]"Draftsmen at Electric Boat Choose to Affiliate with UAW," *Daily Labor Report,*
No. 152 (August 6, 1982), p. A-1.
[4]"Marine Draftsmen Strike Electric Boat Shipyard in Groton, Conn.," *Daily Labor
Report,* No. 113 (June 10, 1983), p. A-4.
[5]*Ibid.,* p. A-4.
[6]"Electric Boat Hires 400 Replacements for Draftsmen at Connecticut Shipyard,"
White Collar Report, Vol. 54, No. 9 (August 26, 1983), p. 179.
[7]*Ibid.*

charges against General Dynamics grew both in importance and press coverage.

The first of these charges arose out of the November 15 death of Harvey Lee, a 32-year-old driver mechanic at the company's Center Line, Michigan plant. Lee died from cardiac arrythmia triggered by the fumes from Genesolv D, the solvent used for cleaning M-1 tanks. In previous months, several others had been injured by the cleaner; at least two of these men suffered heart arrhythmias after potentially fatal contact with Genesolv D.[8]

UAW Vice President Marc Stepp "blasted" General Dynamics, the federal Occupational Safety and Health Administration (OSHA), and Michigan-OSHA, and noted that the union had warned all three about the potential dangers of the solvent after the earlier accidents. He went on to charge that company practices were "a willful disregard of known protective procedures," and he called for a full investigation into General Dynamics' behavior and the practices of the OSHA groups.[9]

Meanwhile, activity continued at the bargaining table, but appeared to focus on job security for the strikers rather than the hoped for wage increases. In January 1984, the strikers, who had dwindled to 1,400, formally rejected any return without job guarantees for all of them.[10]

The Escalation of the Campaign

The official campaign was announced on February 1, and focused on branding General Dynamics as "anti-labor and anti-taxpayer." UAW President Owen Bieber declared that the effort would "expose the chronicle of General Dynamics' greed and abuse to the American people, and to the workers at GD installations all across the country."[11] He charged the company with:

> ... massive ripoffs of American taxpayers through the sale of materials to the Pentagon at outrageous and unjustifiable prices; of chronic abuse of the Defense Department's procurement bidding process; of acquiescence in the questionable practices of various GD executives; of needless endangerment of workers' lives at GD facilities; and of grossly irresponsible conduct in collective bargaining leading to an eight-month strike at its Electric Boat subsidiary in Groton, CT.[12]

---

[8]"News From the UAW" press release issued, November 16, 1983, pp. 1–2.
[9]*Ibid.,* p. 2.
[10]"Electric Boat Gives Strikers Deadline For Returning To Work," *Daily Labor Report,* No. 27 (February 9, 1984), p. A-3.
[11]"News from the UAW," February 1, 1984, p. 1.
[12]*Ibid.*

Unfortunately for General Dynamics, several of the union's charges were already receiving attention from government agencies and the mass media. The so-called "massive ripoffs" were symbolized by "12-cent" allen wrenches which allegedly were sold to the Air Force for $9606.00 each.[13] The practices of P. Takis Veliotis, the former top executive in the firm's Connecticut and Massachusetts shipbuilding operations, were also noted. Veliotis fled to Greece in 1982 after being indicted on seventeen counts for his role in an alleged kickback scheme with subcontractors.[14]

Poor health and safety practices were criticized for the deaths of two workers over thirteen months. Before the end of the UAW campaign, the state of Michigan would charge General Dynamics with involuntary manslaughter and willful violation of state safety standards in connection with the death of Harvey Lee.[15] The indictment was dismissed in October 1984.

In its charges concerning collective bargaining practices, the union invoked the "anti-taxpayer" theme once again. One spokesman cited a company negotiator's alleged statement that the extra expense of replacement workers was unimportant because it could be billed to the government on a cost-plus basis. There were no substantive labor relations charges against the firm, and the NLRB rejected the UAW's claims of bargaining in bad faith.[16]

General Dynamics responded to these accusations and the threat of a broader campaign with both denials and positive action. According to one company official:

> [The statements attributed to Mr. Bieber are] outrageous, slanderous, irresponsible and completely without merit . . . [Bieber's] statements certainly do not indicate in any sense the determination to negotiate in good faith the difficult issues surrounding the unfortunate marine draftsmen's strike at Electric Boat.[17]

Less than a week after the announcement of the campaign, General Dynamics ran a series of advertisements in Connecticut and Rhode Island newspapers to give the strikers a February 10 deadline for returning to work. The firm announced that 500 openings would be held for union members who returned before the deadline, and prom-

---

[13]*Ibid.*, p. 2.

[14]*Ibid.*

[15]*Ibid.*, p. 3.

[16]"UAW Charges General Dynamics With Obstruction and Disregard For Worker Safety Before House Panels," *Daily Labor Report*, No. 120 (June 21, 1984), p. A-14.

[17]"UAW Announces Campaign Against General Dynamics, Citing Boat Strike, Safety Abuse, High Prices," *Daily Labor Report*, No. 22 (February 2, 1984), p. A-7.

ised several improvements in compensation. A lump sum of seventy-five hours worth of wages would be paid after twenty days' work, and a payment for sixty hours would be made ten days into a worker's second year back on the job. Wages would rise 3 percent at the start of the third year. Pension benefits would rise from $12 to $13 per month for each year of service immediately, and would go to $14 in the second year.[18]

The union's next major action was to orchestrate a March 3 rally and march at General Dynamics headquarters in St. Louis. The UAW estimated that 1,000 General Dynamics workers from twelve different unions protested along with supporters from church, women's, anti-war and community groups. The previous charges were reiterated and signs bore messages such as:

Stop Killing People
I'm a Taxpayer and I'm Mad
General Dynamics' Scabs at Groton Must Go

At the rally, UAW Vice President Stepp declared that "General Dynamics will rue the day it took on the UAW."[19]

While the rally drew only minimal attention from the press, 800 union draftsmen were crossing the Electric Boat picket line along with 800 new hires. Furthermore, the company warned that even if the strike ended, there would be room for only 200 of the strikers.[20]

The UAW next planned to bring the IUD's "Coalition to Clean Up General Dynamics" to the company's annual meeting in May in order to "greet the shareholders with a list of embarrassing demands from workers, taxpayers, women, and others."[21] Unfortunately for the protesters, once the firm heard of the plan, it had the meeting moved to another location. Several unionists were still able to attend the meeting and were allowed to speak. On one occasion, a union leader asked the shareholders to "rise in a moment of silence for Harvey Lee."[22] Of the 200 people present, only the protesters rose.[23]

Since the union's coalition was frustrated by the switch in the meeting location, it held a "Concerned Shareholders Meeting" on

---

[18]"Electric Boat Gives Strikers . . . ," p. A-3.
[19]Jeff Stansbury, "Company Without a Conscience," *Solidarity,* March 1984, p. 13.
[20]"A Harder UAW Push on General Dynamics," *Business Week,* March 26, 1984, p. 35.
[21]Jeff Stansbury, "Catching Up with General Dynamics," *Solidarity,* June 1984, p. 9.
[22]*Ibid.*
[23]*Ibid.*

May 2. The charges against the firm were repeated by a variety of different sources, including representatives from:

The National Organization for Women
The Religious Committee on Labor Relations
The Missouri Citizen/Labor Energy Coalition
Catholic University
The Sierra Club
The Sisters of Loretto[24]

Once again, the union failed to attract significant media coverage.

In June, the UAW's efforts shifted to politics for the final leg of the campaign. During an appearance before the Labor Relations and Health subcommittees of the House Labor and Education Committee, Bieber asked the legislators to "require more acceptable behavior by General Dynamics." In addition, he took the opportunity to cite the need for the campaign:

> When a company can charge outrageous prices, when it pays no income tax while making more than 30 percent return on equity, when it has a cozy relationship with its main customer, and when it can pass along as a reimbursable expense the cost of opposing improved working conditions, then the deck is stacked against the worker and they must look beyond the bargaining table to correct the situation.[25]

The Settlement

The corporate campaign against General Dynamics which began in February 1984 was ended six months later by a collective bargaining agreement which ended a fifteen month strike by UAW-represented Draftsmen, Designers and Clerical Workers against the Company's Electric Boat Division. That agreement was not described by either party as an agreement to end anything more or different from a normal, if prolonged, labor dispute as opposed to a corporate campaign. Nonetheless, there does appear to have been something unusual about the settlement (Attachment 1). Specifically, after announcing in February 1984 that it had only 500 openings for any returning strikers and reducing that number to 200 in March of that year, the company agreed in August 1984 to rehire

---

[24]*Ibid.*, pp. 10–11.

[25]"House Digs at General Dynamics Sins," *UAW Washington Report*, Vol. 24, No. 25. (June 22, 1984), p. 1.

700 still striking workers at the expense of replacements hired during the strike.[26] It is not clear, however, the extent to which that "unusual" settlement might have been prompted not by the campaign, but by the fact that as early as March 1984, "The UAW is already predicting a stormy confrontation next year, when its contract expires for 5,600 workers who assemble the M-1 tank, one of GD's largest government projects."[27]

[26]"News From the UAW," press release issued August 24, 1984, p. 1.
[27]"A Harder UAW Push on General Dynamics," p. 36.

ATTACHMENT 1

NEWS UAW
FROM THE

Public Relations and
Publications Dept.

8000 E. Jefferson Ave.
Detroit, Mich. 48214

DAVE MITCHELL Director
(313) 926-5291

INTERNATIONAL UNION, UNITED AUTOMOBILE, AEROSPACE AND AGRICULTURAL IMPLEMENT WORKERS OF AMERICA

FOR RELEASE: Immediate, Friday, August 24, 1984

UAW CITES IMPACT OF CLEAN-UP CAMPAIGN IN
SETTLEMENT WITH GENERAL DYNAMICS

UAW President Owen Bieber and Vice-President Marc Stepp, who heads the UAW's General Dynamics Dept., said today that the union's widely publicized Campaign to Clean Up General Dynamics had a "significant impact" in settling a 15-month strike by members of UAW Local 571, the Marine Draftsmen's Association, in Groton, CT.

"Considering the initial hardline stance of the company," Bieber and Stepp said, "there can be no doubt that concern about its image and the fear of more adverse publicity forced General Dynamics to soften its stance on the return-to-work and wage cap issues in Groton."

The members of Local 571 voted by a 2 to 1 margin yesterday to accept a tentative agreement worked out last week calling for nearly 700 strikers to return to their jobs at GD's Electric Boat facility, which makes Navy submarines. The agreement calls for the removal of strikebreakers hired to replace the strikers, for modification in proposed new rate maximums and for a general raise in the third year of the contract.

The UAW's Campaign to Clean Up General Dynamics, announced by Bieber last February and coordinated by the AFL-CIO's Industrial Union Department, focused on the firm's arrogance in labor-relations, its dismal health and safety record and its abuse of taxpayers through overcharges on spare parts and possible fraud in certain weapons contracts with the Pentagon. The symbol of the campaign was a tiny 12-cent allen wrench, widely worn as a lapel pin, which General Dynamics tried to sell to the Air Force for $9,600.

General Dynamics...2

The Campaign featured a bus caravan of Groton strikers to all UAW-represented GD plants, appearances at the annual meetings of GD and of companies whose boards include GD officers, major demonstrations in St. Louis and Chicago, and a Concerned Public Shareholders meeting held one day before the company's own meeting in May and highlighting the specific concerns of women's, peace, environmental and civil rights groups along with those of General Dynamics workers.

The Campaign stimulated a joint hearing of the Labor Relations and Health and Safety subcommittees of the House Committee on Education and Labor this June. General Dynamics was the sole subject of the hearing, and its labor and safety policies were critized by representatives of several unions as well as by Mary Ann Lee, the widow of a General Dynamics tank plant worker who was killed last November due to the company's careless use of a fluorocarbon solvent. Michigan Attorney General Frank Kelly has since brought charges of criminal negligence against the firm because of that incident.

Bieber and Stepp said they believe the campaign had a substantial impact on the UAW-General Dynamics relationship and that it helped encourage governmental action regarding defense contractor abuses.

They emphasized that the UAW continues to urge oversight committees in the House and Senate as well as the Justice Dept. to "pursue aggressively and with all deliberate speed" their investigations of possible fraud, involving hundreds of millions of dollars, in General Dynamics' handling of an attack submarine contract in the mid-1970s.

General Dynamics...3

"General Dynamics has settled some matters with us, but continuing public scrutiny is needed to insure public confidence in GD as the recipient of multibillion-dollar defense contracts," Bieber and Stepp said. "Workers who are also taxpayers know that waste and fraud endanger their long-term job security along with endangering the national security," they added.

The UAW leaders thanked all those unions and other groups which participated in or supported the General Dynamics Campaign and expressed the hope that the successful effort would benefit other unions which negotiate with the company. They also noted that the Industrial Union Dept. will continue to assist in coordinated bargaining efforts with respect to General Dynamics.

# # #

PL/cb
opeiu494/M-3
8/24/84-82

Litton Industries

Litton Industries is a large advanced electronics company, which, in the words of the Industrial Union Department (IUD) of the AFL-CIO, "describes itself as a high technology company... whose various businesses are tied together by the common thread of technological innovations and advanced products, processes and services."[1] The IUD characterization of Litton Industries was made in conjunction with a 1981 financial review of the corporation which reported annual sales of almost $5 billion (of which approximately 20 percent was attributable to foreign operations) divided as follows by major product groups:

1) Advanced electronic systems	17%
2) Business systems and equipment	15%
3) Electronics and electrical products	22%
4) Industrial systems and services	23%
5) Marine engineering and production	15%
6) Paper, printing and publishing	8%

The IUD's financial analysis included a detailed breakdown of products and performance by product groups which provided ample testimony to the diversity of the company's operations in both identity and clientele. The first lesson to be learned from that detailed analysis is that many Litton businesses did not operate solely under the Litton name but continued to utilize their original firm name after acquisition. The second lesson is that Litton Industries was most definitely not a consumer products corporation but had significant defense contracts which accounted for about 25 percent of its sales compared with 5 percent for its consumer products— microwave ovens. The remainder of its sales were spread across a broad range of industrial and commercial markets.

The IUD's financial analysis of Litton included a section on "employment and organizational status" which stated that Litton employed an estimated 60,000 workers at seventy-nine principal plants in twenty-nine cities in the United States.[2] IUD records

---

[1] Industrial Union Department, AFL-CIO, "Litton Industries, Inc." Analysis distributed at a meeting in Columbus, Ohio, October 30, 1981, p. 1.

[2] *Ibid.*, pp. 11-12.

reflected that 21,300, or 35 percent of those 60,000 workers, were covered by collective bargaining agreements. Overall, thirty Litton locations were unionized, with the largest being Ingalls Shipbuilding in Pascagoula, Mississippi, where 10,000 workers were covered by four agreements. Excluding those workers and supervisory employees, the IUD estimated that "approximately one of every four organizable Litton workers outside of Pascagoula was unionized." That percentage was about twice the percentage for Litton's electronic and electrical components group where, in the words of the IUD, "current organizing and first contract battles are occurring, namely, Athens, AL, Huntington, IN, and Sioux Falls, SD."[3]

Finally, the IUD analysis also included a section on "Directors and Officers" which reported that of the twelve members of the Board of Directors, two were current and two were former Litton officers.[4] Three of the remaining eight members were retired executives, three were academicians, and two were active chief executive officers of other firms. By 1983, the number of directors had been expanded to fourteen, but the Board's character had not changed, as three members were current Litton officers, two were retired Litton officers, four were academicians, three were retired executives, and two were active chief executives.

The Origin of the Campaign

The Litton campaign grew out of the frustration of a single union in its efforts to secure an initial collective bargaining agreement at one Litton plant. The union was the United Electrical, Radio, and Machine Workers (UE), a union which left the CIO in 1950 under charges of Communist domination. The plant was Litton's Sioux Falls, South Dakota, microwave oven production facility.

The Sioux Falls plant opened in 1977 and quickly became the target of a UE organizing drive. That drive bore fruit in September 1980, when the UE narrowly won a National Labor Relations Board (NLRB) representation election. Negotiations over an initial contract began in October of that year. When no substantial progress toward an agreement had been made by the end of 1980, the union staged a demonstration in Sioux Falls in January 1981 to protest that lack of progress. In February 1982, union negotiators told their company counterparts of the union's intention to "do a number on the company" and began its campaign.

---

[3]*Ibid.*, p. 11.
[4]*Ibid.*, p. 13.

The UE's campaign over the following six months was concentrated in Sioux Falls, but extended to other communities in which the union had locals. The union first launched a postcard campaign, asking members of its own locals to send preprinted postcards to the chairman and chief executive officer of the corporation urging the company to adopt a more conciliatory stance in its negotiations with the union. That was followed by demonstrations at appliance dealers, conducted for the purpose of encouraging them to write to the corporation to protest its labor policies. Finally, the union solicited letters to the corporation from political figures, urging a quick conclusion to negotiations.

In May, the company terminated three employees for cause. The union immediately filed unfair labor practice charges, alleging that the firings were motivated by the union activities and support of the three individuals. The union also sought the aid of local civic and religious leaders in protesting the firings, resulting in an open letter from the Sioux Falls United Brotherhood Council to the company and community expressing its concern over the "justice and fairness" of the firings. When that letter evoked no response from the company, the union sought broader community involvement and support by holding a "community conference" on Litton's labor policies in September 1981. That conference was not well attended and did nothing to alter the company's stance at the bargaining table. Subsequently, the discharge of the three employees was upheld by an administrative law judge of the NLRB, as well as by an agency of the state of South Dakota.

The Expansion of the Campaign

The UE saw the first anniversary of its representational victory at Sioux Falls pass without a contract and without apparent success or prospect of success in forcing the company to an agreement through its campaign. The UE clearly was unwilling to undertake strike action in an attempt to force an agreement and unable, on its own, to generate sufficient public pressure on local management to force it to accede to the union's demands or on corporate management to induce it to pressure local management to settle. Thus, the UE had no power on its own to break the impasse in negotiations other than to modify its demands and admit its weakness. Its only alternative to that highly repugnant action was to seek outside assistance in its efforts to pressure corporate management.

The UE's most likely natural ally in its battle with Litton was the larger labor movement from which it was an outcast. If it was to effectuate an alliance with the AFL-CIO and gain its support despite its outcast status and continuing radical ideology, it would have to create some compelling common ground. The AFL-CIO clearly would not lend its weight to the UE over the issue of a contract at Sioux Falls. Some broader institutional issue or cause had to be found.

In the course of its campaign, the UE had sought the support of local unions at other Litton plants, generally without notable success. In the course of that effort, however, it did uncover other unions which had experienced organizing or bargaining setbacks at Litton locations. That common experience provided the common ground on which the affected unions could meet to at least discuss their Litton problems. That did indeed happen on October 30, 1981, at an IUD-Litton conference in Columbus, Ohio. That meeting reportedly was attended by representatives of six AFL-CIO locals— from the International Association of Machinists and Aerospace Workers (IAM), International Brotherhood of Electrical Workers (IBEW), International Union of Electrical, Radio and Machine Workers (IUE), International Union of United Automobile, Aerospace and Agricultural Implement Workers of America (UAW), United Steelworkers of America (USW), Graphic Communications International Union (GCIU)—and two independent unions—from the UE and the International Brotherhood of Teamsters.

At that conference two papers were distributed and discussed. The first was the IUD's analysis of Litton operations cited above. The second was a "Report to Delegates, IUD-Litton Conference, October 30, 1982, Litton's Labor Policy," apparently prepared by the UE. That report purported to review labor problems at nineteen Litton locations over the past decade in support of its opening allegations that:

> Litton Industries has a long history of abusive labor policies and labor law violations. Over the years, a pattern of conduct has emerged that makes one thing clear: *no* group of Litton workers, even where there is currently a stable relationship, is safe from company union-busting.[5]

That claim was the first step in what was to be the UE lobbying campaign "to have organized labor make Litton's labor practices a major focus of union activities in the 1980s." The first evidence of that effort was the informal agreement of the six AFL-CIO unions at the October meeting to lend their individual moral support to a national UE corporate campaign against Litton. Shortly after that meeting, the chief executive officer of Litton received a letter from

---

[5]Document in author's possession.

Ray Rogers in which he alluded to the possibility of a corporate campaign if Litton did not mend its ways.

The Escalation of the Campaign

The national campaign against Litton did not actually broaden until mid 1982. In December, 1981, the UE distributed "an open letter to Litton shareholders" at the company's annual meeting focused almost exclusively on the Sioux Falls situation. In April, the Coalition of Labor Union Women (CLUW), at the request of the UE, staged a protest at corporate headquarters during its convention in Los Angeles over the Sioux Falls problem. It was not until July 1982 that the UE changed the focus of the campaign from Sioux Falls to Litton's larger labor record and a truly national coordinated campaign began.

The key to any corporate campaign is an allegation of morally reprehensible corporate conduct. Clearly, the Sioux Falls situation did not meet that test, nor did the individual problems of the six other unions. What was needed was a vehicle for suggesting far more pervasive and perverse corporate behavior. Fortunately for the UE, the work of Professor Charles Craypo provided allegations of just such behavior—allegations which constituted a vehicle for solidifying the UE's alliance with the labor movement and establishing a plausible public interest issue.

In 1975, Craypo, then associate professor of labor studies at Pennsylvania State University, published an article entitled "Collective Bargaining in the Conglomerate, Multinational Firm: Litton's Shutdown of Royal Typewriter," in which he concluded that unions were at a severe disadvantage in bargaining with such firms.[6] One year later, Professor Craypo submitted a paper entitled "Litton Industries as a Repeat Violator of the National Labor Relations Act" to the U.S. House Committee on Labor in conjunction with its early consideration of so-called "labor law reform." In that paper, he alleged that an examination of twenty-eight NLRB complaints filed against various Litton divisions since 1963 "leads to the inescapable conclusion that since the early 1960s Litton has pursued a policy of flagrant, systematic and calculated lawlessness in its aggressively anti-union policy."[7] In February 1982, Professor Craypo, then associ-

---

[6] Charles Craypo, "Collective Bargaining in the Conglomerate, Multinational Firm: Litton's Shutdown of Royal Typewriter," *Industrial and Labor Relations Review*, Vol. 29, No. 1 (October 1975), pp. 3-25.

[7] Charles Craypo, "Litton Industries as a Repeat Violator of the National Labor Relations Act," paper submitted to the Subcommittee on Labor-Management Rela-

ate professor of economics at Notre Dame, revised and updated that paper in the form of a "working paper" of the economics department of the university in which he reiterated his earlier allegation—an allegation quoted on all leaflets used in the campaign thereafter.[8]

The Craypo Report claimed that between 1963 and 1981 the NLRB issued forty-two complaints against Litton operations, resulting in nineteen findings of violations of the law, thirteen voluntary settlements, and ten dismissed complaints. Those figures were widely cited in press coverage of the Litton campaign. Such citations, in turn, were used in union literature and on one occasion by Professor Craypo himself.[9] The company prepared its own analysis of the data in the Craypo Report and found several major factual, technical and conceptual errors (Attachment I). Strategically, however, it chose not to engage in a debate over the details of the report but to focus on its implications that Litton was anti-union by pointing out that there were few, if any, ongoing labor disputes at Litton subsidiaries, and that such subsidiaries had recently negotiated and renegotiated contracts at more than twenty locations in a period of two years.

Armed with the allegations of the Craypo Report, the UE led its coalition of labor allies into a three-pronged attack on Litton during the latter half of 1982. The first line of attack involved an attempt to convince the general counsel of the NLRB that Litton Industries should be treated as one centrally-controlled enterprise under labor law rather than as an array of separate entities. The second line of attack was to convince Congress that Litton was unworthy of government contracts. The third line of attack was to involve religious and community action groups in the protest of Litton's labor policies.

In July and August, the UE claimed that "union supporters rallied at N.L.R.B. regional offices throughout the country to back up a formal union request that the board institute a strong, company-wide approach in dealing with Litton."[10] Whether such rallies did

---

tions of the U.S. House Committee on Labor, February 19, 1976 and published in, *Oversight Hearings on the National Labor Relations Act* (Washington, D.C.: Government Printing Office, 1976), pp. 125-39.

[8]Charles Craypo, "Litton Industries as a Repeat Violator of the National Labor Relations Act," working paper, Economics Department, University of Notre Dame, February 1982.

[9]Charles Craypo, Jerold Paar, and Mary Lehman, "Litton Industries' Pattern of Labor Law Violations," report submitted to the Subcommittee on Labor-Management Relations of the U.S. House Committee on Labor, on April 20, 1983, p. 2.

[10]Lance Compa, "How to Fight a Unionbusting Conglomerate," *The Nation*, July 16, 1983, p. 40.

indeed occur throughout the country is an open question, but they did occur in Hartford and Minneapolis. In any event, on August 5, 1982, "representatives of a number of labor organizations met with members of the [Board's] General Counsel staff regarding Litton Industries, Inc." to express their view "that the Board's handling of Litton cases is inadequate."[11]

July and August also produced an exchange of correspondence between members of Congress and the corporation. That exchange was initiated by a letter from Representative Burton (D-Cal) requesting a corporate response to charges levelled against it by the UE. The company did respond, as requested. That response, in turn, produced an answer from Representative Simon (D-Ill) after the sudden death of Representative Burton, containing the UE's rebuttal of the corporation's response and the congressman's claim that there was strong and growing sentiment in Washington that labor law violators should not be rewarded with government contracts.

The first signs of religious group interest in Litton's labor policy also emerged in July and August 1982, in the Minneapolis area. In July, the Catholic Archdiocese wrote to express its concern over Litton's labor policies. In August, the Greater Minneapolis Council of Churches entered the picture, and by December, so had the Interfaith Center for Corporate Responsibility, which claimed to have played an important role in seeing that a shareholder proposal regarding corporate labor policy was placed on the agenda for the corporation's 1982 annual meeting. At that meeting, according to the UE, "hundreds of Litton workers and their supporters demonstrated" and "a shareholder resolution criticizing Litton's labor relations (which the company had fought to keep off the agenda) was sharply debated ... though it was eventually voted down."[12] Litton claimed the demonstrators, with few exceptions, were not Litton employees but paid demonstrators.

The close coordination between Representative (now Senator) Simon, the office of the general counsel, and the UE was evident in March and April of 1983. On March 1, Representative Simon introduced H.R. 1743 to debar repeated labor law violators from holding government contracts. On March 10, the general counsel of the NLRB issued instructions to regional offices to search their files for all Litton cases for a special study of the corporation's records. On

---

[11]NLRB internal memorandum from Richard A. Siegel, deputy assistant general counsel to Joseph E. DeZio, associate general counsel, subject: Litton Industries, May 17, 1983, p-1.

[12]Compa, "How to Fight a Unionbusting Conglomerate," p. 40.

April 20, subcommittee hearings were held on H.R. 1743 at which the unions involved in the campaign testified basically against Litton. On that same day, a protest rally was held at George Washington University to persuade Litton director Professor Jayne Spain not to resign but to effect change in corporate labor policy. It was at the hearings on H.R. 1743 that the corporation was first formally given "the dubious distinction of having displaced J.P. Stevens as America's No. 1 labor law violator"[13] by the UE.

The unions' two Washington initiatives barely moved over the summer of 1983. In May, the staff of the general counsel of the NLRB completed their review of Litton cases and concluded that "it is [not] possible to reach any firm conclusions regarding the control exercised by Litton Industries, Inc., over the labor relations of its subsidiaries or divisions. Nor is it possible to conclude either that Litton Industries, Inc. is virulently anti-union or is a notorious labor law violator as the Unions claim. Our review of the cases does, however, raise certain suspicions ... "[14] Nevertheless, on the basis of those suspicions, the staff recommended in September the institution of special procedures to monitor and respond to the concerns and requests of labor organizations. Such special procedures were instituted by the general counsel by memorandum to NLRB regional offices on October 31, 1983—strangely, the same day that H.R. 1743 was voted out of House subcommittee.[15]

During the first nine months of 1983, the UE moved its campaign to the campus. Rallies were held by the UE and its allies at Stanford and the University of Southern California, as well as George Washington University, in an attempt to pressure the corporation's academic directors, one of whom turned out to a non-voting advisory director. The result of those and other rallies, in the words of the UE, was to demonstrate "the potential to unite trade unions, the women's movement, the civil rights movement, the peace movement and other activist forces in a struggle against the unchecked exercise of corporate power."[16] George E. Ogle, of the General Board of Church and Society of the United Methodist Church, joined the union roster of those testifying for H.R. 1743 and against Litton. The name of the Catholic Church, in the person of Msgr. George G. Higgins of Catholic University, was injected in an August article in the magazine

---

[13]Tamar Lewin, "Litton's Angry Labor Conglomerate," *New York Times,* April 24, 1983, p. Fl.

[14]NLRB internal memorandum on Litton Industries, May 17, 1983, p. 6.

[15]NLRB Office of the General Counsel memorandum to all regional directors, subject: Litton Industries, memorandum GC 83-18, October 31, 1983.

[16]Compa, "How to Fight a Unionbusting Conglomerate," p. 41.

America, lauding the campaign as "the best opportunity... to give concrete support to working people in their struggle to organize and at the same time contribute to the longer-range goals of labor law justice and corporate social responsibility."[17] Finally, on September 14, the IUD formally joined the fray, in a press conference, by naming Litton Industries to its "dishonor roll of labor law violators," suggesting that it "may be this nation's number one labor law violator."[18]

The attempt to vilify Litton was fairly well spent by the end of October 1983. At that point, the corporation was, in the view of a majority of a Democratic-controlled House subcommittee, presumptively worthy of debarment; in the view of a Democratic-appointed general counsel for the NLRB, not totally above suspicion as being centrally-controlled; and in the view of the IUD, worthy of recognition as possibly the nation's leading labor scofflaw. In the view of Msgr. Higgins, the corporation was in violation of the papal encyclical "On Human Labor"; and in view of Mr. Ogle of the Methodist Church, characterized by a "sharp class consciousness" on which "both the local management and the representatives of the corporate office appear to agree."

The company's response to its vilification was one of low-key denials. The company declined to testify on H.R. 1743 and took the position publicly that the debarment effort was unjustified and would "not get off the ground."[19] The company's public response to the NLRB's actions was that its record before the NLRB was not a significant one and the general counsel's memorandum was "not anything all that new."[20] Its continued public response to charges of

---

[17]George C. Higgins, "The Litton Campaign: Unions United," *America*, August 27, 1983, p. 88. For further insight into Msgr. Higgins' role, reference is made to an unpublished public relations case study entitled "Dinosaur War: Litton Industries v. United Electrical Workers of America," prepared by Mary Ann Elliott, a student in 1984. In this case study Elliott reconstructs an interview which she conducted with Msgr. Higgins on April 19, 1984. In this interview, Msgr. Higgins states that he wrote the article about Litton for *America* because:

> The unions wanted it. They wanted someone in the Catholic community because they wanted clergy involvement in the Sioux Falls thing. They felt it would be a breakthrough if the story were told in a responsible Catholic publication. The approach was that then they could use reprints in their publicity campaign.

When asked how he knew so much about the Litton situation, Msgr. Higgins replied:

> Actually, Lance (Compa, Washington UE representative) did most of the work. I had asked what I could do to help get the word around.

[18]Industrial Union Department news release, November 16, 1983.

[19]"Testing a New Weapon Against Litton," *Business Week*, December 27, 1982, p. 32.

[20]"Labor Escalates its Campaign Against Litton," *Business Week*, November 21, 1983, p. 51.

being anti-union was to cite its existing bargaining relationships, i.e., the lack of a labor dispute with anyone besides the UE and its regular, peaceful negotiations with a wide variety of AFL-CIO unions. Behind the scenes, the company took the same passive stance, with the possible exception of filing a Freedom of Information Act request with the NLRB for all materials in its file. The company's response, in the view of the company, was a product of the lack of a discernible impact on directors, shareholders, employees, customers or the public, as manifested in director or shareholder meetings, sales—particularly of microwave ovens—or letters from the public (as opposed to media inquiries).

The newness of the "vilification" campaign led to some optimistic predictions regarding its outcome and implications for the future course of labor relations. The *New York Times* stated that "the union campaign against Litton is emerging as the prototype for a new labor strategy to organize giant conglomerate corporations."[21] Msgr. Higgins stated that "if the Litton campaign continues to grow, and if the American people tire of the abuses of corporate power, we may be in a position after the 1984 elections to take giant steps forward to genuine labor law reform."[22] The most ambitious vision, however, was expressed by the UE, which saw the campaign as a model for "the development of an effective force to counter the power of multinational corporations"—a force which would require that American workers "reach out to overseas workers—including those in the left-wing unions of Europe, South American, Asia and Africa"—as well as a force against the exercise of corporate power domestically, as exemplified by Litton's cost overruns, policy against cooperating with EPA inspections, and practice of plant closings and product line relocations which "make clear the need for democratic controls over investment decisions."[23]

The Elevation of the Campaign

In November 1983, the IUD formally assumed control and leadership of the Litton campaign on behalf of the now nine AFL-CIO unions supporting the cause of the UE.[24] That change in leadership

---

[21]Lewin, "Litton's Angry Labor Conglomerate," p. Fl.

[22]Higgins, "The Litton Campaign: Unions United," p. 88.

[23]Compa, "How to Fight a Unionbusting Conglomerate," p. 41.

[24]The nine unions were: 1) Graphic Communications, 2) International Association of Machinists and Aerospace Workers (IAM), 3) International Brotherhood of Electrical Workers (IBEW), 4) International Union of Electrical, Radio, and Machine Workers (IUE), 5) Metal Trades, 6) United Auto Workers (UAW), 7) Carpenters, 8) Paperworkers, 9) United Steelworkers of America (USW).

surfaced on November 16, when the IUD held a press conference in Washington to announce that "labor, clergy join forces in National Litton Campaign." At that press conference, Howard D. Samuel, president of the IUD and now "chairman of the National Litton Campaign" was joined by Msgr. Higgins, "longtime official of the National Catholic Conference," in announcing that "representatives of labor and the religious community have joined together in ... plans for new activities designed to highlight the anti-worker actions of Litton Industries."[25] Specifically cited were a resolution to be voted on at the Litton shareholder meeting on December 10 and plans for a mass protest rally at the site of the meeting.

The decision of the IUD to take over the leadership of the campaign from the UE reportedly reflected the fact that "over the past few months ... Litton angered other unions," as a result of which "several AFL-CIO unions asked the IUD to take charge."[26] Subsequent events, however, suggest that the decision was prompted by the fact that the scope and direction of the campaign under the UE's leadership was angering or at least embarrassing the AFL-CIO and several of its unions, most notably the Metal Trades Council, which held bargaining rights for 10,000 Litton workers at Ingalls Shipbuilding.

The disaffection of the AFL-CIO unions with the UE's leadership of the campaign stemmed from several sources. There was reason to suspect that the UE's only goal was to force a settlement at Sioux Falls, a suspicion given credence by the UE's admission in late 1982 that if Litton signed a contract there, "the question of us playing a leading role (in the campaign) would have to be reviewed."[27] In mounting a campaign to that end, the UE appeared willing to sacrifice the interests of other unions, especially those at Ingalls whose jobs were at risk should debarment become law—a risk publicly discounted by the UE.[28] Above and beyond such mundane considerations was a growing ideological schism created by the UE's growing acceptance of the peace movement as an ally in its crusade against Litton. That "radicalization" of the campaign created an ideological gap between the "hawkish" AFL-CIO and the "pacifist" UE on defense issues. It also exposed ideological differences within the AFL-CIO and between the AFL-CIO and major religious groups.

---

[25]Industrial Union Department, National Litton Campaign, news release, November 16, 1983.

[26]"Labor Escalates its Campaign Against Litton," p. 51.

[27]"Testing a New Weapon Against Litton," p. 33.

[28]Compa, "How to Fight a Unionbusting Conglomerate," p. 40.

That latter difference surfaced in November of 1983, when it was reported that "leaders of the nation's major Protestant and Jewish organizations are withdrawing their support of union organizing campaigns, strikes and boycotts" because "religious leaders are angered by the refusal of top AFL-CIO leaders to defend the churches against right-wing assault" on their positions on foreign policy.[29]

The rift between the AFL-CIO and major religious groups did not prevent the participation of religious representatives in the planned protest at the Litton shareholder meeting on December 10. The union theme for that protest was "Litton Makes Misery—We Can Make a Difference." The program for the rally called for speeches by Howard Samuel, Msgr. Higgins, and Joyce Miller of the CLUW, as well as two alleged Litton victims, interspersed among an invocation by a pastor of an American Methodist Episcopal church; an Old Testament reading by a rabbi; a Litany for Justice by the executive director of Southern California Ecumenical Council; a magnificat by the president of Church Women United; a Litany for Directors by the director of the Church and Society Network, West; and a benediction by a Catholic priest.

The focal point of the rally was to focus attention on and presumably encourage adoption of the following shareholder resolutions to be voted upon at the Litton annual meeting:

> Whereas the right of employees to organize and bargain with their employer in good faith, has long been recognized in our country and has been part of the ethical foundation of our religious life as expressed, for example, by the Social Principles of the United Methodist Church, which state: "We support the right of public and private ... employees and employers to organize for collective bargaining into unions and other groups of their own choosing. Further, we support the right of both parties to protection in so doing, and their responsibility to bargain in good faith within the framework of the public interest."
>
> Whereas we believe shareholders as part owners of the corporation should be mindful of the statement of John Paul II (On Human Work): "They (The means of production) cannot be possessed against labor, they cannot even be possessed for possession's sake, because the only legitimate title to their possession is that they serve labor, and thus ... that they should make possible ... the universal destination of goods and the right to common use of them." In order to better serve the common good of shareholders and employees alike:
>
> Be it resolved that the shareholders request the Board of Directors of Litton Industries form a Board Committee to develop a corporate

---

[29]Harry Bernstein, "Church and Union Leaders Cross Swords on Foreign Policy Questions," *Los Angeles Times*, November 21, 1983, p. 1.

code of conduct guaranteeing the right of employees to organize and maintain unions and affirming the principles of collective bargaining in good faith. This Committee shall seek outside counsel including from community, religious, business and labor leaders and shall submit the code for Board approval by December 1984. The code shall be printed in the next quarterly report and copies shall be sent simultaneously to all employees. Costs shall be limited to amounts deemed reasonable by the Board.[30]

That resolution was voted on at the shareholder meeting and endorsed by 2.45 percent of proxies voted. That was an improvement over the 1.9 percent vote in favor of a resolution the year before which called for an accounting of money spent by the corporation defending itself against unfair labor practice charges, but still fell short of a union self-set goal of 3.0 percent. The 1983 vote came before the corporation's chairman had characterized the proposal as "unworkable and unnecessary" and "counterproductive for both parties" and suggested an alternative approach. That alternative was a five-member study group, composed of two company and two union representatives and a neutral chairman, which would report on "the allegations of unions and others against the company, how collective bargaining and industrial relations between the company and its unions can be improved, and how productivity can be improved through our joint efforts."[31]

Three representatives of the National Litton Campaign, addressed the meeting after the chairman made his proposal—Howard Samuel, Joyce Miller, and Msgr. Higgins. All reportedly "condensed their planned remarks and welcomed [the] offer."[32] One unofficial ally of the campaign, the Rev. George Ogle, director of the Department of Economic and Social Justice of Church and Society of the United Methodist Churches, reportedly "expressed some caution about Litton's offer and said he hopes the resolution of this dispute will be more than a pledge to obey the law."[33]

After the shareholders' meeting, the representatives of the campaign met and decided to make "a positive" recommendation "to accept the proposal" to the presidents of the participating unions, on the grounds that they were "confident that this is a sincere offer" to be treated "very seriously." By December 12, the participating

[30]Litton Industries, Inc., Notice of Annual Meeting of Shareholders Held on December 10, 1983, shareholder proposal No. II, pp. 20-21.

[31]"Litton Chairman Suggests Labor-Management Study of Charges of Labor Law Violations," *Daily Labor Report* No. 239 (December 12, 1983), p. A-4.

[32]*Ibid.*, p. A-5.

[33]*Ibid.*

unions were reported to have placed a "moratorium" on campaign activities but not to have dismantled the campaign structure.[34] The participating unions quietly accepted the Litton proposal and equally quietly dismantled their campaign structure. The committee was appointed on December 21, 1983 and began its work in January 1984 and issued a report on November 20, 1984 (Attachment 2), by which time a contract had been signed at Sioux Falls.[35]

The Culmination of the Campaign

The National Litton Campaign ended abruptly and completely after the December 10 shareholder meeting. All public pressure from both unions and their religious allies ceased virtually overnight once the proposal for a tripartite committee was made. That committee was the sole tangible result of more than two years of concerted, coordinated union pressure on the corporation to change its labor policies in general and at a number of locations in particular.

The nature of the settlement of the dispute between Litton and the labor movement and the process by which it was reached raise two questions. First, why would the company, after two years of quiet denials, suddenly make a conciliatory gesture in the midst of an annual meeting and protest rally? Second, why would the union movement, after two years of intense effort and considerable expense, so quickly accept the company's "first offer"? The answer to both questions would seem to lie in the fact that the campaign had become bothersome to both, but particularly to the AFL-CIO.

The company characterizes the campaign as a nuisance, but staunchly denies it was a burden in terms of stockholder, customer, or public relations. The cost of the campaign to the company was, in its view, not sufficient to warrant any substantive change in the labor policies of its divisions.

The unions have given no public insight into the reasons for their precipitous withdrawal from the campaign, but it is suggested that the institutional costs of the campaign had come to outweigh any potential substantive gains likely to be won by attempting to carry the campaign to its logical conclusion. To the extent that any substantive gains were dependent on government action, the AFL-CIO's prospects for success in the Reagan Administration were definitely

[34]*Ibid.*, p. A-4.
[35]"First Contract Reached at Sioux Falls Litton," *UE News*, Vol. XLVI, No. 12 (September 10, 1984), p. 1.

not good. More importantly, continued pursuit of such gains through the campaign would be economically and ideologically divisive within the union movement in an environment in which union solidarity was and would continue to be at a premium. At the heart of the problem was the unwillingness of the Metal Trades Council to have its 10,000-worker unit in Pascagoula held economic hostage to a 1,000-worker unit in Sioux Falls and the unwillingness of the "moderate" AFL-CIO to be held ideologically hostage to the "radical" UE and its activist allies.

As is often the case in labor relations, the unions emerged from their campaign with something that could be called a "victory," while the company escaped with something that could be called a "non-defeat." A contract settlement was reached at Sioux Falls which represented a "victory" for neither party. Otherwise, there has been no evident change in the company's labor relations policy or posture.

ATTACHMENT 1

In 1975, Professor Craypo had written an article entitled "Collective Bargaining in the Conglomerate, Multinational Firm: Litton's Shutdown of Royal Typewriter," in which he had purported to analyze the closedown of a Royal Typewriter plant in Springfield, Missouri. For source material for the article, he relied heavily upon material provided by the union which was involved in the controversy which arose from that plant closing. In this article, Craypo concluded that organized labor was at a disadvantage in dealing with "conglomerate, international firms" and he offered concrete suggestions to unions to help them "to offset this bargaining disadvantage." In 1976, Craypo testified before the House Sub-Committee on Labor-Management Relations in support of the labor-sponsored "Labor Reform Bill," and submitted a report in support of that ill-fated legislation. In that report, Craypo purported to analyze 28 NLRB complaints issued against various divisions of Litton. The very first case which he analyzed, however, did not involve a Litton Division, but another company with a similar name. In 1982, he revised his report, correcting certain errors in it, but adding additional errors. For example, he analyzed as an NLRB case what in reality was an arbitrator's award. In 1983, Craypo again revised his report and submitted it in conjunction with his testimony before the House subcommittee on Labor-Management Relations in support of the labor-sponsored "Debarment Bill." Craypo has also testified before the same subcommittee in support of the labor-sponsored "Plant Hostage Bill." In addition, he has personally appeared at "anti-Litton" rallies or meetings organized by the UE, and his picture appears in the May 2, 1983 edition of the *UE News*, where he is identified as part of a "union delegation." In December of 1982, he participated in a TV talk show arranged by the UE, but declined to characterize "Litton's labor relations record because there was nothing to compare it with," although in two previously distributed reports he had made scathing condemnations of Litton even though such reports contained no comparative data.

In the various reports on Litton, Craypo made certain assumptions and reached certain conclusions which bear analysis. First, he assumed Litton's parent corporation was "a single employer" with many divisions and was therefore responsible for any unfair labor

practices engaged in by any division. For years there has been an
established NLRB procedure and body of law dealing with "the single employer" issue, i.e., whether two or more seemingly separate
employers are "a single employer" for labor relations purposes. The
"single-employer" concept is used by the NLRB in assessing liability for unfair labor practices (*McEwen Manufacturing Company*, 172
N.L.R.B. 990, 998-999) and in ascertaining whether an alleged separate employer falls within the secondary-boycott protection of the
National Labor Relations Act (*Los Angeles Newspaper Guild, Local
69*, 185 N.L.R.B. 303, 304-305). The "single-employer" body of law
has existed at least since 1957, according to the *NLRB Twenty-First
Annual Report*, pp. 14-15 (1957). That procedure normally requires
an allegation and supporting proof that the allegedly separate
employers are "a single employer." In his latest report, Craypo
referred to 42 cases where NLRB complaints had been issued
against various divisions of Litton during the period 1963 to 1981.
In no case was there an allegation that Litton, the parent corporation, was "a single employer" with any division, although in one case
involving a plant in Springfield, Missouri, a post-hearing finding
was made that Litton was a single employer with Royal Typewriter
Company (*Royal Typewriter Company*, 209 N.L.R.B. 1006 (1974)).
Nevertheless, in 41 of the 42 cases cited by Craypo, there was no
finding of "a single-employer" relationship.

In his various reports, Craypo analyzed NLRB *complaints* which
had been issued against various Litton divisions over a period of
close to twenty years, in many cases assuming or arguing that the
mere allegation in the complaint constituted a finding of a violation.
In some instances, Craypo argues a violation occurred even though
the Board or the court had actually found there was no violation. For
example, Craypo refers to a case involving the Mellonics Division of
Litton as one where the Board found a violation which was either
upheld in the Federal Court of Appeals or was not appealed, when in
reality, the Federal Court of Appeals ruled in favor of the employer
in the case (Memorandum Opinion, Case 83-7542, United States
Court of Appeals for the Ninth Circuit, *National Labor Relations
Board v. Litton Mellonics Systems Division, etc.*, dated June 28,
1984). As another example, Craypo refers to the Erie Marine Division of Litton and states the company had discharged a worker "who
the company now had reason to believe was a covert union orga-
nizer," when in reality, the NLRB had specifically ruled the particular employee had been legally discharged for a serious safety violation (*Erie Marine, Inc.*, 192 NLRB 793 (1971)). In another example,
Craypo discussed the Utrad Division of Litton and stated "threats

had been made by a plant 'foreman' before" an NLRB election, when in reality, the Court of Appeals for the Seventh Circuit held the company had not been guilty of the illegal threats (*Utrad Corporation v. NLRB*, 454 F.2d 520 (1971)). In analyzing the *Landis Tool Co.* case in his report, 190 N.L.R.B. 757, Craypo argues that a letter sent by the company during an election campaign constituted "illegal behavior," when in reality, the Board's trial examiner in the case had specifically held the same letter was not unlawful. In fact, in that case, the trial examiner had reviewed at least 13 pieces of campaign material issued by the company and had concluded " . . . that (Landis') literature neither violated Section 8(a)(1) of the Act, nor did it taint the election atmosphere as to preclude employees from exercising a free choice in the election" (*Landis Tool Company*, 190 N.L.R.B. 757, 762). In analyzing a Board case involving the Guidance and Controls Systems Division of Litton in his report, Craypo states that an employee "was threatened in connection with his testimony in an upcoming Board proceeding," when in reality, the Court of Appeals for the Ninth Circuit held no unlawful threat had been made by the company (*Guidance & Controls Systems Division v. NLRB*, reported in 79 *Labor Cases* 11791). Two examples illustrate the manner in which the Craypo report fits into the UE's corporate campaign. In his report, Craypo refers to layoffs and plant closings at two Litton divisions in support of his argument that Litton divisions engage in "illegal behavior" during union organizing drives. In each of the cases, however, an administrative law judge had specifically held, with Board approval, that the layoffs and plant closings were not illegally motivated (*Sturgis-Newport Business Forms, Inc.*, 227 N.L.R.B. No. 199; *Litton Mellonics Systems Division*, 258 N.L.R.B. No. 84). In analyzing the *Royal Typewriter Case*, Craypo claims the company closed a plant in Springfield, Missouri in order to undermine an incumbent union, when in reality, an administrative law judge, the Board, and the Court of Appeals all agreed the plant closing was lawfully motivated by economic considerations (*Royal Typewriter Company v. NLRB*, 533 F.2d 1030). In discussing the *Monroe* Case in his report, Craypo asserts the Monroe Division undertook "anti union initiatives" by granting a unilateral increase in wages and benefits, when in reality, the Court of Appeals for the Fourth Circuit had reviewed the case and found the "record shows without contradiction that Monroe was economically justified in granting the wage and benefit increases" (*Monroe v. NLRB*, 460 F.2d 121).

Another significant assumption made by Craypo in his report is that a legitimate inference of illegal activity may be drawn from cases which are settled by the parties. Fifteen of the NLRB "complaints" analyzed by Craypo in his report were settled by the parties without any trial ever taking place or any final decision being issued. Craypo's insistence that an inference of illegal conduct can be drawn from complaints which are settled without a trial or decision seems to fly in the face of established Board and court precedent. On the contrary, the Board and courts have gone out of their way to establish the principle that no finding of unlawful conduct can arise from the settlement of a complaint. In *Southwest Chevrolet Corporation,* 194 N.L.R.B. 975, the Board stated:

> The Board has uniformly held that settlement agreements . . . have no probative value in establishing that violations of the Act have occurred and may not be relied on to establish either union animus or a "proclivity" to violate the Act.

The Courts have also adopted this approach to settlement agreements:

> A settlement agreement does not amount to a finding or admission that respondent has committed an unfair labor practice . . . The Board concedes that such agreements are most often prompted by a desire to reach an amicable disposition of the matter without the need for expensive and time-consuming hearings and court reviews . . . *NLRB v. Bangor Plastics, Inc.,* 392 F.2d 772, 775.

Among the forty-two complaints issued against Litton Divisions which Craypo reviewed are a number of complaints issued as part of the appeals procedure in representation cases. The National Labor Relations Act gives the Board authority to act in two principal areas. The first area is in the prevention of unfair labor practices. The second area deals with representation elections. In the latter area, the Board holds secret-ballot elections and resolves disputes, should they arise, over the conduct and results of those elections. In the unfair labor practice area, the Board acts as the appellate court, so as to speak, in reviewing decisions of the administrative law judges who conduct the hearings on complaints issued by the general counsel of the Board. The National Labor Relations Act specifically provides that any person aggrieved by a Board's decision in an *unfair labor practice case* may appeal to a Federal Court of Appeals. No such direct method of appeal exists, however, with respect to Board decisions in *representation or election cases.* Instead, an employer wishing to appeal a Board decision in a representation or election case is required to follow the circuitous route of refusing to recognize the union, which then must file an unfair labor practice charge against the employer alleging a refusal to bargain. The Board's general counsel must then file a "complaint" against the employer and the Board must issue a decision finding the employer has committed an unfair labor practice by refusing to recognize the union. The employer may then appeal that decision to the Federal Court of Appeals, which will then review the validity of the Board's decision in the *representation case*. In other words, according to the procedure provided in the National Labor Relations Act, an employer desiring to appeal a Board decision in a representation case is required to engage in what is recognized as a technical refusal to bargain with the union. It is then, and only then, that the Federal Court of Appeals will review the action of the Board in a representation case (See *Funs, Inc. v. NLRB*, 150 F.2d 84).

In his report, Craypo argues that a pattern of illegal behavior begins in Litton Divisions "when unions try to organize Litton employees." However, in only one case of the many analyzed by Craypo covering a period of almost twenty years was an election declared invalid because of company behavior. Further, of the forty-two complaints analyzed by Craypo, excluding the technical violations required as part of the appeal process, only nine ultimately resulted in findings against Litton Divisions, and in just five of those cases was a union organizing drive in effect.

ATTACHMENT 2

REPORT OF JOINT IUD-LITTON COMMITTEE TO FRED O'GREEN, CHAIRMAN AND CEO, LITTON INDUSTRIES

November 20, 1984

On December 9, 1983, Mr. O'Green proposed, and the Industrial Union Department AFL-CIO accepted, the establishment of a committee to (1) study the allegations of the unions against the company; (2) determine how industrial relations between the company and its unions can be improved; and (3) recommend how productivity can be improved.

This report follows:

Since December 12, 1983, the Chairman and/or the members of the committee have spent 52 days in meetings, travel, and consultation on this problem. The committee's effort has produced some significant successes, has identified areas of continuing friction and has suggested a variety of continuing activities aimed at diminishing the potential for future problems.

The committee is pleased that it successfully mediated two out of three disputes which were pending at the time Mr. O'Green proposed the committee's formation.

Perhaps the greatest success the committee had was in encouraging the conclusion of negotiations at the microwave facility in Sioux Falls, South Dakota. The United Electrical Workers Union and the company had been in negotiations since the unit was certified in September of 1980. The talks that led to this agreement were intense and arduous. Final agreement might have been achieved earlier, but when a preliminary announcement about the unit's sale was issued, the committee determined that contract negotiations should be suspended in favor of bargaining directed to the effect of the sale. After the sale fell through, the committee encouraged a series of negotiating sessions between the parties which culminated in an August 24, 1984 agreement.

In the New Britain situation, a day of frank discussion between the parties cleared the air, and the report of the IAM and the company representatives at a later date indicated that our meetings had the effect of commencing a dialogue which has had good results.

While we are proud of the committee's mediation successes, we were not able to bring the parties closer together at the company facility in Athol, Massachusetts, where a work stoppage has been in effect since May 23, 1983. At the committee's request, the parties did make some moves towards settlement, but a final resolution of this conflict has evaded our efforts.

During the period of our mediation efforts the Industrial Union Department (IUD) of the AFL-CIO, and certain of its member unions, compiled an historical review of their view of labor relations at Litton Industries.

The committee met, reviewed, and discussed this material in detail. The discussion was frank, sometimes aggressive, but very worthwhile. The dialogue which ensued clarified, I believe, for each of the parties, the reasons for the misunderstandings between them, and serves as a basis for the recommendations which will be made later in this report on how to improve the relations between the parties.

It is clear that the parties view the nature of their problems from very different perspectives. The unions maintain that Litton's labor relations policies constitute a centrally directed plan to deny them their rights—a belief that the unions feel was buttressed by actions of the NLRB general counsel in urging that Litton cases be consolidated without regard to the division in which they originate. Unions perceive Litton's policies as being out of step with corporate labor relations as practiced by other major corporations. Essentially, their concerns fall into four categories. The complaining unions believe that:

- Litton aggressively discourages employee organization.
- Litton's expressed preference for operating in a non-union environment has resulted in continued frustration of the organizing process.
- The Company's bargaining in contract negotiations is unduly strident—particularly in bargaining on first contracts. The unions also believe that Litton's bargaining approach frustrates the continuation of harmonious relations at facilities which were already organized when acquired by the company.
- Litton's reliance on legal appeals in union certification situations is intended less as an exercise in legal thoroughness than as an effort to destabilize and thwart union activities.

The company, however, maintains that its industrial relations practices are totally within the law and claims that it has an essentially unblemished record insofar as violations of labor law may be involved. The company also asserts that under the National Labor Relations Act, it is perfectly legal for the company to inform employees of their right to remain unorganized, and that so long as it does not sponsor or initiate decertification efforts, or unilaterally withdraw recognition of a union without proof that an employee majority so desires, or threaten job loss or product line movement, or withhold investment to undermine union support, it is acting legally.

Litton states categorically that it operates on a decentralized basis, with its divisions preferring to operate without unions. The company notes that this preference for a non-union atmosphere is legal and that this right to express its opinion is allowed by law. In defense of this position, Litton points out the following:

- Litton divisions are primarily responsible to the parent for operating a profitable enterprise. Labor relations are essentially a divisional responsibility, although support from headquarters is available upon request.
- Litton's divisions bargain hard in their contract negotiations. In recent times, the necessities of business have directed the company to use the bargaining process to seek new and changed procedures intended to offset the effects of recession and growing foreign competition. The company observes that the unions have been unable or unwilling to consider the economics of the many Litton divisions.
- The company feels that isolated instances or disputes are being used inappropriately to describe the company's labor relations posture. In the past two years, there have been 24 contract negotiations that were resolved without any dispute. It also notes that at its largest unit, Ingalls Shipbuilding Division, the excellent relations between the company and the Metal Trades Department of the AFL-CIO are an example for all union and company units to follow.

In an early position paper, the Chairman stated to the committee that in our deliberations we wanted to be realistic, not idealistic. He further stated that it would serve no useful purpose to retry old issues. As our function was to fact-find, it was incumbent on us to understand the nature of the problem and make recommendations to improve the situation.

As mentioned earlier, the different perspectives of the parties may have magnified actions by the one party into glaring abuses in the view of the other. The Litton divisions may have, in exercising their preference for union-free operations, committed excesses in some of the operating units—all intended, no doubt, as doing a job for the company. Where elections have been won by a union, there has also been a tendency on the part of the company to exhaust the various legal remedies provided by the National Labor Relations Act before concluding contract negotiations. This has eliminated or delayed meaningful dialogue between the parties, and has broadened the areas of misunderstanding.

There have been a few situations where the position of the parties has been inflexible to the degree that no settlement can be reached. This has created a situation which has frustrated both parties tremendously, and has, unfortunately in those cases, convinced both parties that it is impossible to deal one with the other. Clearly this, for the long term, can do neither party any good.

It must be pointed out that Litton has been, in recent years, a company undergoing a change in its major businesses. The determination has been made that it will ultimately be an advanced electronic defense, high-tech, and resource exploration and geophysical services company, and that those businesses which do not fit in will be divested. As we look at the history of some of the problems between the parties, some can be attributed to the upset which occurs when employees are understandably concerned, and a legalistic position intended to prevent anything from happening which could alter the intended action is the response.

With this as a backdrop, then how can relations between the parties be improved? Your committee makes these recommendations:

1) We feel considerable understanding between the parties has resulted from the formation of this committee and the dialogue which has resulted. We recommend that you constitute the committee for a year, with the charter to meet semiannually to review relationships and matters of mutual concern. The charter should include an opportunity for the committee to report to you personally.
2) Dialogue between the parties should be carried on down through the various company and union organizations so that both organizations understand that:
- The various company policies and intentions are to:
- Allow each division to exercise, in a legal fashion, its right to promote its position on union representation.
- Bargain in good faith for a mutually acceptable contract when a union has been certified as an election winner. This does not prevent either party from filing objections to the conduct of the election. However, both parties should recognize that such objections, if frivolous, tend to damage a constructive relationship between them.
- Recognize and meet with a temporary grievance committee until the first agreement is negotiated.
- Otherwise, act in accordance with the rules and rights of collective bargaining as established by the National Labor Relations Act.
- The interest of the corporation and its various companies is to live in harmony with its employees. The operations must, however, operate profitably and competitively, and they need the understanding and cooperation of the employee group to accomplish this and, at the same time meet the needs of the employees.
- Employee actions which are legally acceptable activities in an organizing campaign and in conformity with established division

rules are not reasons for discipline, discharge, layoff, or suspension. Both parties agree that illegal actions or those which do not conform with established division rules cannot be condoned or supported.

3) Plant closing and product line movements have a serious impact on all workers, and are particularly difficult for those whose lifetimes have been spent in the organization. We recommend, then, that when such occurs, Litton divisions develop, with the unions involved, programs intended to ameliorate the adverse effects of the job loss.

4) There are some unfair labor practice charges being litigated. Litton divisions believe they will win these cases, and so do the union representatives. In view of the fact that much of that which brought about the formation of this committee grew out of the numerous NLRB actions between the parties, we suggest the parties meet to review their positions and make a good faith effort in each instance to see if there is a basis to settle all or part of the pending cases. The committee should be available to assist in these efforts if requested by either of the parties.

Not only Litton, but also a wide sector of American industries, have been subject to unusually profound challenges in recent years. Deregulation, sharply rising foreign competition, recessions effects, technological advances and sectoral shifts, all must be adjusted to today if a business is to survive. The people side of the business world often resists necessary change.

This report is also to include recommendations as to how productivity could be improved. As we discuss this problem it becomes clear that again we have a problem of perception. The company feels that the improvement of labor relations and the improvement of productivity are synonymous. And this may be so. For their part, the unions understand that reasonable improvements and productivity are a fact of industrial life, but their effect on workers must be reasonable as well. In consideration of this point of view, we recommend the following:

1) It is clear that among the reasons for successful labor relations and a productive work force at the Ingalls Shipbuilding Division is the interest and contribution of the Metal Trades Department—AFL-CIO in the business problems of the Division, and their efforts to help the company business. We suggest the IUD be urged that with its obviously excellent research facilities, and with its ability to communicate broadly to the various labor unions, to study the problems of Litton's various businesses with the cooperation of the company (i.e. machine tools) and to make this information known to its member unions. With understanding should come better relations and improved productivity.

2) Labor unions should always be sensitive to the value of cooperation. An adversary relationship is not generally productive or successful

in meeting the needs of the work force. Indeed, Samuel Gompers once wrote, "It is not the mission of the industrial groups to clash and struggle against each other. Such struggles are the signs and signals of a dawning comprehension, the birth pangs of an industrial order attempting through painful experience to find itself and to discover its proper functioning. The true role of the industrial groups, however, is to come together, to legislate in peace, to find the way forward to collaboration, to give of their best for satisfaction of human needs." We suggest the IUD be requested to disseminate information to affiliated unions, which will be helpful on this score.

A good starting place might be the Ingalls Shipyard story.

3) The company believes that a change in certain contract provisions will improve productivity. The company also believes that contractual changes impacting productivity can best be accomplished in an atmosphere conducive to cooperation and understanding. The parties believe that all this must be worked out with due recognition of the fact that people's lives and futures are involved. We suggest there be created a Litton—IUD-AFL-CIO study committee on contract proposals to meet the needs of today's work place. Each party should contribute to the agenda.

The committee should be chaired by a neutral and be given its assignment to complete in no more than nine months. It should report the results of its efforts to Mr. O'Green; President Howard Samuel of the IUD; and the Presidents of Litton-affiliated unions. Clearly, there is an opportunity for much constructive and original work to be done in this area. Smart people away from the pressures of negotiations should be able to recommend alternative solutions to problems which will satisfy each of the parties. Nothing recommended would be binding, and this in itself should encourage creativity.

To me, as Chairman, this has been an exciting and stimulating experience. The opportunity to work with four highly intelligent and extremely able men has been an exciting opportunity. To be able to rationally search for alternatives to a knotty series of problems, while not always providing solutions, has, I believe, opened the door to an improved relationship between the company and its labor unions. In the future, intelligent application of the things we propose should continue to improve that relationship.

Mr. O'Green, the company Chairman, said that Litton is a different kind of company and I believe that. He has also said that Litton's strength lies in its decentralization with sufficient controls so that if things go wrong they will surface quickly to be identified and then corrected. It is not unusual for companies that are strong operationally and financially to conclude that, therefore, the people side of the business is properly attended. It does not necessarily follow that good operators are good communicators.

We believe that with the assurance of the alignment of operating units with managements beliefs, the unions will be convinced that the company's policies and practices are directed to a successful business-labor relationship. Concomitantly, we believe that our productivity recommendation should serve to bring about a helpful mutuality of effort which will serve both parties well.

Respectfully submitted,
Paul W. Kayser
Chairman

For the Company:

M.J. Diederich, Jerry St. Pe

For the Industrial Union Department:

Elmer Chatak, Edward Fire

Louisiana-Pacific

Louisiana-Pacific is the second largest lumber products company in the United States. It operates some 100 plants nationwide. Its basic product is lumber for the construction industry—a market in which it competes with such giants of the timber industry as Weyerhaeuser, Boise Cascade and Georgia Pacific. Unlike those three firms, Louisiana-Pacific did not in 1983 own extensive timber land but secured its timber by bidding for cutting rights to government-owned land. Also unlike those firms and many of its other competitors, Louisiana-Pacific is not extensively involved in the production of pulp and paper and is, by comparison, a relatively specialized lumber company.

The Cause of the Campaign

The proximate cause of the corporate campaign against Louisiana-Pacific (L-P) was a bargaining impasse in its 1983 negotiations involving its western lumber operations. Those operations encompassed a total of twenty company plants located in Northern California, Oregon, and Washington. The cause of the impasse was a refusal by the company to follow the 1983 "pattern" set by the Big Seven of the western wood products industry.

The western wood products industry in 1983 employed a total of 150,000 to 180,000 employees of which only about one-third (50,000–60,000) were unionized. The unionized producers in the industry were divided into a three-tier bargaining system. The seven largest producers bargained on a multi-employer basis and were expected to set the pattern for the industry. The second tier of the industry encompassed those not so large firms which elected not to participate in multi-employer bargaining, but which were expected to follow the pattern set therein in the individual company's contracts. The third tier encompassed some 70 small companies which historically bargained on an "unbound" multi-employer basis through the Timber Operators Council against the pattern set in multi-employer negotiations.

The 1983 round of negotiations took place in an environment of depressed demand for lumber from the construction industry. That condition created some serious economic problems for those (smaller) producers which did not own their own timber and were "stuck" with bid commitments to the federal government for timber made when demand was strong. (Those commitments, if called by the government on schedule, would have left most of the industry bankrupt.) Those problems did not substantially affect the largest producers which reached an agreement in multi-employer bargaining in early 1983 that called for wage increases of 8.5 percent over the life of the three-year agreement. Those problems, however, did affect smaller producers resulting in substantial resistance to the pattern. The leader of that resistance was L-P, although it was not alone since the third tier of unionized companies also broke with tradition and abandoned multi-employer negotiations in favor of company-by-company bargaining in search of their own special deals.

L-P withdrew from multi-employer bargaining prior to its 1983 negotiations and informed its unions that it not only would not be party to multi-employer bargaining but also would not be party to multi-plant bargaining for its western operations. Thus, L-P's 1983 negotiations were conducted on a plant-by-plant basis to the extent that any such negotiations took place prior to contract expiration. At the outset of those negotiations, the company made it clear that it would not simply follow the pattern set in Big Seven negotiations. Instead, it proposed a two-tier wage system under which entry-level wage rates would be reduced for new employees and all other job rates frozen for the duration of a one-year contract. The union flatly rejected that offer and indicated that "it could hardly wait to strike the company" which it did in June 1983. The company took the strike and after a few weeks began to hire permanent replacements and resume operations. As a result, "violence [broke] out sporadically at many of the struck plants" requiring the company to spend "$5 million during the strike for increased security, repairs to damaged equipment and legal costs."[1] Despite such violence, the company was able to staff nineteen of its twenty operations with a combination of permanent replacements and strikers who elected to return to work rather than be replaced, and by June 1984 was able to "produce as much as the market demands." Indeed, the company was able to produce more than a still slumping market demanded as evidenced by the fact that it had some active workers on layoff as of the summer of 1984. By that time, the company had "won" decertification elections in nine of its twenty struck plants, although most of those victories were still being contested.

---

[1]Patricia A. Bellew, "Lumber Firm Wins Big Fight with Strikers," *Wall Street Journal,* June 26, 1984, p. 37.

The Boycott

The corporate campaign against L-P formally began in December 1983 when the AFL-CIO and the United Brotherhood of Carpenters and Joiners of America (UBC) launched a nationwide consumer boycott of L-P's wood products. The UBC played the lead role in the campaign by virtue of the fact that the 1500 workers on strike at L-P were members of the Western Council of Lumber Production and Industrial Workers (LPIW) which was an affiliate of the UBC.

In order to effectuate its announced boycott, the UBC established "L-P Support Committees" in each of its 1800 locals with "the responsibility of coordinating and conducting regular boycott activities at retail lumber yards and stores selling L-P's wood products."[2] By March of 1984, the union reported that such support committees, in conjunction with other labor organizations, were conducting "boycott activity on an ongoing basis at over four hundred outlets throughout the country."[3] At that time, the UBC claimed that "the boycott activity has produced a very positive response from the consuming public" and that "responding to the expressions of consumer support for the boycott, retailers at many locations have ceased selling L-P wood products."[4]

The boycott activity typically began with a letter to a retailer from the UBC informing him of the existence of the dispute and the union's plan "to commence lawful noncoercive boycott activities" at his store. (Attachment 1) The outlet would then be subject to picketing and consumer handbilling. (Attachment 2).

A special focus for boycott activity was L-P's new waferboard product, a plywood substitute which was a high margin profit product for L-P. The company at the time was perceived to have "embarked on an ambitious waferboard expansion program, with the hopes of doubling its present waferboard capacity by 1985."[5] In its effort to target waferboard for boycott activity the UBC "identified the present distribution system for L-P's existing waferboard facilities" in Wisconsin, Maine, and Texas and intensified its boycott activities in "cities such as Houston, Minneapolis, Chicago, New York, Indianapolis, and major New England cities."[6]

---

[2]"Carpenter's L-P Strike Campaign," handout distributed at a Wall Street rally, March 22, 1984, p. 1.
[3]*Ibid.*, p. 2.
[4]*Ibid.*
[5]*Ibid.*
[6]*Ibid.*

In June 1984, the UBC reported that "the product boycott presently is being conducted in 20 states with approximately 400 lumber and building product retailers picketed on a weekly basis."[7] The company consistently has claimed that the boycott has had little effect on its sales and the *Wall Street Journal* in June 1984 seemingly agreed when it reported that the boycott "has apparently had little effect."[8]

The Wall Street Approach

On March 22, 1984, the UBC took its corporate campaign to Wall Street in the form of a noon rally at the New York Stock Exchange following a morning of publicity leafletting in the financial district. In announcing that action, the UBC indicated that it was designed "to show Louisiana-Pacific we will be taking action from Main Street to Wall Street"[9] to gain justice and increase public support for the campaign.

Prior to that rally, the UBC had written to a major insurance company which was the largest L-P stockholder to inform it of the dispute and to suggest that it was in a unique position "to exercise informed discretion and independent judgment as to how the present dispute might best be resolved."[10] The union also had written to a major bank which was signatory to a credit agreement with L-P to inform it of the dispute and the boycott, citing a section of that credit agreement providing that the bank was to be promptly apprised of any strike involving 1,000 or more L-P employees which continues for more than thirty days. Neither of those financial institutions responded to the invitations to become involved in the dispute, but one small San Francisco Money Fund, Working Assets, did become involved in the form of a letter to L-P in which it indicated that it "will not purchase prime commercial paper of Louisiana-Pacific Corp. because your company has been placed on the National AFL-CIO 'Do Not Patronize' list" and that it "will notify our shareholders of your company's violation of our social and economic investment criteria, and ask that they not purchase your products."[11]

7"News From UBC," press release, issued in Washington, D.C., June 26, 1984, p. 2.

8Bellew, "Lumber Firm Wins Big Fight . . . ," p. 37.

9"News from the UBC, press release, March 20, 1984, p. 2.

10Letter from Mr. Patrick J. Campbell, General President of the United Brotherhood of Carpenters, to Mr. Edward B. Rust, President and Chief Executive Officer, State Farm Mutual, dated February 6, 1984.

11Letter from John C. Harrington, Vice President, Working Assets, to Mr. Harry A. Merlo, Chairman and President, Louisiana-Pacific Corp., dated March 30, 1984, p. 1.

The Shareholder Approach

The UBC also supported the formation of a L-P Workers for Justice Committee (L-PWJC) comprised of striking L-P workers who were also company shareholders. The purpose of the L-PWJC was to communicate with other L-P shareholders on issues relating to company operations. Three such issues were raised by the L-PWJC in the form of proposals to the company's 1984 shareholders meeting. Those three proposals were:

> 1) Strike Impact Accounting: The proposal requested that L-P quantify for shareholders the cost of the strike to the company in terms of increased production costs, and decreased sales and profits related to the strike...
>
> 2) Independent Board of Directors: The second proposal concerned the composition of the L-P Board, a majority of which is composed of individuals with past or present employment, business or financial relationships with the company...
>
> 3) Compensation Committee: The third proposal sought to reconstitute the Board's executive compensation committee of which Mr. Harry Merlo, L-P's chairman and CEO is chairman.[12]

In search of support for those proposals, the L-PWJC provided "solicitation material to the holders of 26 of the company's 33 million outstanding shares."[13] That material cited the fact that "financial analysts have identified multi-million costs for L-P related to the strike" as well as "numerous costly legal infractions involving L-P which were attributed to the lack of a strong independent board" and "repeated instances where Mr. Merlo has benefited handsomely from decisions of the compensation committee."[14] The shareholder response to that solicitation was, in the view of the union, "very positive, with the L-PWJC representing over 2 million shares at the May 14 annual meeting in Rocky Mount, North Carolina."[15]

The UBC, as part of its shareholder approach, planned a mass rally for May 14 in Rocky Mount—a place described by the union as "one of the most unlikely and inaccessible spots ever picked for a major corporate annual meeting."[16] The union characterized the choice of Rocky Mount "as part of a strategy to hide from the public, the media, its own shareholders and the family of organized labor."[17]

---

[12]"Carpenter's L-P Strike Campaign," pp. 2–3.

[13]*Ibid.,* p. 2.

[14]*Ibid.,* p. 3.

[15]*Ibid.,* p. 2.

[16]"News from the UBC," press release issued in Washington, D.C. May 9, 1984, p. 1.

[17]"It's Showdown Time for the Louisiana-Pacific Corporation and Its Chief Executive, Harry A. Merlo," flyer distributed at the annual shareholder meeting, May 14, 1984, p. 2.

In order to counter that strategy, the union conducted a "Reckoning at Rocky Mount" for which it "recruited some 400 participants from a variety of community, union, church and civil rights organizations, among them Rev. Joe Lowery, president of the Atlanta-based Southern Christian Leadership Conference (SCLC)."[18]

The "reckoning" began with a pre-meeting rally and "trial" of Louisiana-Pacific as a first step "in bringing this billion-dollar corporate outlaw to justice."[19] It then proceeded to the annual meeting which the SCLC packed with its supporters. At the meeting Rev. Lowery was to present one of the resolutions and representatives of the IUD, the National Council of Churches, and environmental and senior citizens groups were to speak on behalf of the L-PWJC proposals. The union and its supporters were successful in "disrupting" the meeting but not in securing passage of the L-PWJC proposals. Undaunted, the union then indicated that:

> The L-PWJC will continue to communicate with L-P shareholders, with the focus on L-P's continuing difficulties. Special emphasis will be given in the communication process to large institutional shareholders holding significant positions in L-P stock and which handle union pension funds.[20]

The Governmental Approach

In March the UBC stated that, "we will be making our case against L-P not just to the consuming public, but also to the investing public, shareholders, government officials and regulatory agencies."[21] The first step in the union's efforts to involve the government in its campaign was to link its Wall Street rally to hearings by the New York State Assembly Labor Committee on the "Plight of the Collective Bargaining System."[22] That was followed by city council resolutions in two of L-P's plant sites to support the strike. The final step in the politicization of the dispute was a successful effort to get the Labor-Management Subcommittee of the House Education and Labor Committee to launch a "preliminary investigation of the company's use of Urban Development Action Grants from the U.S. Department of Housing and Urban Development to help finance its waferboard ... facilities in the states of Minnesota, Michigan and Mississippi."[23]

18"News From the UBC," press release issued May 9, 1984, p. 1.
19"It's Showdown Time ... ," p. 1.
20"Carpenter's L-P Strike Campaign," p. 3.
21"News from the UBC," press release issued March 20, 1984.
22*Ibid.*
23"Carpenter's L-P Strike Campaign," p. 3.

The union on two occasions utilized environmental regulatory agencies in an attempt to pressure the company. In early 1984, the union claimed that "an air permit challenge by the Colorado State Council of Carpenters and environmental challenges have slowed the progress of the Montrose, Colorado, [waferboard] facility."[24] In May 1984, the union was able to enlist the aid of the Sierra Club in opposing an L-P request for a variance from the requirement of secondary treatment of wastewater at its Samoa, California, pulp mill from the Environmental Protection Agency (EPA).

The issue of L-P's racial policies was raised only once and was not a major element in the campaign. The union did, however, attempt to secure data on the composition of L-P's workforce from the Office of Federal Contract Compliance Programs (OFCCP), but was unsuccessful. The union's effort to contact shareholders in 1984 produced a request from it to L-P to supply a list of the names and addresses of all shareholders. The company replied that it would permit the union access to its records of shareholders, but that the union would have to bear the burden of copying those records. The result was a protracted legal hassle in which the Securities and Exchange Commission was heavily involved.

The company's decision to hire permanent replacements and operate the struck plants left the union vulnerable to decertification elections. In an effort to forestall or prevent such elections, the union sought and secured "a standing order from the National [Labor] Relations Board [NLRB] to file what is called an 'unfair labor practice' complaint against L-P for 'bad faith bargaining.'"[25] As long as that order stood, decertification elections could not be held. In May 1984, the acting general counsel of the NLRB revoked that order, paving the way for immediate decertification elections in 9 plants. The union threatened to challenge the general counsel's action in court, but was unsuccessful in so doing.[26]

The Results of the Campaign

The UBC admits having spent $4 million on its campaign against L-P and has little to show for it. Its boycott undoubtedly has had some adverse effects on company sales and possibly on L-P stock prices, but it is impossible to separate any such effects from the broader effects of the industry's basic economic problems. In any

---

[24]*Ibid.*
[25]"News From the UBC," press release issued June 26, 1984, p. 2.
[26]*Ibid.*

event, it is clear that the union has not achieved its goal of "busting the company."

The company admits having spent some $5 million to enable it to operate its struck plants, but denies that the corporate campaign, per se, has had a discernible effect on its sales, costs or profits. It will, however, admit that the campaign has been a managerial and legal bother, particularly with respect to the "proxy fight" and government regulation. Any such bother has been more than offset by its "victories" in decertification elections. By June 1986, the company had won 16 such victories with two others awaiting certification by the NLRB. At that time, a rerun election was pending in one other unit and one unit was no longer in operation.

ATTACHMENT 1

PATRICK J. CAMPBELL,
GENERAL PRESIDENT

UNITED BROTHERHOOD OF CARPENTERS
AND JOINERS OF AMERICA
101 CONSTITUTION AVE., N. W.
WASHINGTON, D. C. 20001

February 3, 1984

Eugene Planing Mill
306 Lawrence Street
Eugene, OR 97401

Attn: Store Manager

Dear Sir:

This is to inform you that the Western Council of Lumber Production and Industrial Workers, United Brotherhood of Carpenters and Joiners of America, AFL-CIO, has a labor dispute with Louisiana-Pacific Corporation. We are beginning a nationwide consumer boycott of Louisiana-Pacific Corporation's products.

Based on information we have received, we have determined that Louisiana-Pacific Corporation's products are sold at your store, and we plan to commence lawful, noncoercive boycott activities at your store and a number of other stores where Louisiana-Pacific Corporation's products are sold. We intend to engage in lawful publicity, including consumer picketing and leafletting to ask the public not to buy Louisiana-Pacific wood products wherever they are sold.

We have no dispute with your Company and the public will be so informed. If, in fact, you do not distribute any Louisiana-Pacific products, please let us know as soon as possible.

The Western Council and the Louisiana-Pacific Corporation employees we represent have made every effort to reach a fair and equitable agreement with the Company. Enclosed please find instructions to pickets and instructions to coordinators. Finally, also please find a copy of the leaflet which will be distributed. If any of the information in the leaflet is incorrect or you learn of any violations of these instructions, please notify the undersigned so that the matter can be corrected.

We regret any inconvenience which this consumer boycott may cause you as the boycott expands in the coming weeks, but we are determined to secure justice for the employees we represent. You may wish to contact Louisiana-Pacific Corporation at 503/221-0800 for further information about the dispute.

Sincerely,

General President

PJC/js:hp
opeiu #2/afl-cio

enclosures

193

ATTACHMENT 2

Here's Why We Ask You . . .

Please Don't Buy
L-P Wood Products

Because L-P, a billion-dollar company, a giant in the industry, has *unfairly* forced over 1,500 of its employees out of their jobs by refusing to observe the modest industry-wide collective bargaining settlement agreed to by its competitors—large and small.

Because L-P seeks an *unfair advantage* over its competitors at the expense of its employees, with no benefit to the consumer.

Because, even though L-P employees accepted a wage freeze, L-P wants *even lower pay* standards.

Because L-P is being *unfair* to its working people and the communities where they live.

That's Why We Ask the Consumer . . .
- You decide what's fair.
- If you believe in fairness, Please Don't Buy L-P Wood Products.

We, the employees of Louisiana-Pacific and the United Brotherhood of Carpenters, say:

THANK YOU!

L-P's Unfair Wood Products

L-P makes and sells lumber and lumber products; plywood; waferboard; particleboard; hardwood; floor systems; and insulation. L-P brand names include: L-P Wolmanized; Cedartone; Waferwood; Fibrepine; Oro-Bord; Redex; Sidex; Ketchikan; Pabco; Xonolite; L-P-X; L-P Forester; L-P Home Centers.

But No Inconvenience for You
Please Buy Fair Wood Product

You don't need to buy L-P. There are plenty of quality wood products on the market. Other *fair* manufacturers make products comparable to those of *unfair* Louisiana-Pacific.

Here are a few of the hundreds of fair, responsible companies selling wood products at the same price as L-P—or in some cases, even lower:

Boise Cascade; Champion International; Crown Zellerbach; Georgia-Pacific; Publishers Paper; Simpson Timber; Weyerhaeuser; Williamette; Bohemia; Pope and Talbot; Roseburg Lumber and many others.

Please Note: We have no dispute with this wood products distributor. Our dispute is with Louisiana-Pacific, a manufacturer.

APPENDIX VI

Consolidated Foods-Hanes Division

The corporate campaign against Hanes and its parent company, Consolidated Foods Corporation (CFC) which is now Sara Lee, was not strictly speaking a union corporate campaign. The campaign was conducted by two nuns who were members of the Sisters of Divine Providence with the aid or guidance of the Interfaith Center for Corporate Responsibility (ICCR). The Sisters of Divine Providence is headquartered in San Antonio, Texas, and is a member of the Texas Coalition for Responsible Investment which in turn is a member of the Interfaith Center. The two members of that order who led the campaign were at the time assigned to do community work in Bennettsville, South Carolina, as members of the Connective Ministry Across the South which is sponsored by the Glenmary Commission on Justice. At the same time those two sisters were on the volunteer staff of the Southerners for Economic Justice—an organization formed in 1976 by the Amalgamated Clothing and Textile Workers Union (ACTWU) to generate support for its organizing efforts at J.P. Stevens. Except for that affiliation, there was no visible connection between the corporate campaign and the labor movement.

The fact that the ACTWU did not play a visible role in the campaign did not mean that it was not an interested party or that it did not aid the nuns in their efforts. The ACTWU played an instrumental role in the development of the data on which the sisters built their case and in the analysis and refutation of a report challenging that case. From the viewpoint of the company, or at least of one Hanes plant official, the two sisters were clearly working with, if not for, the union. An allegation to that effect brought a sharp rebuttal from the head of the Sisters of Divine Providence indicating that the two sisters were simply "concerned about the issues of industrial health and about women's, consumers' and workers' rights . . . concerns of our Congregation for all people; they are consistent with the teachings of our Church and, we believe, with the moral values of all persons of ethical conviction of whatever religious denomination."[1] That

---

[1]Letter from Sister Mary Margaret Hughes, Superior General, Sisters of Divine Providence, to Mr. John H. Bryan, Jr. Chairman of the Board Consolidated Foods Corporation, dated December 4, 1982, p. 1.

195

rebuttal elicited an equally pointed response from Hanes in which the company indicated that its employees had volunteered the information "that the Bennettsville Sisters were contacting Hanes employees and among other things offering to help our employees contact union organizers."[2]

The Background of the Campaign

In 1979, Hanes' 10 plants with a total of 16,000 employees became a major organizing target of the ACTWU. By November of that year, the union had won a representation election at the Hanes plant in Galax, Virginia. The company challenged that victory charging that the union had committed numerous unfair labor practices. That challenge produced a threat from the union to mount a boycott against the company. That threat led to an agreement between the company and the union to await and abide by the decision of the circuit court. That decision was handed down in May 1982 and invalidated the union's victory.[3]

In 1980, while the company's case was pending, the Occupational Safety and Health Administration (OSHA) appeared on the scene to investigate the high reported incidence of tendinitis and related disorders (TRD) in Hanes facilities. The result of that investigation was a 1981 agreement between OSHA and Hanes containing "provisions proposed voluntarily by Hanes" calling for corrective actions which "were underway at Hanes long before the OSHA agreement."[4] Specifically, the company had retained an ergonomics consultant to assist it in the redesign of work stations and work motions to reduce the risk of TRD. The process/program of corrective action was acceptable to OSHA and was continued under the agreement with OSHA.

The Beginning of the Campaign

The corporate campaign against Consolidated Foods came as a surprise to the company. Its first clue that something might be about to happen came just before its annual shareholders' meeting in October 1982 in the form of a letter to its CEO, John Bryan, from Sister Imelda Maurer, Sisters of Divine Providence, requesting a

---

[2]Letter from Mr. Philip R. Curriers, President Hanes Hosiery, to Sister Mary Margaret Hughes, Superior General, Sisters of Divine Providence, dated January 12, 1983, p. 1.

[3]Hanes Corp. v. N.L.R.B., 677 F.2d 1008 (4th Cir. 1982).

[4]Letter from Mr. John H. Bryan, Jr., Consolidated Foods Corporation to Sister Imelda Maurer, Connective Ministry Across the South, dated November 4, 1982, p. 1.

meeting to discuss "problems relating to tendinitis and other industrially related illnesses, the rights of women employees, the rights of workers to organize, the issue of Consolidated Food Corporation food prices and CFC food consumer's concerns related to health and nutrition."[5] The corporation did not respond to that request and no meeting was scheduled or held with Sister Maurer during the week of October 25, 1982. That was the week of the shareholders' meeting—a meeting attended by, among others, Sister Maurer and Father Dahm of ICCR.

At that meeting Father Dahm spoke against the reelection of Robert Elberson, who had been the CEO of Hanes prior to its acquisition by Consolidated Foods, to the CFC Board of Directors. Sister Maurer then introduced some Hanes employees to provide testimony on the terrors of tendinitis. A second issue raised by Sister Maurer at the meeting was one of discrimination against women, specifically with respect to the direct store delivery operations of Hanes. The response of the chairman and CEO to the accusations of Sister Maurer was that there was no problem. That position was formally reiterated one week later in a letter to Sister Maurer from Mr. Bryan in which he responded to the questions she had raised at the meeting and concluded "that there is simply no basis in fact to the charges made by you and your associates at our Annual Meeting."[6] That letter prompted a response by wire within the week and by letter in January of 1983. In that letter Sister Maurer made it clear that tendinitis was her central issue and indicated that "It is your unwillingness to meet with us that compels us to pursue other measures for redress of this problem."[7]

Those other measures actually had begun before the annual meeting. The Hanes problem had been aired at an October 1982 meeting of the Catholic Committee of the South. As a result of that meeting, the corporation received a large number of complaining letters from a host of Catholic orders and several other religious and civic groups and a few threatening letters from trustees of retirement systems. Noticeably absent were letters from labor unions. The standard company response to such letters was a letter accompanied by the original written rebuttal of Sister Maurer's charges sent after the shareholders' meeting.

---

[5]Letter from Sister Imelda Maurer, Connective Ministry Across the South to Mr. John H. Bryan, Jr., Consolidated Foods Corporation, dated October 19, 1982, p. 1.

[6]Letter from Mr. John H. Bryan, Jr. to Sister Imelda Maurer, dated November 4, 1982, p. 3.

[7]Letter from Sister Imelda Maurer to Mr. John Bryan, dated January 13, 1983, p. 2.

The war of the written word went on for almost five months, from November 1982 to March 1983, with neither side making any discernible progress. By the end of February the corporation was blessed by a diminishing stream of protest letters and an encouraging number of supportive letters from Hanes employees. At the same time, however, it was beset by an increasingly nervous board of directors, particularly its outside directors, many of whom had been approached directly. In addition, there was some evidence of institutional sales of blocks of corporation stock in lots not large enough to affect price but large enough to be disquieting. Thus, by mid-March both sides were at the end of their respective ropes.

The Escalation of the Campaign

The stalemate reached by mid-March was broken by the end of the month by a new initiative on the part of Sister Maurer. That initiative involved the creation of a "Citizens Commission on Justice at Hanes" composed of a number of noted activists including such individuals as Bella Abzug, Julian Bond, Gloria Steinem, and Studs Terkel, as well as representatives of the Southern Christian Leadership Conference, the National Council of Negro Women, the National Organization for Women (NOW), and Women Against Pornography.

On March 11 Sister Maurer wrote to Mr. Bryan to invite him to a meeting of the commission to be held in Chicago of March 21. On March 16, Mr. Bryan wrote to Sister Maurer declining her invitation and inviting her to meet with the corporate vice-president of Human Resources to discuss the Hanes situation. Sister Maurer did not avail herself of that opportunity and the Commission met as scheduled on March 21.

The press was invited and did appear at the Commission meeting where it and the Commission members were presented with a report on the Hanes/Consolidated Foods situation prepared by Sister Maurer. In that report Sister Maurer cited the tendinitis problem and the problems of route saleswomen and focused the blame for such problems on Consolidated Foods Corporation's management which she characterized as lacking in "concern for the communities or people affected by CFC-owned companies" and relegating "people to mere objects in a vast money-making machine."[8] Sister Maurer concluded her report with the following action recommendations:

   1. A full-scale fact-finding mission that includes on-site investiga-

---

[8]"Report to the Citizens Commission on Justice at Hanes" prepared by Sister Imelda Maurer and presented on March 21, 1983, at Chicago, Illinois, pp. 5–6.

tions in the towns with Hanes plants and that includes the participation of workers, local churches and groups, company personnel and community representatives . . .

2. A broad-based campaign to educate the general public—especially women's, religious, civil rights, consumer, labor, and health organizations—about repetitive trauma disorders at Hanes . . .

3. A well-focused effort to dialogue with, and work in cooperation with, a selection of the company's major stockholders who are also concerned about issues of health and safety.

4. A program to assist in sponsoring a stockholder's resolution(s) that will challenge current corporate policies regarding worker health and safety and treatment of women by CFC-related operations.[9]

The commission meeting received considerable press coverage, but the commission itself did little to implement Sister Maurer's recommendations. In May 1983, a follow-up article in the *Winston-Salem Journal* noted that "a panel of prominent social activists formed to focus attention on working conditions at Hanes Corp.'s Southern textile plants apparently hasn't been up to much since it was launched two months ago." That same article went on to indicate that "so far a consensus seems to be far from developing among the commission members . . . [whose] attitudes range from strident to indifferent."[10]

The corporation did not respond passively to the formation of the commission. In the face of growing concern on the part of some of its outside directors, particularly those on the board's Public Responsibility committee, an effort was made to counter the potential adverse image effects of a "Citizens Commission on Justice at Hanes." The corporation retained a prominent black consultant to guide that effort. His first initiative was to contact the black organizations represented on the commission to invite them to visit Hanes plants and to make them aware of the possibility that they were not participating in a campaign for social justice but were being used in a union organizing campaign. His second initiative was to do the same with a number of prominent Southerners and seek their active interest in the Hanes situation. As a result of that effort, the company was able to form its own Advisory Council of prominent private citizens of the region in June of 1983.

---

[9]*Ibid.*, p. 11.
[10]John Byrd, "Panel Slow in Investigating Work Conditions at Hanes," *Winston-Salem Journal*, May 22, 1983, p. G-1.

The Transformation of the Campaign

A second dimension of the corporate strategy in dealing with the campaign recommended by Sister Maurer was a decision not to stonewall potential participants in that campaign but to seek to engage them in a private dialogue, thereby hopefully projecting an image of the corporation as being open and concerned. The first major opportunity to implement that strategy came shortly after the commission meeting in the form of a letter from the director of the Social Justice Office of the Sisters of Divine Providence dated March 28, 1983.[11] In that letter, the director, Sister Billeaud, made three information requests of the corporation in conjunction with her role as monitor of "our investments for social responsibility": 1) a description of measures taken and planned to eliminate stressful motions; 2) the EEO-1 data for Consolidated Foods and each Hanes plant; and 3) information on the compensation of female route sales-persons. In addition, Sister Billeaud requested that a study be made of the incidence of repetitive motion trauma disorders at all Hanes plants and that the results of that study be shared with her congregation.

That letter constituted the first showing of a substantive interest on the part of the Sisters of Divine Providence in the issues raised by its member Sister Maurer. The only previous correspondence had been a letter from the head of the order protesting a statement of a Hanes official that the order worked with unions. The corporation saw in this second letter a potential opportunity to substitute a private dialogue with the leaders of the order for a public debate with Sister Maurer and quickly sought to establish contact at that level. In early April, the corporate senior vice-president for human resources flew to San Antonio and phoned the head of the order to request a meeting. That request was reluctantly granted. As a result of the ensuing meeting, agreement was reached to continue private discussions of the order's concerns as an alternative to public confrontation. The responsibility for the conduct of those discussions on the part of the order was delegated to Sister Billeaud.

The Sisters of Divine Providence were only reluctantly drawn into a private dialogue as they seemingly had prepared for an open confrontation over the issues raised in Sister Billeaud's letter of March 28. Nonetheless, they did live up to their commitment to on-going

---

[11]Letter from Sister Theresea Billeaud, Director, Social Justice Office, Sisters of Divine Providence to John H. Bryan, Jr. Chairman, Consolidated Foods Corporation, dated March 28, 1983, p. 1.

private discussions in lieu of public confrontation, although the threat of the latter was always present, making those discussions at times more like negotiations. To further complicate matters, from the viewpoint of the company, the leadership of the order was unable or unwilling to control or to silence Sister Maurer.

The first major development in those discussions was a meeting in San Antonio in mid-May to address the concerns stated in Sister Billeaud's initial letter. The order was represented at the meeting by an interesting array of individuals from three distinct constituencies: 1) the Sisters of Divine Providence (Sister Billeaud), 2) the Connective Ministry (Sister Maurer) and 3) the Interfaith Center on Corporate Responsibility (Dara Demmings) and its local affiliate—the Texas Coalition for Responsible Investment. The appearance of a representative of the ICCR suggested to the company that it was the target of a classic ICCR corporate campaign in which shareholder resolutions play a central role, as indeed proved to be the case. The agenda for the meeting suggested that campaign was focused on two issues—the incidence and impact of TRD and equal pay and equal opportunity. In that context, there was one hidden agenda item—unionization—represented, in the view of the corporation, by Sister Maurer and the Connective Ministry which it believed was financed by the ACTWU.

The central topic of the first meeting was the tendinitis issue and the order's request for information on the incidence and impact of TRD. The company focused attention on the incidence issue, which was consistent with its previously stated position that the problem, while not trivial, was not widespread. Sister Billeaud's earlier request for an incidence study also was discussed.

Subsequent to that initial meeting, the company announced formation of a medical task force composed of nine doctors with specialized knowledge in the area of TRD to undertake an extensive study of the situation in Hanes plants and to issue a comprehensive report of their findings. Also subsequent to that first meeting, the company launched a study of the earnings of route salespersons which disclosed, fortuitously, that on average women earned slightly more than men.

The appointment of the medical task force had to be well received by Sister Billeaud. It was not similarly welcomed by Sister Maurer or by the labor movement in the person of Joyce Miller who was reported by the media to have made a comment about a boycott by women's groups after a July 14, 1983, Washington hearing. That comment produced an influx of protest letters from Hanes' largely female workforce to organizations such as NOW, which opened

another avenue for the dialogue for the corporation. The result was
an August 1983 meeting with the president of NOW in which the
corporation presented its side of the story on the tendinitis and
equal pay issues as well as some new issues raised by Sister Maurer
in the interim. It is not at all clear that organizations such as NOW
were seriously contemplating joining the campaign against Hanes,
but it is clear that they did not in fact do so.

Meanwhile, Sister Maurer was at work raising issues regarding
the methodology of the medical task force and making accusations
regarding company intimidation of employees asked to participate
in its study. Those issues and accusations were embodied in letters
to the board of directors, to the chairman of the task force, and to
the company's ergonomics consultant, all of which were made available to the media. The questions raised by Sister Maurer inevitably
had to be discussed as part of the dialogue with the Sisters of Divine
Providence and were not finally laid to rest until a meeting was
arranged in San Antonio with the full membership of the task force
in the fall of 1983. Well before that meeting, however, the cause of
Sister Maurer had become secondary in the discussions/negotiations
between the corporation and, in its view, the Interfaith Center.

The corporation's perception that it was the target of an ICCR
campaign led it to establish an independent dialogue with that organization through Dara Demmings. By September, that dialogue
made it clear that ICCR's primary interest was EEO data and that it
was preparing to press that interest through a shareholder resolution. At the same time it became clear through the on-going dialogue
with the Sisters of Divine Providence that release of the medical
task force report to it and other shareholders would also be a potential subject of a shareholder resolution. Finally, Sister Maurer's constituency was also heard from in the form of a proposed resolution
regarding Hanes ads from the Women Against Pornography. The
corporation was prepared to fight this last issue before the Securities and Exchange Commission on the grounds of relevance, but
nonetheless agreed to meet with representatives of the organization.
The other two threats were taken far more seriously resulting in
intensive negotiations which ultimately were successful in averting
shareholder resolutions and a confrontation at the 1983 shareholders
meeting.

In August, while those negotiations were going on, the company
was approached by Peter Jennings of ABC television who wished to
do a piece on the Hanes situation for a Labor Day special report. The
corporation's basic strategy of avoiding the appearance of stonewalling dictated that it accede to such a request. In anticipation of that

possibility, the key executives of Consolidated Foods and Hanes had been given special training in dealing with unfriendly interviews. Such training proved helpful but not essential in the case of ABC because, after seeing the situation first-hand, Mr. Jennings decided that the company deserved credit not criticism. CBS television also contacted the company and sent researchers to investigate plant conditions. They too concluded that there was nothing sufficiently wrong to warrant a story and departed the scene. That was most fortuitous as the consultants who trained the executives in interview techniques advised them against talking to representatives of the CBS program, *60 Minutes.*

In September, the corporation succeeded in reaching agreements with Sister Billeaud and Ms. Demmings under which both agreed to withdraw their proposed shareholder resolutions. In exchange, the corporation agreed to provide a copy of the tendinitis study to any shareholder who requested one and to publish basic EEO data in its annual report. With those two issues settled, the 1983 shareholder meeting was remarkably quiet. The same was true in 1984.

The Waning of the Campaign

The campaign against Consolidated Foods and Hanes was effectively but not technically ended by the time of the shareholder meeting in October 1983. At that time, the tendinitis study had yet to be released. The final report of the medical task force was published in November 1983. That report generally confirmed that the incidence of TRD was limited, as the company had contended, but indicated that the problem was real, as the company had recognized. As a result of the study, the company has expanded its ergonomics program, instituted a physical conditioning program, and is considering mandatory work breaks.

The results of the study and subsequent company action were acceptable to the Sisters of Divine Providence, but not to Sister Maurer. With the aid of the ACTWU's occupational safety and health staff she prepared a report challenging the integrity of the members of the task force and the validity of their methodology, findings, and conclusions. That "counter-report" was issued in March 1984, but received little public attention.[12] Undaunted, the Bennettsville Sisters have continued to leaflet Hanes plants urging workers to write to the CEO of Consolidated Foods detailing their

---

[12]"We All Know What's Making Us Sick," Connective Ministry Across the South's response to Hanes Medical Task Force Report, 1984.

health problems. In addition, they have accused the company of fighting worker compensation claims for TRD. That accusation attracted the attention of their order which in turn attracted the attention of the corporation which found that its insurance carrier was dragging its feet in dealing with such claims. That situation was corrected and by the fall of 1984 the processing of such claims had been expedited to the point where the corporation was receiving congratulatory letters from the religious community.

The Results of the Campaign

The corporate campaign against Consolidated Foods has to be viewed as a victory for the religious community as represented by the Interfaith Center in that it did result in the corporation making public data on the composition of its workforce and the incidence of tendinitis. That victory, however, was not necessarily a defeat in equal measure for the corporation. The data released were not damaging to the corporation in its efforts to deal with this potential problem, not only in its Hanes operations but in its other operations characterized by rapid repetitive motion.

The corporate campaign against Consolidated Foods can hardly be characterized as a victory for Sister Maurer, unless one assumes that her goal was simply to force the company to do what it was already doing—admit the existence of and address a tendinitis problem. The campaign did result in some further workplace improvements and some more expeditious compensation for TRD victims, but it did not result in the indictment of the corporation as an uncaring crippler of legions of workers or as a callous exploiter of female employees. In that context, it is interesting to note that many of Hanes' female employees apparently felt that they were being exploited by Sister Maurer when she talked of launching a boycott through the women's movement. The reaction of those employees to that suggestion, in the form of protest letters to not only women's organizations but to Catholic bishops and at least one cardinal, provided ample testimony to the double-edged character of the boycott sword. In this case, the women's groups proved highly sensitive to that fact. The religious community, however, did not, as may be judged by the following statement in a letter to the corporation:

> I am well aware of the contribution of the Hanes group to the economy of the small, southern communities where they are present in the states of North Carolina, South Carolina and Virginia. However, it has been the posture of the churches teaching that the individual comes before any profit and that the dignity of the person is primary in the economic venture.

The question of whether or not the union movement, most notably the ACTWU, will benefit from the campaign which it quietly encouraged and assisted remains to be seen. On the one hand, the campaign and study had to sensitize workers to the threat of tendinitis which might well create an organizing issue for the union, particularly if workers believe that the company is unconcerned. On the other hand, the study and the actions it has encouraged may serve to demonstrate that the company is concerned and will take care of them. The first test of whether the campaign gave the union a viable organizing issue or deprived them of one came in a November 11, 1984, representation election at the Galax, Virginia Hanes plant—the same plant in which the union won an election in 1979. The union lost that election by a vote of 669 to 359.

INDEX